D0079370

Swinburne and His Gods

The Roots and Growth of an Agnostic Poetry

MARGOT K. LOUIS

McGill-Queen's University Press
Montreal & Kingston • London • Buffalo

PR
5513
.L6
1990

© McGill-Queen's University Press 1990
ISBN 0-7735-0715-9

Legal deposit first quarter 1990
Bibliothèque nationale du Québec

Printed in Canada on acid-free paper

This book has been published with the help of a
grant from the Canadian Federation for the Humanities, using funds provided by the Social Sciences and
Humanities Research Council of Canada.

Canadian Cataloguing in Publication Data

Louis, Margot Kathleen, 1954-
  Swinburne and his gods

  Includes index.
  Bibliography: p.
  ISBN 0-7735-0715-9

  1. Swinburne, Algernon Charles, 1837-1909—
Criticism and interpretation. I. Title.

PR5513.L69 1990   821'.8   C89-090257-7

Contents

Texts and Abbreviations

References to Swinburne's text are by the letter designating the appropriate edition, followed by volume and page number (e.g., *P*1:3 for *Poems*, vol. I, p. 3). Unless otherwise indicated, line-enumeration is from *Swinburne: Selected Poetry and Prose*, edited by John D. Rosenberg (New York: Random House 1968). Wherever possible, I use the editions of Swinburne's lyrical and dramatic work proofread by the poet himself in 1904–5.

B   *The Complete Works of Algernon Charles Swinburne*, Bonchurch edition, ed. Edmund Gosse and Thomas James Wise, 20 vols. (London: Heinemann 1925–7)

L   *The Swinburne Letters*, ed. Cecil Y. Lang, 6 vols. (New Haven: Yale University Press 1959–62)

LB   *Lesbia Brandon*, ed. Randolph Hughes (London: Falcon Press 1952)

P   *The Poems of Algernon Charles Swinburne*, 6 vols. (London: Chatto & Windus 1904)

T   *The Tragedies of Algernon Charles Swinburne*, 5 vols. (London: Chatto & Windus 1905)

WB   *William Blake: A Critical Essay*, ed. Hugh J. Luke (Lincoln: University of Nebraska Press 1970)

Acknowledgments

I am grateful to Elizabeth von Klemperer, for stimulating my interest in a great and neglected poet; to W. David Shaw, for his patience and tact when this book was first trying to take shape; and to my family, for their support and encouragement.

French quotations are translated in the notes; I should like to thank Mary Shelton for her valuable advice on these translations. I am obliged to Charles Beer for editing the manuscript so carefully. Kathryn Kerby-Fulton and Gordon Fulton provided invaluable help in proofreading.

During the years I worked on this book, I was supported in part by a series of SSHRC doctoral fellowships, and by a Queen Elizabeth II Ontario Scholarship; I am very happy to express my gratitude for this assistance.

Parts of this book have been previously published, in a slightly different form, in *Victorian Poetry*, *Victorian Newsletter*, and the Newsletter for the Midwest Victorian Studies Association.

I dedicate this book to the memory of my mother, and to my father.

Swinburne and His Gods

Introduction

The subtlety and precision of Swinburne's religious polemics have never been fully appreciated. Nobody has yet examined in any detail the poet's early devout Anglo-Catholicism, and his violent repudiation of Christianity after his "deconversion" at Oxford; but consideration of his High Church background will show that his attacks on orthodox Christianity were at least well informed. Moreover, a careful analysis of the way in which he manipulates sacramental imagery within his lyrics and dramas proves that his criticism of High Church sacramentalism is at once radical and exact. Swinburne suggests that the analogical universe of Keble and Newman expresses the self-contradictory, self-destructive violence inherent in the natural world: the Christian God is Time, disguised as Eternity.

According to the High Church theorists of the Oxford Movement, the world that we see constitutes a sacramental system of meaning, a vast analogy created and organized by God to express His love and wrath. God alone makes and is meaning: the significance of His sacramental system is stable, and accessible to all who are rightly attuned to its divine harmonies. Swinburne's rebellion against conventional theocentricity manifests itself most forcefully at the point at which the sacramental systems of nature, language, and the Church interconnect through the ritual of the Eucharist; as J. Hillis Miller puts it, "The Eucharist was the archetype of the divine analogy whereby created things participated in the supernatural reality they signified."[1] For approximately a decade after his "deconversion" (1857–67), Swinburne's work expressed a deep pessimism, a bleak faith that the universe has been created and organized by a god whose name is time, or change, or pain – and all these names are one name, in which all language is summed up. In Swinburne's eucharists of violence, the eaten God is transformed into a diabolical maw, a consuming fire that sheds darkness visible rather than light. Throughout the Judaeo-Christian literary tradition, it has been customary to present the enemies of Jerusalem as distorted parodies of Jerusalem herself; in Swinburne's extension of this strategy, God becomes indistinguishable from his own black distorted shadow. The mode of demonic parody, adopted from the Bible and from Christian tradition, is central to Swinburne's early verse.

But the poet refuses to rest in the "turbid nihilism" of his early pessimism. Hillis Miller has shown that there are several modes of reacting to the "disappearance of God": apart from "diabolical nihilism," one may adopt the agnostic piety of Tennyson or Mansel, or the atheistic humanism of Feuerbach or George Eliot; or one may attempt to reduplicate the Romantic feat of creating a new system by which the divine and the human are integrated (12–14). As Swinburne experiments with various alternatives to the Christian sacramentalist vision, he develops eucharistic images of harmony which suggest that sacramental systems are created and organized by humans, rather than by God. Yet how can a human being generate meaning and value from a world intrinsically void of both?

In the political poetry of 1867–76, and especially in the volume entitled *Songs before Sunrise*, Swinburne asserts boldly that man makes meaning. He posits an Idealist deity who attains to self-realization through human republican activity; only in the Republic to be can the order and meaning of nature become fully real, self-aware. Swinburne proclaims this Neo-Hegelian vision dogmatically, in the mode of Romantic prophecy; as we learn from his essay *William Blake* (published 1867), Romantic prophecy to Swinburne is a mixture of myth and didactic allegory, with the emphasis on the latter. But Swinburne's experiments in the prophetic mode lead him gradually toward a more organicist aesthetic, focused more closely on myth; and William Rossetti's 1869 edition of Shelley stimulates Swinburne to a fresh examination of radical Romanticism, which in turn leads him to a clearer understanding of Romantic poetics.

At this stage, Swinburne's central concern is with the power of imaginative action, as it resists, exploits, or conquers time. In the humanistic ideologies developed through the Romantic prophecies of *Songs before Sunrise*, time is conquered through time; the apocalyptic Republic, to be attained through the self-sacrifice of political radicals working in time, is the true meaning of the apparently meaningless world of changing "things." More subtly, the conquest of time through time is achieved in the Apollonian mythopoeia of Swinburne's next period (1876–84). To celebrate another artist's triumph over time is to reenact it – to replay it, but in a different key. The technique of celebration, as developed in *Songs of the Springtides*, makes it possible for the dead letter of another's text to become a new song.

Yet the reconciliations of *Songs of the Springtides* depend on a two-edged word which can curse as well as bless. The ambiguity of the word illuminates the ambiguity of time. Is a triumph over time really possible? At best, each such victory is transient, *ad hoc*, questionable. In his last period (1884–1909), Swinburne recognizes as much, and claims no more for each triumph over time than that it is a persona's – or, in the elegies, a friend's – experience. The interaction of mind and nature, or the extent to which each mirrors the other, now displaces his interest in the specifically poetic imagination. At the same time, as Swinburne examines the experience of the individual mind more and more closely, his confidence in its self-sufficiency wanes. The "divine" source of meaning is no longer immediate and incarnate in poetic language, but becomes an unknowable mystery; words point toward that radiance which would give them life and meaning, but can only evoke instead of incorporating the deity. In *Songs of the Springtides*, Swinburne moved toward the meditative mode of the Greater Romantic Lyric; in *Astrophel* (1894), he exploits the Greater Romantic Lyric and the elegy, in the spirit of an agnostic vividly aware that myth may be unreliable as an epistemological tool. In the finest of his late lyrics, Swinburne's scepticism turns every divinity into what one might call a nonce-god, a god created for the moment only. He deliberately narrows his focus to immediate experience; whether this experience functions as a metaphor for divinity, or as divine in its own right, or whether it is simply mean-ingless, is a question left open in the end. In this way Swinburne's work develops from anti-Christian polemic, through Romantic prophecy and the humanistic celebration of imaginative power, to a genuinely agnostic poetry.

This brief summary of my argument should suggest both what I am attempting to do, and what I shall refrain from attempting. John D. Rosenberg and Jerome J. McGann have demonstrated, el-oquently and finally, that Swinburne's poetry deserves to be taken seriously; I shall not endeavour to defend what requires no defence, nor, generally, shall I even attempt to praise what is fully worthy of praise.[2] This is not an evaluative polemic. I am simply concerned to elucidate the ways in which Swinburne's poetry works, and the course of Swinburne's development as a poet.

CHAPTER ONE

Demonic Parody and the Great Whore

SWINBURNE AND THE HIGH CHURCH

[J]e foule aux pieds les préjugés de mon enfance, je les anéantis, cela m'échauffe la tête. (Sade, *Oeuvres*, 21:78)[1]

Swinburne's Romanticism has been much discussed, but too little attention has been paid to the impulse which drives him to Romantic art. Nobody has yet examined in any detail the poet's early devout Anglo-Catholicism, and his violent repudiation of Christianity after his "deconversion" at Oxford; and yet it is obvious that Swinburne joins the "Church of Blake and Shelley" long after he leaves the Church of Christ. In fact, Swinburne devotes himself at length to sustaining and developing the Romantic tradition because that tradition offers an alternative to Christianity, or (as Abrams puts it, more exactly) "a displaced and reconstituted theology" and "a secularized form of devotional experience."[2] The poet may indeed have been predisposed to Romanticism by the efforts of Keble and his followers to "theologize" Wordsworthian Romanticism.

His family background, as he observed, was "quasi-Catholic" (L3:13): "[w]ithout going very deeply into theology," says Gosse, the Swinburnes "threw in their lot with Newman and Keble" during the poet's childhood, "and their Anglicanism took a warmer and vivider colouring." His mother's letters express her unpretentious piety; and Swinburne's intimate knowledge of the Bible was due to her training.[3] It would seem too that she introduced him to Newman's Anglican sermons. In 1828, Swinburne's aunt, Elizabeth Swin-

burne, had married John William Bowden, Newman's close friend;
and through her Lady Jane Swinburne later sent Newman a token
of gratitude for his sermons, which had been "so great a help to her
and hers." (Transmitting this message to Newman, Mrs. Bowden
added that Lady Jane was "very good, but alas! it is only your old
sermons that she reads.")[4] Moreover, as we shall see, there is evidence that Swinburne became well read in the works of other literary
figures of the High Church, such as J.M. Neale and Richard Chenevix
Trench.

Swinburne lost his faith at Oxford, in 1858 or 1859, and never
regained it. We have almost no documentation for the period in
question – Swinburne's letters, otherwise so frank about his
thoughts and feelings, say as little about his loss of faith as they do
about his "lost love" (John Nichol's mixture of Carlylean and Millite
liberalism was probably the main contributing factor).[5] In Swinburne's case, therefore, our interest must focus not on his deconversion, but on his continued use of the motifs and concepts of his
childhood faith throughout his later poetry; on his manipulation of
Christianity in order to undermine it. His mature view of the Church
was never more explicitly declared than in his letter to E.C. Stedman
in February 1874:

Having been as child and boy brought up a quasi-Catholic, of course I went
in for that as passionately as for other things (e.g. well-nigh to unaffected
and unshamed ecstasies of adoration when receiving the Sacrament); then
when this was naturally stark dead and buried, it left nothing to me but a
turbid nihilism: for a Theist I never was; I always felt by instinct and perceived by reason that no man could conceive of a *personal* God except by
brute Calibanic superstition or else by true supernatural revelation; that a
natural God was the absurdest of all human figments; *because* no man could
by other than apocalyptic means – i.e. by other means than a violation of
the laws and orders of nature – *conceive* of any other sort of divine person
than man with a difference – man with some qualities intensified and some
qualities suppressed ... But we who worship no material incarnation of any
qualities, no person, may worship the divine humanity, the ideal of human
perfection and aspiration, without worshipping any God, any person, any
fetish at all. Therefore I might call myself if I wished a kind of Christian (of
the Church of Blake and Shelley), but assuredly in no sense a Theist. Perhaps
you will think this is only clarified nihilism, but at least it is no longer turbid.
(*L*3:13–14; italics Swinburne's)

Theologically, we can see precisely where Swinburne diverged
from the writers of the High Church. To the writers of the High

Church, the natural world itself may constitute a quasi-sacramental system, at least to those who can "read" it aright.

THERE is a book, who runs, may read,
   Which heavenly truth imparts,
And all the lore its scholars need,
   Pure eyes and Christian hearts.
         ....
Thou, who hast given me eyes to see
   And love this sight so fair,
Give me a heart to find out Thee,
   And read Thee everywhere.
        (John Keble, "Septuagesima Sunday")[6]

Keble is speaking of the natural world; but to Richard Chenevix Trench, a High Churchman influenced by the Oxford Movement, human language similarly offers a revelation of God's nature, of our alienation from God through sin, and of our dependence upon Christ's redemptive sacrifice and God's sustaining grace. Trench asserts confidently that words are "not arbitrary and capricious signs, affixed at random to the things which they designate, ... but ... stand in a real relation to them," and that language itself testifies both to man's "divine birth" and to "the depth of his fall." The history of the word *self-sufficiency* demonstrates our increased understanding (thanks to Christianity) of man's dependent situation:

The word in Greek exactly corresponding to our 'self-sufficient' is one of honour, and was applied to men in their praise. And indeed it was the glory of the heathen philosophy to teach man to find his resources in his own bosom, to be thus sufficient for himself ... But the Gospel has taught us another lesson, to find our sufficiency in God: and thus 'self-sufficient,' to the Greek suggesting no lack of modesty, of humility, or of any good thing, at once suggests such to us.[7]

In 1867 Swinburne specifically criticized Trench's theocentric assumptions, with regard to this point.

[Archbishop] Trench has pointed out how and why a word which to the ancient Greek signified a noble virtue came to signify to the modern Christian the base vice of presumption. I do not see that human language has gained by this change of meaning, or that the later mood of mind which dictated this debasement of the word is ... indicative of any spiritual improvement; rather the alteration seems to me a loss and a discredit, and the tone of thought which made the quality venerable more sound and wise than that which declares it vile. ("Matthew Arnold's New Poems," B15:72n)

Swinburne's much-advertised paganism is thus connected with a very precise objection to the Church. The precision of his polemics is due, no doubt, to his intimacy with Anglicanism throughout his boyhood; his religious training was reinforced in three vicarages, for at different times through his boyhood he was sent to reside with clerical tutors. Of these, the most important – the most impressive to Swinburne, and the most eminent in later years – was James Russell Woodford, later the bishop of Ely. This clergyman had a vivid sense of his priestly calling, and considered the administration of the Eucharist "the highest part of his office"; here, he insists, the priest "most closely imitates the action of our ascended Lord behind the veil." To be sure, Woodford keeps within the bounds of the Thirty-Nine Articles. The Eucharist constitutes no repetition of Christ's sacrifice; it is merely a "Memorial" and a "shadow" of the Passion. On the other hand, Woodford is never weary of stressing the need for frequent attendance at Communion, for the Eucharist is the instrument whereby a "special gift of grace" is communicated; the "sacramental Mysteries" must never be "evaporated into mere acts of man ... or become mere superfluous and uncertain signs of that which God's decree has already given." Woodford never confronts the issue of the Real Presence, but there can be no doubt that to him a rationalist interpretation of the Eucharist appears more dangerous than the doctrine of Rome. Emphatically, the sacrament is a vehicle of grace, operating "to bring souls into contact with the reconciliation, and to sustain them in union with it."[8]

Swinburne's confession that his early religious enthusiasm extended "well-nigh to unaffected and unshamed ecstasies of adoration when receiving the Sacrament" (L3:13) suggests that he had absorbed something of Woodford's reverence for "sacramental Mysteries." In this context, we can see that Swinburne's negative use of eucharistic imagery, later on, was meant to produce that sense of liberation which comes from desecrating old sanctities. More importantly, the frequency of such images in his prose and verse reflects a "quasi-Catholic" conviction that this sacrament is the true centre, the essence of Christian worship. Thus Swinburne's negative eucharists implicitly criticize what he perceives as the central expression of Christian devotion; the doctrine of that Atonement which the ritual memorializes, the concept of that supernatural redemption which the ritual mediates, and the very concept of sacramental mediation – all are tacitly censured.

At the same time, the poet happily exploits the emotional connotations of the Eucharist to sanctify the various deities which he evolves for himself. And in his positive transformations of the Eucharist, he commonly emphasizes the very aspects of the sacrament that Woodford stresses. Except in the political "eucharists," the element of sacrifice – and even the sense of communion with one's fellow-human (central in Positivist "sacraments") – are subordinated to the idea of a mysterious union with the divine. (It is true that in Swinburne the divine and the human are often one and the same; but in a *A Song of Italy*, for instance, humanity is primarily the eaten and redeeming god, and only secondarily the group of recipients to be redeemed.)

It is possible that Swinburne's early "ecstasies of adoration" were intensified by the influence of Newman's veneration for the Real Presence. "We eat the sacred bread, and our bodies become sacred; they are not ours; they are Christ's; ... they are inhabited by His Spirit; they become immortal." We shall see that the assumptions underlying such a passage as this have left their traces in Swinburne's poetry; we shall also see that Swinburne increasingly focuses his hostility on the doctrine of transubstantiation, a dogma which Newman in 1836 thought carnal and rationalist, "a substitution of something earthly for a heavenly mystery."[9] Swinburne appropriates and expands on this argument, implying (as Victor Hugo does in *Religions et Religion*) that all dogmatic Christianity displays a carnal habit of mind, a kind of materialism. Thus the content of Swinburne's attacks on Christianity, as well as the rhetorical strategies employed in such attacks, are largely determined by his early intimacy with the High Church, and with its clergy.

Nothing amused him more than the proceedings of the Church Congress when that ecclesiastical assembly held its meetings at the Albert Hall; or perhaps I should say that nothing amused him so much as the letters appearing in ... the *Daily Telegraph* commenting on those proceedings ... The letters from curates on such subjects as "The Cure of Souls" and "Disheartened Clergy" he read and re-read. He caught the ordinary Oxford-bred curate's brassy tone with wonderful accuracy.[10]

The final sentence is significant. Swinburne's talent for parody is generally recognized; but critics have overlooked the crucial importance of parody in his anti-Christian polemics. Gosse described him once as an "evangelist turned inside out,"[11] because of his proselytizing vehemence and his style's obvious debt to the Bible. But that debt is still greater than most critics have supposed. No one has yet discussed Swinburne's wholesale appropriation (and transformation) of the Bible's demonic imagery. As Frye has lately pointed out, nations antagonistic to Israel, and the gods of these nations, are presented in both Testaments as demonic parodies of the true God and his apocalyptic Kingdom: the temporary success of the heathen darkly foreshadows that eternal glory.[12] Swinburne not only turns the demonic parody against Christianity – for instance, the Christian Church becomes the Whore of Babylon, the demonic parody of the true Bride of the Redeemer, in "Before a Crucifix" and "Locusta" – but transforms such demonic figures as the Great Whore, as radically as William Blake in the *Marriage of Heaven and Hell* transforms the image of Hell.

Swinburne's acquaintance with biblical typology came from his High Church training, as Ruskin's from his evangelical upbringing. The Oxford Movement brought into High Church culture the habits of typological reading which had always formed an essential part of evangelical culture; Woodford and William Sewell (a friend of the Swinburne family from 1844 on) both evoked "the principle of the typal relation of the dispensation of the Law to the dispensation of the Gospel."[13] Like Ruskin, Swinburne derived from this principle an aesthetic which stressed "*both* the formal elements of the beautiful and its deeper theological significance."[14] But Swinburne chooses to translate the traditional symbolic patterns of Christianity in his own way. In his play *Marino Faliero*, for example, the Latin hymns chanted by the monks (brilliant pastiches of the mediaeval hymns in Trench's *Sacred Latin Poetry*) have much less authority than the running commentary on those hymns, provided by the hero. In *Bothwell*, the traditional patterns of biblical typology are ruthlessly reorganized around the figure of Mary Stuart; she, rather than Christ, is at once the final meaning and the source of all "types." The radically revised typology of *Bothwell* is the focus of my next section, which functions as an introduction to Swinburne's equally subversive transformations of the sacrament.

RESHAPING TYPOLOGY

> ... [Glencairn]
> Unmoulds her God and mints and marks him new
> And makes his molten chalices run down
> Into strange shape and service. (*Bothwell*, v.i, t3:207)

The criticism of the last thirty years has retrieved the typological vision. D.W. Robertson and Rosemond Tuve first revived it for medieval and seventeenth-century studies; more recently, George Landow and G.B. Tennyson, among others, have shown how for

Victorians this method still revealed, to Tractarian and to Low Church evangelical alike, a "universe of divinely instituted order." The Low Church tended to emphasize the typological interrelation of historical events; the High Church, the sacramental economy of ecclesiastical ritual and of the natural world. But we have seen that the Tractarians accepted the typological method, and both parties assumed that the form and meaning of the universe have their source in God, and that the typical and sacramental systems both find their centre in Christ's redemptive Sacrifice; thus God's creative and com- passionate action at once creates and constitutes meaning.[15]

Swinburne exploits typology freely, but his eucharistic imagery is more richly and radically innovative than his secularization of such common types as the Pisgah vision or the bruising of the serpent's head. Yet in his most ambitious dramatic work – the trilogy of plays (*Chastelard, Bothwell,* and *Mary Stuart*) on the life of Queen Mary of Scotland – Swinburne does refashion the symbolic system that we call typology, in a manner at once systematic and original. In this sequence Swinburne begins by transforming the figure of Mary Stuart into a type of the Great Whore, and destructively criticizes two antagonistic forms of Christianity by showing that the god of their worship is really identical with His own demonic parody; then gradually, as the work progresses, Mary is revealed in a new light as a symbol of the human power to create our own order, to construct meaning. In the first case, Swinburne inverts traditional typology to undermine the system; later in the work he so drastically rearranges traditional typology, that the reader's very concept of meaning is radically altered.

In *Chastelard* (composed between 1858 and 1863, and published in 1865), the Scottish Puritans soon establish the point that Queen Mary Stuart, like Aholibah in the prophecy of Ezekiel, is typologically related to the Great Whore of Revelations. The physical savagery of Ezekiel's parable of Aholibah makes it especially suitable for Swinburne's purpose. Aholah and her sister Aholibah are figures of destructive and self-destructive lust; so God tells Aholibah,

Thou shalt drink of thy sister's cup deep and large: thou shalt be laughed to scorn and had in derision; it containeth much.

Thou shalt be filled with drunkenness and sorrow, ... with the cup of thy sister Samaria.

Thou shalt ... break the sherds thereof, and pluck off thine own breasts. (Ezek. 23.32–4)

Taking Aholah as the type of Mary de Guise, and Aholibah as the type of her daughter Mary Stuart, the citizens echo this passage very

closely (T2:125–6), with a vindictive passion which has sadistic un-
dertones. Even in Swinburne's early works, the church – Catholic
ecclesia or Presbyterian Kirk – is founded on a Sadic lust for cruelty.
In *Rosamond* (1860), Queen Eleanor was spurred on to murder Rosamond by a choir-boy's Latin hymn, which ran, in part:

[God] empties and refills the bitter chalice with the same hand. He makes
the eyes sore with much unsatisfied weeping; he orders that the shining
breasts should be gnawed by the tooth, bruised by the hand ... (*Rosamond,
T1:270–3; my translation)[16]

Eleanor drove home the point that the hymn was touched by her
own sadistic jealousy, when she cried, "I do thank God, / I praise
the wording of his prayer, will ... / Be married to his love, my purpose
making / Such even wing and way with his" (T1:273). And Mary
Stuart in *Chastelard* is more confidently and greedily sadistic than
either Queen Eleanor or the Scottish citizens; she watches Chastelard's execution with shining eyes and throat stretched out (v.iii,
T2:151), just as the heroine in one of Swinburne's prose pieces contemplates her lover's hideous death: "her lips had the look of laughter and her eyes shone and smiled; all her face was warmed and lit
with pleasure" (*LB* 180). Mary more than justifies her subjects' criticism of her; they cannot conceive the fullness of her wanton savagery, the extent to which she fulfils the type of the fatal whore.

In Ezekiel, Aholah and Aholibah are allegorical figures of Samaria
and Jerusalem, who have gone whoring after strange gods; they
thus anticipate the Great Whore of Revelations, a composite of all
those nations that have "lived deliciously" with idols. "For all nations
have drunk of the wine of the wrath of her fornication ...: in the
cup which she hath filled fill to her double" (Rev. 18.9, 3, 6). When
the Whore is identified with Babylon, mother of harlots (Rev. 17.5),
theological infidelity is united with political tyranny, with domi-
nation and enthralment. Since zealous Protestants of Mary's era
invariably identified the Whore as a prophetic type of the Roman
Catholic Church, and since Mary Stuart was the supremely visible
representative of that Church in Scotland, it was inevitable that she
would be associated with the Whore.

Now, the Whore is the demonic parody of the true Bride of Christ,
which is the Church of God. In *Chastelard*, however, the Great Whore
has no counterpart; there is no true Bride, and no true Church. We
might even say that *Chastelard* offers us the Bible with everything
but the demonic parodies excised. The difference between Mary and
her subjects, between Catholic and Puritan, even between Great

Whore and avenging God, is one of degree, rather than of kind. In the end all parties serve the creative power "Who wrought so miserably the shades of men / With such sad cunning (T1:287)."

In the elegiac sequence *In Memoriam*, and elsewhere, Alfred Tennyson had struggled toward an image of marriage which would be reminiscent of Christ's marital relationship with the Church, and which would therefore convey some assurance of a divinely-ordered harmony. Swinburne, by contrast, established the figure of the adulterous wife as the type of order's collapse, the image which best conveys the divine dissonance of the world. Guenevere and Iseult, debased in Tennyson's *Idylls*, are glorified in Swinburne's *Tristram of Lyonesse*; Mary Stuart is similarly glorified in *Bothwell* (1871–4). In this enormous closet play, she begins as the murderess we saw in *Chastelard*, but becomes something more as the drama proceeds: she is a source of an order which she continually re-creates.

At the end of Act II, Darnley is about to be murdered by Mary's associates, and at her command. He gradually apprehends her purpose – in scene xix, through a dream; in scene xxi, through the reading of a psalm. Darnley's nightmare reveals Mary first as a demoniac siren ("about her all the reefs were white / With bones of men whose souls were turned to fire"); next, he dreams of a "garden walled," in which "one ... like a god in woman's flesh" gives him fruit

> As red as fire, but full of worms within
> That crawled and gendered; and she gave me wine,
> But in the cup a toad was; and she said,
> *Eat*, and I ate, and *Drink*, and I did drink,
> And sickened ... (T2:414–15)

The biblical parataxis emphasizes the ritual quality of the dream; the Gothic imagery makes this ritual at once material and infernal. Here Mary Stuart is the antitype of Eve, who gave her husband the fruit of death; but she is also a dark parody of Christ, as she administers a corrupt and poisonous eucharist. Instead of suffering a sacrificial death to redeem the spouse she loves, as Christ does, she enforces the death of her own spouse. Darnley does not realize the full significance of his vision until he learns to interpret Mary through his reading of that "deadly scripture," Psalm 55 – the psalm *Exaudi, Deus* – as it appears in the Book of Common Prayer. Quoting verses 2, 4–8, and 12–15 almost word for word, and preserving their parallel constructions, Darnley converts the Psalmist's case into a type of his own.

Nor is it an open enemy, he saith,
Hath done me this dishonour: (what hath put
This deadly scripture in mine eye to-night?)
For then I could have borne it; but it was
Even thou, mine own familiar friend, with whom
I took sweet counsel; in the house of God
We walked as friends. Ay, in God's house it was
That we joined hands, even she, my wife and I,
Who took but now sweet counsel mouth to mouth
And kissed as friends together
....
                    ... O God, God,
I know not if it be not of thy will
My heart begins to pass into her heart,
Mine eye to read within her eye, and find
Therein a deadlier scripture. (T2:435)

The dream, the Prayer Book, and the Queen's face progressively bring Darnley to the true consummation of his marriage: the ineluctable Sadic union of "The slain and slayer, the spoiler and the spoiled," as Knox later puts it (IV.vii, T3:186). Foreknowing his death, Darnley sees God and his murderers as indistinguishable: "hands [God] hath, / Their bloody hands to smite with, and her heart / Is his toward me to slay me" (T2:437). Another doomed and raving murderer – Guido Franceschini in Browning's *The Ring and the Book* – in his last moments perceives a saving power in his victim;[17] Darnley, instead, sees a devilish God in his own slayers. To him, his queen has become the very Demon of heaven; Scripture itself reveals her, and she is the true antitype of its types.[18] Yet the Mary of *Bothwell* also transcends Scripture, creating a new system of types centred on her own unstable will. Ironically, this heretical vision is provided by John Knox's sermon in Act IV, scene vii. After listing those who have loved the Queen to their ruin – Hamilton, Gordon, Chastelard, Rizzio, Darnley, and Bothwell himself, that antitype of Cain – Knox defines Mary, in a series of rhetorical questions, as the force which has created and organized the form and meaning of these doomed men's lives:

What were they but as shadows in the sun
Cast by her passing, or as thoughts that fled
Across her mind of evil, types and signs
Whereby to spell the secret of her soul
Writ by her hand in blood? What power had they,

What sense, what spirit, that was not given of her,
Or what significance or shape of life
Their act or purpose, formless else and void,
Save as her will and present force of her
Gave breath to them and likeness? (T3:183–8)

In this important passage, Mary appears at first as a Berkeleian divine mind, containing her lovers as the mind contains its passing thoughts. But this model of God's creation is promptly replaced by one more likely to be familiar to Knox: the model of the creator *ex nihilo* who appears in Genesis – who makes man in his likeness, and gives him breath. In both models, however, the Queen creates the "types and signs" through which she is revealed; her lovers are flickering shadows, men of clay animated by her power. The effect of the Berkeleian simile is to enlarge her, temporarily at least, so that she becomes the sole reality. But more striking still is her appearance as the source and significance of a typological system. If her creation were merely a demonic parody of God's creation, hers ought to have its apocalyptic counterpart; yet in Knox's sermon God exists only in opposition and in reaction to Mary's evil action. God is only the Accuser, the avenger of blood.

Knox's sermon is a closed circuit of rhetorical questions answered by Knox himself, and Mary's destructiveness provokes an equally destructive response from her subjects: "Fire for the murderess! cast her bones in the lake! / Burn, burn and drown!" (IV.vii, T3:192). The vicious circle of cruelty and avenging cruelty is personified in Mary Beaton, who will bring about Queen Mary's execution at the end of the trilogy in revenge for the execution of Chastelard. To the Queen, Beaton at the end of *Bothwell* is "a type ... and sign / Incognizable" (v.viii, T3:284). In time the "incognizable" significance of this ominous signifier will become determinate and cognizable; but that significance is determined entirely by Mary Stuart's actions and attitudes. All that Beaton does or is, then, is shaped and made meaningful by the Queen.

The typological system which Swinburne sketches around his central figure is not a stable structure of signs in accepted and traditional relationship, but an arrangement of events that become significant by shadowing forth the Queen's fluid "will and present force." Even Knox forgets that typology is created by God through the medium of history, and presents type and antitype as contemporaneous within a semiotics created by a strange deity. The system of typology becomes a symbolic system developed by a poet-wanton, a Whore who creates these symbols as mirrors to reveal to herself "the secret of her soul." She too must learn to read these symbols, learn to discover what she should "hope or fear to learn" from the types of which she is the antitype. She is a god in the process of self-discovery; as such she can be compared with the evolutionary Idealist deity of Neo-Hegelian philosophy. But she is also – and, in Swinburne's drama, more importantly – the simply human poet; man, or rather in this case woman, creates meaning.

Swinburne chooses to glorify the adulterous wife, and to deify the Great Whore, not only because of his personal devotion to "our Lady of Pain," but because the demonic element must be incorporated into the new deity; hell must be, not merely married to, but integrated with, heaven. For the instability of this woman-god's nature is the basis of the new typology; there is no more striking way of demonstrating the disappearance of the old order, which gives way now, not to a new order, but to a creative and destructive activity, perpetually trying to discover its own nature. By deifying the Whore, Swinburne announces the death of the old, Christian order; by allowing Knox (of all people) to show how Mary rearranges the typological system about herself, Swinburne shows that the new perception of meaning must be at once less time-bound and more fluid than Christian order. Swinburne detested Ibsen, and yet one might say that to Swinburne, the human mind is very like Nora in *A Doll's House:* a wilful wife determined on her own voyage of self-discovery. Mary Stuart shows us how the mind should slam the door on her heavenly Bridegroom.

CHAPTER TWO

The Sacrament of Violence

The value of the sacramental vision is twofold. It permits us to see the sacred by means of the ordinary; and by the same token it imbues the ordinary, the material, with at least a faint reflection of celestial light. The affinity of Keble's sacramentalism with Wordsworthian Romanticism lies chiefly in this sense of the world as an "organic whole charged with divine meaning";[1] the crucial difference between Keble and Wordsworth lies in Keble's failure to see how, for the early Wordsworth at least, the source of "celestial light" is problematic. The caution and uncertainty with which Wordsworth approaches the problem; the tendency, in such poems as the Intimations Ode, to present the individual human imagination as the source of meaning – these are wanting in Keble's Wordsworth. In *Natural Supernaturalism*, Meyer Abrams has shown how Wordsworth transforms the traditional Christian concept of Christ's marriage to His Church. The marriage of mind and nature, in the Prospectus to *The Recluse*, is endowed with all the apocalyptic harmony of the Lamb's wedding in Revelation; and through this new, quintessentially Romantic sacrament, we commune with the external world and shape the sacredness of "the common day" (Prospectus, 55). The instability of this marriage becomes the major theme of nineteenth-century poetry, and remains so long after Wordsworth withdraws to celebrate a more conventional union.

In Christian tradition the soul of the worshipper, or of the worshippers, is the Bride; in the Prospectus to *The Recluse*, as in Hölderlin's *Hyperion* and Shelley's *Prometheus Unbound*, the mind is the active Bridegroom.[2] Swinburne's androgynous god-whores at once embody and exaggerate this inconsistency between the two traditions; they are types of a Bride who proclaims her own autonomy and courts what she creates. And, just as the typological system becomes malleable in her hands, so too the sacraments are reshaped, reordered – made instruments of a new and infirm deity. She may invent a eucharist of murder, and make the sacramental union of marriage a Sadic wedding of victim and aggressor; she may undermine the sacramental vision and the principle of analogy, replacing them with a universe of magical identities and violent, pre-Derridean dissolutions.

Yet the divine whore – as emblem of the formidably free human imagination – does not spring full-grown from Swinburne's brain at the beginning of his rebellion against the Church. On the contrary, Swinburne begins by presenting humanity as the honourable child, or innocent gallant lover, of a world best figured by the murderous mother, or the queenly *femme fatale*. In *Atalanta* and *Poems and Ballads*, a pessimistic, anti-sacramentalist vision of language itself is one aspect of a broad and bitter pessimism: God and nature are formidably hostile. When we have understood this, we can properly assess the resonance of Swinburne's eucharists of murder, wherever they appear, and whether they are served by Christian priests or by a goddess who celebrates and consumes herself. We can also comprehend more fully the charges which Swinburne brings against the Christian vision, and against the language of the Church.

THE TRADITION OF BLASPHEMY

As the Venus of the Horselberg, the god-whore, triumphant rival of Christ, undermines not only Tannhäuser's morals but his faith in analogy as well. The knight rejects the meaning of the miracle which is the very centre of the legend as Christians have presented it:

> Yea, what if dried-up stems wax red and green,
> Shall that thing be which is not nor has been?
>   Yea, what if sapless bark wax green and white,
> Shall any good fruit grow upon my sin? ("Laus Veneris," P1:24)

Yet the rejection of analogy is only one aspect of Swinburne's attack on Christianity. Far more important to the early work is his ruthless exploitation of demonic parody; what is it that makes possible the apotheosis of the Whore? The answer may lie in the examples provided by Baudelaire and Sade. True, Baudelaire's "joyeuse Messe noire" of misers, jilts, critics, and sensualists[3] bears little resemblance to Swinburne's far more violent sacraments; for Baudelaire condemns the shabby hypocrisies of the world, and Swinburne the cruelty and violence of God, His Church, and His Creation. But Swinburne's interest in demonic parody seems to have been powerfully reinforced by Sade's monumental (if mechanical) endeavours to set Simeon Stylites on his head, and by Baudelaire's exaltation of dark parody, in "Les Litanies de Satan" – a lyric which Swinburne praised very highly – and in the first eleven stanzas of "L'Imprévu."

Sade, it is true, disappointed Swinburne. Misled by Dumas, Swinburne had hoped to find the great pornographer pursuing "l'idéal de l'esprit infini dans la torture de la matière bornée"; he found instead "a typical monk," "a very serious Simeon Stylites – in an inverted posture" (L1:55–8). Sade is concerned almost exclusively with "la matière bornée." Early in *Justine*, la Dubois avers that "il n'y a de vrai que les sensations physiques"; Coeur-de-Fer describes humans as "portions d'une matière vile et brute"; and Clément supplies the *reductio ad absurdum*: to shred a human body is only to make "d'une portion de matière oblongue … trois ou quatre mille rondes ou carrées."[4] As Mario Praz observes, Sade "empties his world of all psychological content except the pleasures of destruction and transgression, and moves in an opaque atmosphere of mere matter" (106). Sade's language is equally dominated by a concern with quantity, number, and extension rather than by emotion or sensory impression (as Clément's remark suggests). By contrast, Swinburne in *Atalanta* or "Anactoria" will evoke a universe of energy in flux, and of complex and intense emotion. "In the infinite spirit is room / For the pulse of an infinite pain" ("Satia te Sanguine," P1:87).

Yet Sade's most audacious reversals are seminal for the finest of Swinburne's early achievements. The world of infinite pain, presented in these early works, is clearly based on the Sadic vision as Swinburne understood it: "'Nature averse to crime? … it is by criminal things and deeds unnatural that nature works and moves and has her being … Friends, if we would be one with nature, let us continually do evil with our might. But what evil is here for us to do, where the whole body of things is evil?'" (WB 158n).

In "Anactoria" (1863–5), Sappho achieves a kind of harmony with this vicious nature, as she longs, in tormented cruelty, to devour her lover: "That I could drink thy veins as wine, and eat / Thy breasts like honey!" (111–12). Her denunciation of God's similar "melancholy lust," later in the poem (155–58), seems on the strength of the manuscript evidence to be an "after-thought," an interpolation; yet this passage is essential to the logic of the poem as a whole. Sappho is one of Swinburne's complex goddesses: terrible, yet human, vulnerable; victim as well as tormentor. On one hand, she shares God's cruelty; on the other, she suffers with the tormented natural world.[5] Like the yearning waters, she is "sick with time as these with ebb and flow" (225–7); the earth, she says, "Has pain like mine" (233–6); God has made her even as these natural objects which are "woven as raiment for his word and thought" (243–4). And her art, which will "waste" the days of men's lives "With gladness and much sadness and long love" (279–80), is similarly in harmony with a vicious heaven and a suffering earth. Even her triumphant immortality as a poet is a torment and a weariness; for the last ten lines of the poem lament that Sappho's fiery pain can never be allayed, "Till time wax faint in all his periods" (299). Art, love, the natural world, and all are miserably animated by what Swinburne in *Atalanta* calls "The supreme evil, God" (1151) – a formulation unmistakably recalling Sade's definition: "un être moral non créé; éternel, non périssable; ... le plus méchant, le plus féroce, le plus épouvantable de tous les êtres."[6] Swinburne's antitheistic pessimism is far subtler and more thoughtful than Sade's; yet, it is safe to assume that, without the stimulus of Sade's example, Swinburne's dark vision would never have reached its culmination in *Atalanta*, where a tortured mother-goddess reveals the most damaging powers of poetic language.

ATALANTA AND THE LANGUAGE OF DIVISION

For one word hath a heart of fire
And one the likeness of a lyre.[7]

Of all Swinburne's early works, *Atalanta in Calydon* is the most explicit in its analysis of language. The text is profoundly concerned with the nature and the powers of language; and Swinburne's strategies reinforce and develop his theory of "the word." Two major styles are employed in *Atalanta*. The first is soothing, rational, and expository, and is used by characters attempting to veil the irrational hostilities which motivate the tragedy. But this language betrays its own nature, and reveals itself at last as inconsistent. The second style expresses hostility, division, and pain more frankly, with a frightening lyrical vigour which recalls the very cadences of sacred language; for *Atalanta* reveals a god of pain and division, a "supreme evil" embodying the violence of time. However we name this god, our language, if it is to be accurate and expressive, must share in his divisive power: "words divide and rend" (1203). It is the chorus, "Who hath given man speech?" that most clearly defines the deity;

and a close analysis of other crucial passages within the text fully supports the sombre antitheism of the chorus. Degenerate versions of the detached Epicurean deities celebrated by Lucretius, Swinburne's "high gods" are as malicious as the gods of "The Lotos-Eaters," and more actively so. They "Lay hands" on the poison, "stir" it, "hold it to our lips and laugh" (1102-7). But the gods of Tennyson's poem seem to be merely projections of the lotos-eaters' irresponsibility; divine amorality conveniently justifies the mariners' self-indulgence. The Chorus of virgins in *Atalanta* seem to be more reliable than Tennyson's singers, however.[8] The antitheistic resentment of Swinburne's Chorus is not personally motivated, and the maidens qualify their flights of fancy cautiously. "For now we know not of them," they remark, after describing the gods' malicious activity (1130); and the "one" person whom they imagine attacking "The supreme evil, God" (1131, 1151) begins his polemical flight by crying, "When hast thou seen? ... / None hath beheld him, none / Seen" (1132-6). The maidens are equally agnostic in the third chorus, when they observe that they "know of" the disastrous effects of love, but that the goddess Love is beyond comprehension or description: "thee / Who shall discern or declare?" (827-8).

God, the "high gods," and Love are all personifications of the single dynamic force that destroys the protagonists: a force to be apprehended only through its hideous effects. Artemis too, "treble in [her] divided deity" (4), is an aspect of this force; so too is her brother Apollo, invited early in the play to "burn and break" (21). All the divided manifestations of destructive energy are unified by Swinburne's diction – by his use of such verbs as *rend, break,* and above all *divide*.[9] They are also united by the image of the consuming fire which finally divides Meleager ("For as keen ice divided of the sun / His limbs divide," 1989-90).[10] The implication is that our myths reveal the central truth of our experience, the disintegration which proceeds everywhere and always. We may well doubt the personality, the individual existence, of God or of gods; but there is no room for scepticism about the cruelty of life and change, the bitterness of mortality. According to Christianity, an incarnate deity has taken man's mortality upon himself to give mortals a share in immortality; the Lord's Supper reenacts or commemorates this divine sacrifice, in which the bread of life is broken and eaten. In *Atalanta*, this pattern is reversed. The "high gods" refuse the draught of time, lest they too should become mortal: "Therefore they thrust it from them, putting time away" (1114). Unwilling to "grieve as men, and like slain men be slain" (1129), they administer this poisonous wine to us alone; and, instead of God's descending into the material world to destroy and transfigure it, a figure arises in the material world to realize our worst dreams of the gods.

In a Greek tragedy, we would expect the presiding goddess (Artemis, in this case) to appear at the end – as Athena does in *Erechtheus* (*P*4:408–11) – placing the dramatic action in a theological or, at least, an ethical context. In *Atalanta*, however, the only theophany is achieved within a human's madness. After Althaea has heard of her brothers' murder at the hands of her son, the Chorus attempts to console her by describing the prenatal union between Meleager and herself, a union which they describe in eucharistic terms: the child eats and drinks his mother. They urge that this union should and must endure; Althaea points out that her son has already broken it, and presently (we assume; but there are no stage directions) goes to burn the brand that is identified with her son's life. The Chorus sings the ode to fate, and Althaea emerges raving, proclaiming herself divine ("You strong gods, ... I am as any of you") and declaring that she feeds on "flesh / Made of [her] body" (1864–5, 1870–1).

John O. Jordan truly describes this theophany as a "horrifying reversal" of the former "communion"; the mother devours her son in "a ritual of human sacrifice" more shocking than the infanticide in "The Witch-Mother." The shared identity of mother and child has now been explicitly "cloven apart" ("The Triumph of Time," *P*1:37) into two halves: man the victim and mother/God the devourer. Here, as elsewhere, Swinburne "helped prepare the age for *The Golden Bough*'s great mother goddesses and their ambivalent relationship to their worshippers."[11] But Althaea too is divided, "broken" (1508), "severed from [her]self" (1943), "a spoiler and a spoil, / A ruin ruinous" (1777–8) – Hertha collapsing in on herself. The Miltonic allusion in 1704 ("My spirit is strong against itself") prepares us for Althaea's suicidal murder, and for the Chorus's lament, "The house is broken" (1806): "O lastly over-strong against thyself! / A dreadful way thou took'st to thy revenge" (*Samson Agonistes*, 1590–1). But Althaea is neither liberator nor phoenix. If she is in harmony with nature, as she suggests in her apostrophe to the earth, nature itself is a vicious circle, a self-consuming ouroboros. And language – her language, and also the language of the Chorus – is equally sinister. For, directly or indirectly, all speech expresses the destroying power which, as we have seen, is the essential principle of *Atalanta's* universe; "words divide and rend" (1203).

Consider first the Chorus's description of the bond between mother and son:

Nay, for the son lies close about thine heart,
Full of thy milk, warm from thy womb, and drains

Life and the blood of life and all thy fruit,
Eats thee and drinks thee as who breaks bread and eats,
Treads wine and drinks, thyself, a sect of thee;
And if he feed not, shall not thy flesh faint?
Or drink not, are not thy lips dead for thirst?
This thing moves more than all things, even thy son,
That thou cleave to him; and he shall honour thee,
Thy womb that bare him and the breasts he knew,
Reverencing most for thy sake all his gods. (1676–86)

In the first and most famous chorus ("When the hounds of spring
are on winter's traces," 65–120), the maidens began by praising Artemis the chaste huntress, and ended by evoking an erotic hunt;
this, according to Mark Siegchrist, was the "first hint ... of the polarized self-contradiction of human life."[12] Now, again, their words
betray them. They seem to be describing a harmonious symbiotic
relationship, a love unalterable from the moment at which the child
begins to live in the womb. Yet, if we look more closely at the lines,
we find that their tendency is divisive. The child's effect on his
mother is described in purely negative terms: he drains, eats, drinks,
breaks, and treads her; but if he does not eat or drink she starves.
She depends on his eating her.

The Chorus's language reveals and conceals the secret violence in
the bond between mother and son. The violence is partly suppressed
by the evocation of comfort and affection at the beginning of the
passage ("*close* about thine heart," italics mine; "Full," "warm"). The
eucharistic metaphor, too, partly conceals its own violence, through
its venerable associations. The words *cleave* and *sect* contain a similar
duality. *Cleave*, in this context, means "adhere," but the verb has of
course a more sinister meaning ("divide"), employed in the account
of Meleager's kin-slaying (1543–4). The word *sect* implies at once
that Meleager is made out of Althaea and that he has already been
"cut away from her";[13] as the *OED* reads the line, he is in fact a
"cutting" ("Sect," *sb*.2), a plant separated from its original stem. This
separation Althaea recognizes, when she points out to the Chorus
that their conclusion in 1684–6 is inaccurate; far from honouring her
and "Reverencing ... all his gods," he has not revered "his gods nor
[Althaea's] own heart / Nor the old sweet years nor all venerable
things" (1688–9). The consequence of Meleager's independence is
expressed in Althaea's raving after she has burnt the brand:

Ho, ye that wail, and ye that sing, make way
Till I be come among you. Hide your tears,
Ye little weepers, and your laughing lips,

Ye laughers for a little; lo mine eyes
That outweep heaven at rainiest, and my mouth
That laughs as gods laugh at us. Fate's are we,
Yet fate is ours a breathing-space; yea, mine,
Fate is made mine for ever; he is my son,
My bedfellow, my brother. You strong gods,
Give place unto me; I am as any of you,
To give life and to take life. Thou, old earth,
That hast made man and unmade; thou whose mouth
Looks red from the eaten fruits of thine own womb;
Behold me with what lips upon what food
I feed and fill my body; even with flesh
Made of my body. Lo, the fire I lit
I burn with fire to quench it; yea, with flame
I burn up even the dust and ash thereof. (1856–73)

In the earlier passage, the lines move slowly, weighed down by
frequent spondees and trochees, and by a dense crowd of monosyllables; the heavy motion suggests the substantial presence of the
infant, the weight in the mother's womb. The Chorus uses the present tense, to persuade Althaea that Meleager's prenatal bond with
her still exists. Indeed, their mode of discourse throughout the passage is persuasive and conciliating, a mixture of rhetorical questions,
insinuating reminders and revisions of Althaea's experience, and
advice timidly expressed in a dependent clause and in the subjunctive ("That thou cleave to him"). And, though ponderous, the metrical motion is fairly smooth and formal; with one exception only, all
the lines are strongly end-stopped.

By contrast, Althaea's speech contains nine heavily marked caesuras and half-a-dozen enjambed lines, her passion tearing at the
barriers of metre; the blank verse is much more rapid and anapestic
than that of the earlier passage. Her assertions are equally abrupt
and violent, interspersed with commands and interjections. The
Chorus's favourite pronoun in the former passage is "thou" in all
its forms; Althaea apostrophizes heaven and earth only to display
herself in her apotheosis, using "I," "mine," "my," or "me" seven-
teen times (as opposed to ten instances of "ye," "you," "thou," or
"thine"), in the language of self-proclamation common to Hertha,
to Moses' God (Exod. 3.14), and to Krishna in the Bhagavad Gita.

Richard Mathews has suggested that the form of *Atalanta* contains
"a confusion which pits the lyric and dramatic elements against each
other much as man and woman or body and soul [are] contrasted
in the action of the play." Concomitant with this formal division is

a rhetorical differentiation between the lyrical "language of the soul, of dream or vision" and a "language of the body, ... of direct action"; Mathews associates these different styles with Northrop Frye's "rhythm of association" and "rhythm of decorum," respectively.[14] What we have seen so far is a rhetorical differentiation between two passages of blank verse, one persuasive and expository, one mythic, passionate, and self-proclamatory. Both contain the "sound-links" and "ambiguous sense-links" which Frye describes as characteristic of the lyrical "rhythm of association"; all Swinburne's poetry is lyrical in this sense. But in Althaea's speech we also find the other characteristics of this rhetoric: sacred paradox[15] and an "irregular, unpredictable, and essentially discontinuous rhythm," the oracular cadence of sacred literature.[16]

I propose to adapt Mathews's analysis as follows. The major rhetorical division within *Atalanta* is that between the mythic language of Althaea's speech and the persuasive discourse of the Chorus's earlier utterance. In the Queen's mythic vision, as we shall see, the tormenting oppositions of the world, "The violent symphonies that meet and kill" ("Genesis," P2:118), are vividly apparent. In the still lyrical but more rational and expository language of the Chorus, an undercurrent of violence remains – and we may note that it betrays itself in the Chorus's allusions to (Christian) religious ritual – but the maidens do create a superficial harmony, a frail vision of perfect union. (We should also notice that the two styles of *Atalanta* correspond to the two functions ascribed to poetic language, specifically, in Swinburne's early prose and poetry. Either words "strike," "sting," "burn their way in," as in the revelations vouchsafed through Sappho's verse and Blake's prophecies; or language is a decorative tissue clothing – or veiling – a "hideous violence," as in Baudelaire's "Une Martyre.")[17]

"Thy double word brings forth a double death," Althaea tells the Messenger (1492). Nature and the gods are "double," ambivalent, giving life and death both; thus when we contemplate any god primarily as the source of life, we deceive ourselves, and when we describe a world of order and unity we deceive others. The psychological counterpart of the world's doubleness is man's duplicity. Much of the dialogue in *Atalanta* is a tissue of lies, or, to put it more kindly, a web of inconsistencies. Althaea knows that the gods are ultimately hostile, as she tells the Chorus on her first appearance (148–60); yet, reasoning with Meleager, she tries to persuade him that sincere and upright behaviour will win divine blessing (466–76), only to contradict herself when she sees that reasoning is vain: "the gods love not justice more than fate, ... / And bruise the holier as the lying lips" (644–7). Her conventional speeches exemplify the "rhythm of decorum," gracious and futile, and also the language of "theological explanation";[18] when such "fair words" (569) and "wise words" (648) fail her, she turns to the "wild and windy words" (694) of passion, which are equally fruitless. The stately Landorian rhythms of her "wise words," with little enjambement and unobtrusive caesuras (see particularly 487–526), are echoed in the smoothness of the Chorus's eucharistic passage; in her "wild words," on the other hand, we find all the enjambement, heavy caesuras, interjections (such as "Lo"), and use of the imperative mood ("Fear thou the gods and me and thine own heart ... take thou thought," 683–99) which we observed in her murderous delirium.[19]

"The tragedy is Althaea's,"[20] and such marked stylistic duality does not characterize the speech of the other dramatis personae – with the exception, of course, of the Chorus. Yet there is inconsistency and self-contradiction in the utterances of Atalanta and Meleager. Atalanta, for instance, asks Artemis to make the day of the boar-hunt the "crown" of all Atalanta's days (893); a little later, she swears by the gods and her own body that she has no wish for "Crowns," or for "the spoil of slain things" (1010). This oath is hardly borne out by events, for she laughs and blushes when Meleager offers her the "spoil" (1522–32). Siegchrist indeed interprets her laughter as a sign that she has no serious interest in the spoil, but suggests it also contains "mysterious intimations" of a "transient vulnerability to love" which reappears later in the play, and which represents a "brief apostasy" from her earlier claims of whole-hearted devotion to Artemis (955–91).[21]

Meleager's inconsistency is more radical. He insists that he does not love Atalanta; he worships her (620–1). Yet he admits at the end that he has "loved" her (2294). Swinburne, associating with the Pre-Raphaelites, knew very well that erotic love is compatible with religious worship. At his death the hero calls for "a *Liebestod* as erotic as Wagner's": "stretch thyself upon me and touch hands / With hands and lips with lips" (2300–1).[22] When he asks Atalanta thus to veil his body (2298), the veil of his own unconscious duplicity is torn away. A still more drastic "doubleness" appears in Meleager's final attitude to Althaea, which in microcosm presents our true position vis-à-vis the gods (or the force that brings life and death). "Mother," he cries, "I dying ... / Hail thee as *holy* and worship thee as *just* / Who art *unjust* and *unholy*" (2220–2; my italics). Here antitimetabole is self-negation, meaning's suicide. As Peckham remarks in relation to this passage, Meleager's "cultural incoherence is never transcended. It is, in fact, only polarized" (291). The incoherence is theological, psychological, and verbal. Gods are, like Atalanta, "Adorable, detestable" (1694); Meleager's love for his mother and hatred for his slayer form an insoluble psychological dilemma; and his expression of that dilemma is a meaningless paradox, a piece of nonsense.

We have seen that much of the persuasive discourse in *Atalanta* is more or less consciously dishonest. In his provocative essay, "Swinburne's Semiotics," Leslie Brisman makes the gap between signifier and signified the central division of the play, the field of battle between Meleager and Althaea. God is the supreme evil "because He is the supreme metaphor, the word furthest from the object world," and yet the freedom that Meleager finds in the gap indicates a liberating "lordship over the world of sensate things" (592, 597). In fact, however, Swinburne's emphasis is less on a gap between words and things than on the senseless violence which is at the dark centre of nature and language both. For Swinburne, as for Baudelaire and Rimbaud, "the transcendence of God has reversed its polarity and has turned into a devouring darkness, the frightening reality of a positive rather than empty nothingness."[23]

Certainly a tragic gap exists between signifier and signified in the Chorus's eucharistic passage and in the persuasive rationalism of 466–568 (Althaea's "wise words" to Meleager). The kind of moral order that Althaea there evokes is hopelessly remote from the disorder of things as they are; the harmonious unity that the Chorus evokes through the image of the eucharist is equally remote from the union of victim and victimizer underlying that imagery. Yet this tragic gap between a verbal world of harmony and a world of disorder characterizes only one style in *Atalanta*. The alternative to such false soothing language is the savage lyrical-oracular verse that "hurts horribly," like the Gothic lyrical ballads sung in *Lesbia Brandon*. In these ballads, as the singer there remarks, words "get teeth and bite; they take fire and burn ... and hurt and delight" (*LB* 148). Such language incorporates the divisiveness of our experience. Meleager's nonsense presents the contradictions of his situation accurately; Althaea's delirium employs a "language of presence" which looks forward to Cassirer's analysis of the "mythical consciousness" for which "there is no such thing as *mere* mimesis, *mere* signification."[24] Consider, for example, these lines:

> Thou, old earth,
> That hast made man and unmade; thou whose mouth
> Looks red from the eaten fruits of thine own womb;
> Behold me ... (1866–9)

In line 1867, not only does the metre force a stress on the syllable *un-*, but also the anacoluthon closing the phrase, "made man and unmade," seems actually to unmake man; the syntactic blank is underlined by the caesura. "Man" has disappeared. The next phrase focuses on the image of earth's red "mouth," a combination of the particular and the mythic as strange and violent as that in 103–4: "the hoofèd heel of a satyr crushes / The chestnut-husk at the chestnut-root." There too the source and its fruit (the root and the husk) are connected by an act of destruction. But the impersonal and accidental quality of the satyr's crushing the chestnut-husk is absent from Althaea's speech. "Fruits" means literal fruit; it also refers, of course, to all that earth produces, all the children of Mother Earth (a reading enforced by Althaea's use of the word *womb*). And it also means achievement, the fruits of one's labour. When Althaea describes Meleager as her "fruit of life," her "travail" (1893–4), she uses "fruit" in both the second and the third senses; earth's travail, like Althaea's, is tragically frustrated by her infanticide. On the other hand, of course, earth's "mouth / Looks red," which implies that she is a vampire – again like Althaea, who sucks up vitality from her son's death ("my cheek is luminous with blood / Because his face is ashen," 1924–5). In Althaea's raving, the phrase, "To give life and to take life" (1866) means exactly what it says: to "give" life means to give some of it away; to "take" life is to take back that portion of vitality into oneself.

It is in this magical sense that Althaea seems to herself to devour Meleager. And her attitude to language is magical. The brand and Meleager's life are indistinguishable: *That is my son ... / Meleager, a fire enkindled of mine hands / And of mine hands extinguished; this is he*" (1893–6; italics mine). The exceptionally elaborate chiasmus emphasizes the hideous symmetry of this self-negation, while the ambiguity of the preposition *of* stresses the fact that this immolation is, indeed, a self-negation on Althaea's part (cp. 1769–70, "I ... / Slay mine own soul"). The brand is Meleager is Althaea, in a dark reversal of that "mystery of archetypal identity" later celebrated by Hopkins ("This Jack, joke, poor potsherd ... / Is immortal diamond").[25] Similarly, Althaea identifies her name with her nature: "My name that was a healing, it is changed, / My name is a consuming" (1944–5).

Here is no gap between words and things. At the same time, verbal magic is not omnipotent. In the height of her delirium, Althaea's emotional division is exaggerated to cosmic proportions: "lo mine eyes / That outweep heaven at rainiest, and my mouth / That laughs as gods laugh at us" (1859–61). The polarities of "delight and grief," which will be partially resolved in "On the Cliffs," are wholly irresoluble in *Atalanta*; indeed, just as the queen's mythic vision presents only a tormentingly vivid image of earth's bestial cruelty, so her lyrical and oracular style "restores," as Brisman puts it, "the energy and violence of language as the energy and violence of nature" (585). Swinburne extends this theme to its limits in his demonic parody of those central concepts of the Christian word: the Logos and the Gospel.

In *Atalanta*, "Good news" involves the announcement of death (the boar's) which is to bring forth a further death: "Fetch sacrifice and slay," Althaea cries gaily, "for heaven is good" (1219, 1229). All the ironic implications of this message-scene are fully realized in the next, as the Messenger brings word of the brothers' death: "A little word may hold so great mischance" (1514) and produce more; as Althaea remarks punningly, "Thy double word [ambiguous message] brings forth a double death [the death of the brothers and the death of Althaea's joy in her son; the death of Meleager, and that of Althaea]" (1492). "[I]n the word," as the Chorus has already pointed out, man's "life is and his breath, / And in the word his death" (1040–1). The "word" in this sense is the opposite of the Logos (the Word which is life and God, John 1.1–4) and of the Gospel (the good news that Christ has died to give us life). And as the Logos represents that reasonable order which in Stoic thought is the essential structure of the universe, this anti-Logos represents the disorder and incoherence which constitute the real structure of the world (or so Swinburne seems to assume at this point). Again, as the Gospel recounts the saving intervention of the compassionate Word, the news of Swinburne's Messenger describes the destructive action of "vain and violent words, / Fruitless" (1549–50).[26]

The Messenger reports the objectification in deed of what has already been made explicit in words. The first half of the play consists largely of a series of confrontations, in which each character defines his or her opinions in opposition to the views of others. And such confrontations usually spring out of an expression of worship. The Chorus's hymn to Artemis makes Althaea snap, "What do ye singing? what is this ye sing?" (121), and she rebukes their sentimental concept of deity (122–82); Atalanta's less orthodox homage to Artemis and Meleager's semi-erotic reverence for Atalanta irritate Althaea and her brothers into proclaiming their own (more conventional) principles of worship (972–5, 906–16, 454–63, 932–50).

Praise of her/his gods, a form of self-definition, increasingly divides each character from the rest. But all articulate speech is a kind of definition, a making of boundaries and of ends (*de* + *finire*). Althaea remembers her son as an infant, when he "moaned / With inarticulate mouth inseparate words" (272–3); but the disastrous coming of Love is applauded by men "that hear / Sweet articulate words / Sweetly divided apart" (750–2). The superfluous adverb "apart" underlines the separation inherent in meaningful language, which must distinguish concept from concept. Yet one might protest that "articulate" also implies a putting together; syntax is after all the arrangement of words in such a way as to show their logical connection. In a sense, any meaningful sentence is a Hegelian synthesis.

Yet there is nothing in *Atalanta* to suggest that language makes it possible for us to triumph in any way over the contradictions about us and within us, the universe that Mathews has described as "an almost Hegelian world of thesis and antithesis, where synthesis is never reached" (48, 35). Althaea, whose mastery over words is generally acknowledged (569–77), falls into silence; Meleager's language collapses into nonsense; Atalanta and the Chorus take refuge in a laconic impersonality (2310–17). The author's pessimism in regard to language seems almost to match his pessimism in other respects. The word is another fatal mother (1043), divisive, a "burning fire" (354). It is the fourth chorus ("Who hath given man speech?") that expresses pessimism most memorably: death is time's brother,

> imperishable as he
> Is perishable and plaintive, clothed with care
>   And mutable as sand,
> But death is strong and full of blood and fair
> And perdurable ... (1047–51)

Here is no such balance of forces as Dylan Thomas evokes in his memorable oxymorons ("green age," "green and dying"). Destruction and division outweigh, or, rather, half corrupt the spring revels of the first chorus. Thus even repetition, apparently a unifying device, may at times signal a drifting apart, as in the Chorus's list of the effects of Love: the "breaking of city by city; / The dividing of friend against friend, / The severing of brother and brother" (838–40). As in the case of Althaea and her son, it is the destruction of love by Love, of affection by passion, that is most poignant. Again, the music of the play provides an apparent unity of mellifluous effect, yet the metrical variations of the choruses are sometimes unsettling (and would have been more so to an educated Victorian audience, accustomed to the symmetry of the Greek chorus). Moreover, the phonetic effects suggest that process of transformation which is central to the tragedy.

Consider, for instance, Swinburne's use of alliterative assonances. We have already seen *warm/womb* and *food/feed* (1677, 1869–70); the play also contains *burn/bone, fields/folds, saying/seeing* (139, 1826, 1268–9), and more, including a cluster of such pairs in the first chorus (*rains/ruins, fresh/flushes, trammel/travelling, fleet/foot* – 89, 99, 98, 106). The crucial example, which directs our reaction to all the others, is of course *flower/fire*, as in Althaea's prophetic dream of her son's death: "I ... saw the black brand burst on *fire* / As a branch bursts in *flower*" (284–5; italics mine). The identity of growth and death is heavily underlined by the *b*-alliteration, the assonance of "brand" and "branch," and the repetition of "burst"; only the change in sound and sense from *fire* to *flower* suggests the tragic difference – to humanity – between the force that melts and consumes and the energy that gives life. It is the difference between the mother from whom her child "drains / Life ... and all [the mother's] fruit" (1677–8), and the mother who burns her child and devours him. But the mother is one and the same.

Language is one more manifestation of the self-negating force revealed in the processes of nature. As there are "moans" in the "bridal measure" (1067), so in the only cheerful choruses are references to "Orion overthrown" (1465), to the arrows of Artemis (73), to feeding and crushing and pursuing (97; 103; 65, 105–20). In a temporal world anticipation and memory darken the happiest songs and the brightest months; "Spring shall be ruined with the rain" (131), and the singing-bird is only "half assuaged" for the slaughtered child (69–70). In a world of aggression and flight, language provides a treacherous weapon (931), an instrument of self-destruction (1029–30, 1201–2). In a world of disorder, persuasive language may create a limited order – "with charmed words and songs have men put out / Wild evil, and the fire of tyrannies" – but words cannot control or extinguish the essential forces of disorder, "the gods and love" (451–3). Only the most intensely lyrical language, the poetry of dream and delirium, can effectively convey the incoherence and disorder of a disintegrating world; and such language is painful to utter, even self-destructive. "Verse hurts horribly: people have died of verse-making, and thought their mistresses killed them – or their reviewers" (*LB* 148). Althaea puts it more simply: "I say this and I die" (1898). And at the end Althaea is silent, while the other main characters and the Chorus take part in an elaborate ritual of lamentation, a glittering mourning-veil flung over "all the pain" (72) and all the hopeless divisions.

THE SWINBURNEAN EUCHARIST

As Althaea's language incorporates the divisive power of a world of pain, so, as we have seen, the image of the eucharist itself can be inverted, in such a way that it presents a god's devouring of human happiness. But Swinburne can do stranger things than this with the sacramental rite. Another glance at *Bothwell* helps us to see the radical freedom with which Swinburne approaches the sacrament of communion. The eucharistic imagery in this drama is extraordinarily fluid, depending for its significance on the shifting, brilliant force that is the Queen. Her moods and her unique experience determine the meaning of the sacrament; resenting Knox's "inquisition" into her marital relationship with Darnley, she can ask if she must "let the common mouth communicate / In [her] life's sweet or bitter sacrament, / The wine poured, the bread broken every day" (*T*2:230). She converts the eucharist to her use as she does all other things: "doubt itself and danger are as food / To strengthen and bright wine to quicken me" (*T*2:294). After her escape from Lochleven, she is intoxicated by the "great drink of freedom; O, such wine / As fills man full of heaven, and in his veins / Becomes the blood of gods" (*T*3:273). This transubstantiation shows how Mary's "divine" power depends on, and reveals, her unscrupulous freedom. A stronger Lady Macbeth, she tempts Bothwell to kill Darnley: "Who would eat bread must earn bread: would you be / King?" (*T*2:325, 383). Bothwell and his victim eat and drink their own ruin, which Mary administers to them as the priest administers the eucharist. Yet she transcends to some extent the mutual destruction she instigates, and feeds alone on nature, danger, and freedom, which image her and display her to herself: a goddess, not self-consuming, but self-nourishing; a "Sun kindling heaven and hell" ("Adieux à Marie Stuart," *P*5:263); a fiery energy that creates and imparts significance. At the end of the Stuart trilogy the murderess, conspirator, and heroine successfully reshapes even the crown of martyrdom to fit her; her Last Supper (*Mary Stuart*, *T*4:195–6) is an impudent creation of transient harmony in the face of her defeat and just doom.

Yet the sacrament in Swinburne's work is more malleable, more wildly diverse, than even Mary can conceive. No less than four major groups of eucharistic imagery can be distinguished in Swinburne's poetry. Contained in the first group are images relating the Eucharist to conspiracy, murder, cannibalism, and vampirism; in the Stuart trilogy Darnley's vision of Mary supplies the greater part of such associations. In his symbolic dream, Mary gives Darnley the food of death; earlier, in *Chastelard*, her Catholic practice becomes an emblem of her divine cruelty. "[Y]ou ... eat holiness," Darnley tells her, "Put God under your tongue and feed on heaven, / ... / And look as though you stood and saw men slain / To make you game and laughter" (*T2*:108).[27] It is not surprising that the second group of eucharistic images, presenting the sacrament of Eros, develops simultaneously with the first group. Erotic and murderous sacraments appear throughout the tragedies; thus the vindictive wife administering a fatal eucharist is the central figure in *Rosamond*, *Bothwell*, and *Rosamund, Queen of the Lombards*, composed in 1858–60, 1871–74, and 1899, respectively. But within the lyrical work such frankly blasphemous eucharists are restricted, almost entirely, to Swinburne's early period.

Just as the sacrament of murder develops side by side with the sacrament of love from the very beginning of Swinburne's poetic career, so the third and fourth groups of eucharistic imagery evolve together. The eucharist of political and social union appears first in *A Song of Italy* (published 1867), and is used for the last time in *Marino Faliero* (1885); the eucharist of art develops from *William Blake* (also published in 1867) to *A Study of Victor Hugo* (1886).[28] These two groups have much in common, as might be supposed from their simultaneous development: in both the eucharist transmits a saving freedom, political or spiritual. In the aesthetic or Apollonian eucharist, of course, the sacramental power is the poetic imagination, while in the political eucharist that power is republican ardour, the divine grace communicated by freedom's martyrs.

Always, however, the poet controls the implications of his imagery very tightly, so tightly that his eucharists effectively criticize the conventions they exploit. The images of the third and fourth groups become progressively less concrete and more drastically reductive, as Swinburne tends more and more toward a (sceptical) idealism; and after the mid-eighties (when his scepticism begins to outweigh his idealism) the eucharist disappears from Swinburne's lyrical work almost entirely, as sacramentalism itself ceases to be a serious concern.

In his earliest works of importance Swinburne presents the world as a closed circuit of destruction, and Christianity as an imperfect revelation – and celebration – of that world; imperfect, because it purports to reveal the love of the self-sacrificing Lamb (just as Mary Stuart, in *Chastelard*, hypocritically pretends to be ready to die for her lover). At the same time, certain Christian views and symbolic patterns are inherently violent, and thus in harmony with nature. In the remainder of this chapter, I propose to show how, employing the sacrament of violence, Swinburne demonstrates this point and elaborates on it. In the following chapter, I explain how he uses the erotic, republican, and Apollonian eucharists to sanctify the various religious attitudes which he presents as alternatives to Christianity. His development first toward and finally away from idealism, which will be charted in more detail in the later chapters, can be traced through the complex evolution of his eucharistic imagery.

THE EUCHARIST OF MURDER

Swinburne's use of eucharistic imagery in a secular context is in itself a defiance of conventional piety, at a time when Tennyson and Dante Gabriel Rossetti altered or expunged their secular eucharists for fear of the public.[29] But his constant creation and re-creation of a murderous Black Mass constitute a radical attack on Victorian sensibilities. Since his negative eucharists are often set in a Roman Catholic context, his explicit references to the Roman doctrine of transubstantiation intensify the blasphemous effect. In *The Queen-Mother* (1858–60), for instance, the Fool threatens to give Huguenots a "sacrament of eye-water and rye-bread / Changed to mere foolish flesh and blood to sup" (*T*1:10). Like so much else in this early play, this joking is not clearly focused; if it is meant to suggest that the Huguenots' troubles and tears will be forgotten in the coming massacre (on St Bartholomew's Day), the conceit seems a little strained. In *Rosamond*, composed concurrently with *The Queen-Mother*, the Fool's eucharistic allusions are more carefully harmonized with the main thrust of the tragedy as a whole.

"The devil kissed me / Mouth on mouth ... / He gave me black wine and sweet / Red fruit and honey-meal to eat" (*T*1:245). While the Fool chants this frivolous mixture of sensuality, diabolism, and nonsense, Eleanor and her accomplice toy with the notion of murdering Rosamond. The connection thus plainly established between sensuality and cruelty is made again, yet more explicitly, in *Chastelard*; Darnley makes the point memorably, by placing it within the context of a brutally materialistic reference to the Mass. Mary's Catholic piety is a pitifully thin disguise for her sadistic lust; indeed, the Protestant jibe contained in the phrase, "Put God under your tongue," suggests not only that the reception of the Host is a ritual debasingly sensuous rather than spiritual in content, but also that Mary can exploit religion in her speech for her own savage purposes.

Swinburne makes these points with insolent bravura, but none of them is very original. Something much more interesting is happen-

ing in one or two of the literary ballads that he wrote during the
composition of these tragedies: for instance, in "The Sea-Swallows,"
an imperfect but haunting work, imagery suggestive of the eucharist
is used to underline the absence of any real communion in the
characters' bleak lives. The refrains which do most to unify the ballad
formally are expressions of division and fruitlessness. The second
burden ("The ways are sair fra' the Till to the Tyne") evokes a painful
separation; the first ("Red rose leaves will never make wine") is
expanded in the third stanza, where it implies that sexual delight is
fruitless and creates no enduring bond, nothing that will nourish or
sustain life:

> Blossom of broom will never make bread,
>   Red rose leaves will never make wine ...
>   (9–10 [my line-enumeration], P1:288–90)

Broom and roses commonly have sexual connotations in Swinburne's ballads. The lovers' intercourse bears fruit in one sense –
the woman bears a child – but she gives birth alone, in the absence
of all traditional signs of community: her "bearing-bread" is grass,
her "washing-wine" water (45–6). The male lover disappears from
the poem after the second stanza, and the interest shifts from the
lovers' relationship to the reaction of the woman's father. This pattern suggests that the ballad may be intended as a Pre-Raphaelite
revision of Blake's "A Little Girl Lost": in both works, moreover,
the lovers are associated with an idyllic natural world (Blake's "sunny
beams," garden, and grass; Swinburne's rowan, grass, broom, rose
leaves, and water); in both, the lovers' meeting and the woman's
confrontation with her father are presented with the minimum of
explanation by the narrator; and both poems end with the father's
expression of dismay and misery. But Blake's narrator makes the
moral of the tale obtrusively explicit:

> Children of the future Age,
> Reading this indignant page;
> Know that in a former time.
> Love! sweet Love! was thought a crime.[30]

This directive to the reader is very different, both in manner and
in content, from Swinburne's hints that erotic passion is fruitless
and full of pain. The paternal figure in Blake is both representative
and victim of religious morality: his glance, "Like the holy book,"
makes Ona tremble, while he himself is shaken by his own "trem-

bling fear" and "dismal care" (27–34). The father in Swinburne's ballad is far more sinister and vindictive, although he too is a victim: it seems that he will murder his illegitimate grandson and then die of grief. In Luke 11.11 Christ asks, "If a son shall ask bread of any of you that is a father, will he give him a stone? or if he ask a fish, will he ... give him a serpent?" The function of this rhetorical question is to persuade the audience, by analogy, that God the Father will give good things to his children who pray to him. But the father in "The Sea-Swallows" offers his grandson "'Fen-water and adder's meat'" for food (19); in opposition to the father of Christ's rhetorical question, this figure would seem to be a living disproof of God's love.

Yet we should not place too great a burden of meaning on a poem which drifts so uncertainly in the space between Symbolist composition and melodramatic narrative. The reference to Christmas and Easter lights in the first stanza, the echoes of Luke 11.11 and (in l.63) of Prov. 28.10, and above all the parallels between Swinburne's ballad and "A Little Girl Lost," all suggest that Swinburne may be using the violence conventional in the ballad to make a serious point about the cruelty inherent in love, in the cult of family honour, and in religious morality; and yet "The Sea-Swallows" carefully calls attention, not to the moral implications of its central action, but to its own atmosphere. The refrain, "Red rose leaves will never make wine," filled with liquids, nasals, breathed sibilants and semivowels, inbues the bleak tale with an air of sad luxury, a decorative and self-indulgent melancholy; while the poem as a whole turns inward at the end to contemplate a mysterious guilt ("'For the pit I made has taken me,'" 63), establishing no communion between reader and narrator, and taking upon itself a fatal, fruitless beauty.

Swinburne has not yet learned to deal with the tension between the decorative poetic language of his Pre-Raphaelite circle and the violent disharmony of both nature and society, as he perceives them at this period. In "The Witch-Mother," another ballad (sung by the formidable heroine of Lesbia Brandon), he solves the problem as Morris does, by using a plainer and more archaic language:

Says – Eat your fill of your flesh, my lord,
  And drink your fill of your wine;
For a' thing's yours and only yours,
  That has been yours and mine.

Says – Drink your fill of your wine, my lord,
  And eat your fill of your bread ... (LB 147–8)

As the wine and bread here are the blood and flesh of the children, slain by their mother and fed to their father, the eucharistic allusion suggested by "wine" and "bread" is overborne by the more obvious reference to Procne and Medea. The passage is less a demonic parody of the eucharist than a reconstruction of pagan cruelty, as the ballad-singer's comments to her own children suggest: "'she killed them, Ethel, both, and put their blood in a little brass dish ... with the blood of a little white chicken, like you: and of a grey pigeon, like Rosamond; and of a yellow kite, like Cecil'" (*LB* 147).

After reading Sade and Baudelaire in 1862, Swinburne's demonic parodies gain startlingly in audacity, and in pointed hostility to Christian sentiment. We have seen the results in *Atalanta*; a text more closely tied to Sade is "Dolores" (1865; *P*1:154–68), that comic mixture of priapic paganism and demonic parody. "Our Lady of Pain" presides over a eucharist of wine made from the foam and froth of pleasure's serpents; the speaker, Dolores' lover and worshipper, serves her and celebrates her as both priest and congregation:

> All thine the last wine that I pour is,
>   The last in the chalice we drain,
> O fierce and luxurious Dolores,
>   Our Lady of Pain. (133–6)

The "new wine of desire" is also the final wine of death, and the "wine shed for me" is in no way redemptive; it only gives power to "cozen / The gods," to cheat them by snatching perverse delight and amusement from the sterile doom of "marriage and death and division" (137–60). Dolores is a mockery of Christ and of his mother, and also of the Church, the Bride of Christ. She is not a "garden inclosed" like the Bride in the Song of Solomon (4.12), but a "garden where all men may dwell" (18); and the tower of ivory, the strength and beauty of the sacred Bride (Song of Sol. 7.4), becomes a Tower of Babel, a type of the presumption which in Gen. 11.3–9 is foiled, but in "Dolores" succeeds: "O tower not of ivory, but builded / By hands that reach heaven from hell" (19–20). Whereas the wanton goddess "Astarte or Ashtaroth" (410) was degraded to mere Whore in the Judaeo-Christian system, the Whore's divinity is now restored to her; and yet it is impossible to take her very seriously, because the poet is burlesquing his own technique. "Dolores" is a black joke, a frivolous offshoot from *Chastelard* and *Atalanta*.

It is in *Songs before Sunrise* that the eucharist of murder is first employed, seriously and specifically, as a rhetorical weapon against the Church. In *Atalanta*, as I have explained at length, pessimism is independent of metaphysics; the world's cruelty continues whether the gods exist or not. In *Songs before Sunrise*, the God whom the speaker denounces is a damaging fiction, a demonic parody of the true Man-God. This volume of political lyrics retains the biblical pattern of sacred original and demonic parody: republican Man is a living and organic heavenly Jerusalem, and the communion of Freedom's enemies is a savage distortion of the true communion which will be achieved when God, king, and priest are thrown down. Thus in "Siena," for instance, political oppression is described in terms of a cannibalistic eucharist-in-reverse ("And one had hunger and is fed / Full of the flesh of these, and red / With blood of these as who drinks wine," *P*2:163), whereas Italy in her political cruci-fixion sheds blood that is a "bitter blessing" to her worshippers (*P*2:168–9). Italy is both Christ and the Virgin, "the true maiden-mother, slain / And raised again" to unite God and man; when her work is done, Time will "Lead the Republic as a bride / Up to God's side" (*P*2:169–70). This vision of apocalyptic harmony appropriately concludes a poem in which the symbols of Christianity appear to be appropriate instruments for a liberal "stump-orator."[31]

Swinburne does not always find the Christian mythos an adequate vehicle for the expression of republican truth; in "Before a Crucifix," indeed, he tests it and finds it wanting. Apostrophizing Christ, he says, "Thy blood the priests make poison of"; the Church is a leprous "bride / Whose kissing lips ... / Leave their God rotten to the bone" (*P*2:86–7; cp. the snake's kiss in the "Hymn of Man"). But he con-tinues to present Christianity as a demonic parody of true religion; thus in the last canto of *Tristram of Lyonesse* we glimpse Truth's "radiant feet ... / Trampling the head of Fear, the false high priest, / Whose broken chalice foams with blood no more," while "The miscreation of [Fear's] miscreant God" cowers overthrown on the "chancel floor." A popular type, the bruising of the serpent's head,[32] is simply transferred to Truth, that "God ... unimaginable of man," while the Christian deity is recast as the demonic serpent, "That shade accursed and worshipped, which hath made / The soul of man that brought it forth a shade ... blood-saturate as its Lord" (*P*4:135–6).

In "Siena" and *Tristram* the demonic eucharist is described in terms which suggest cannibalism or vampirism; we have seen that Al-thaea's eucharist-in-reverse is cannibalistic, but the earliest poem directly linking Christianity to cannibalism is, of course, the Cannibal Catechism, composed c. 1863 for the Cannibal Club. This coarse but exuberant imitation of "Holy Willie's Prayer" satirically celebrates a god "whose meat and drink is flesh in pies / And blood in bowls";

but the ironic focus of the poem wavers from the materialism and barbarous violence inherent in the Eucharist to the doctrines of Election and of Hell and at last, somewhat bathetically, to teetotalism. The Cannibal Catechism is insignificant as literature, but it indicates the kind of joking in which Swinburne probably indulged with Thomas Bendyshe, Richard Burton, and other atheistic members of the club, and it pinpoints the frivolous origin of what becomes a serious argument in Swinburne's anti-Christian polemics.

B y connecting the Eucharist with cannibalism, Swinburne can make the concept of transubstantiation, in particular, seem repellently and barbarously materialistic. We must not confuse the materialistic with the physical: Mary's eucharist of freedom in *Bothwell* is partly physical, since liberty "Becomes the blood of gods" in human "veins," making body and soul divine. But part of Swinburne's definition of freedom is the harmonious union of body with soul in such a manner as to prevent the former from controlling the latter; the diabolical deity of his anti-Christian polemic is the emblem of our fearful bondage to "things," our undue emphasis on the physical, and it is this emphasis which Swinburne calls materialism. The degree to which these assumptions became habitual with him may be seen in his casual comment on the Jenkins case in 1875: "I hope your religious feelings are as much relieved and gratified as my own by the judicial decision forbidding any (so-called) Christian who does not believe in the Devil to eat his God in peace. Qu. [*sic*] would the exalted privilege of theophagy be conceded to a believer in the identity of those two Beings?" (*L*3:49).

Five years later, reviewing Victor Hugo's *Religions et Religion*, Swinburne interpreted that work, with obvious approval, as "an impeachment of all mere materialism," "the militant materialism of Papists and Positivists" both, but chiefly of the former, with their creed "based on deicide and sustained on theophagy." Christianity is "the worst ... surviving form of materialism in the whole world"; "it is implicitly impossible to be a Christian without being a materialist" (*B*13:196–8). Swinburne distorts Hugo's argument slightly – the French poet seems in fact to view scientific materialism as a more dangerous enemy to true religion than orthodox Christianity – but certainly Hugo does attack the tendency in popular religion to adapt infinite deity to our own comprehension: "Il nous le faut visible, il nous le faut mangeable ... / Rénonce, ver de terre, à créer le soleil."[33]

Not only is the Eucharist coarsely materialistic; it represents a cruelty and a meaninglessness which, Swinburne implies, are built into the structure of Christian society. In *Marino Faliero* (1885), no Venetian can avoid "Communion in one sacrament of shame," "the wine of wrong, / The bread of outrage" (*T*5:320). There is a eucharist of Christian violence in the play; there is no eucharist of republican harmony. The Real Presence of immediate evil is equally powerful in *The Tale of Balen* (1896), where the eucharist becomes the symbol of senseless violence. Here Swinburne deliberately departs from his source, Malory, by adding passages which stress the injustice of this world and the emptiness of the next. For example, Balen's virgin companion offers her "stainless" blood to heal a sick woman; yet her altruism does not succeed, as it might, says Swinburne, "Were God's grace helpfuller" (*P*4:204–5). Immediately after this incident, Balen attempts to heal his host's son, and ends by dealing the "dolorous stroke" that ruins "three countries" (*P*4:213). Swinburne takes this opportunity to underline the implied contrast between the Christian scheme of salvation through Christ's blood, and the futile bloodshed which, in *Balen*, seems to be the sole political reality.

> For in that chamber's wondrous shrine
> Was part of Christ's own blood, *the wine*
> *Shed of the true triumphal vine*
> *Whose growth bids earth's deep darkness shine*
>   *As heaven's deep light through the air and sea;*
> That *mystery* toward our northern shore
> Arimathean Joseph bore
> *For healing of our sins of yore,*
>   *That grace even there might be.* (*P*4:213)

The portions I have italicized are Swinburne's additions; and the point of these additions lies in their irrelevance to Balen's situation.[34] The healing supposedly brought by Christ cannot be achieved; Christ makes darkness bright, but Balen and his brother in the next canto pour and drink "the draught of death" in a place "Where darkness cast[s] out light."[35] Their fratricidal combat recalls the destructive universe of *Atalanta*; but the violence they do and suffer is not theirs; they are the innocent puppets of a savage society and of its false God. Joseph of Arimathea brought the Grail and the Lance into Britain "That grace even there might be"; yet the Christian God has no grace for Balen and Balan: "God's own grace / Forsook them" (*P*4:255). The only grace accorded them is a function of Romantic memory: "death's requickening eucharist" restores to Balen the Real Presence of the past. "He drank the draught of life's first wine / Again," and the memory of his childhood "Fulfilled his death with joy"; so, "dying not as a coward that ... dares not look in death's dim eyes," he views the flux and reflux of life steadily, and expects no resurrection (P4:231–2).

The balanced violence of *Balen* appears again in *Rosamund, Queen of the Lombards*, published three years later (1899). Here the eponymous heroine is a spirit of vengeance rather than a character. Her husband, Albovine, forces her to drink from her father's skull at a feast; she complies with secret fury, and later asks him to drink from the same skull at another feast, with her, as a "sign / Of perfect plight in love and union"; this "sacramental draught of love," she avers, will seal their "eucharist of wedlock" (T5:443–4). She forces Albovine's loyal servant to murder him at the second feast, and drinks poison from the skull herself. More than one character identifies Rosamund with God, or with a diabolical God (T5:444, 431–3); but in this tragedy the only god is the law, or symmetrical violence, of action and reaction. Albovine pays for his cruelty with death; so too does Rosamund, crying that all but she and he are innocent. The catastrophe is cathartic, ending in forgiveness (Rosamund's antimetabole suggests a real, if melancholy, harmony in death) and calm of mind: she dies saying, "I pardon thee, my husband: pardon me," and the old councillor Narsetes adds, "Let none make moan. This doom is none of man's" (T5:451).

The world of the late tragedies and of *Balen* is one in which Christianity, working in association with the social order, maintains a reciprocity of violence, symbolized by the demonic eucharist. There is no demon of heaven to fire the whole natural order with pain and cruelty, as in *Atalanta*; and, though the Christian fiction does sufficient harm, it is possible for Swinburne's heroes and heroines to win a limited victory over it: they can die, at least, in the dignity of hope, or memory, or reconciliation. But the language of Christianity adds nothing to such dignity; on the contrary, the sacramental imagery in *Rosamund*, and through most of *Balen*, underlines the tragic pointlessness of the action. It is, however, in Swinburne's last (incomplete) tragedy – *The Duke of Gandia* (composed 1902; published 1908) – that religious language is most ruthlessly criticized.

Intellectually, the play turns on the tension between Caesar Borgia's cold scepticism and his father's superstition. Pope Alexander cannot convince himself that religious language is empty; on the contrary, Caesar's fratricide seems to the Pope to prove God's horrible reality: "O God! Thou livest! And my child is dead!" (B10:402–3. For Caesar, on the other hand, the Eucharist affords a sufficient proof that God is not.

> ... [B]ethink thee what a world to wield
> The eternal God hath given into thine hands

Which daily mould him out of bread, and give
His kneaded flesh to feed on. (B10:406)

"The baker made him," as Lady Jane Grey observed. But, unlike her, Caesar has no more spiritual God to put in place of the Host. He insists that God bade Francesco die, "if God / Be more than what we make him," and the hypothetical clause is contemptuously dismissive (B10:408). God lives on the Pope's lips, he says, and withers in Alexander's silence (B10:394). Caesar finds Christian dogma and symbolism meaningless; in the course of two short scenes, he contrives to sneer at the doctrines of the Immaculate Conception, Papal Infallibility, Providence, priestly absolution, the Harrowing of Hell, the Trinity, effectual prayer, Transubstantiation,[36] and the Atonement:

Was not God – the God of love, who bade
His son be man because he hated man,
And saw him scourged and hanging, and at last
Forgave the sin wherewith he had stamped us, seeing
So fair a full atonement ...? (B10:387)

Swinburne is obviously reworking the speech Hugo had ironically attributed to God in *Religions et Religion*:

– J'ai, jadis, dans un lieu charmant et bien choisi
Mis la première femme avec le premier homme;
Ils ont mangé, malgré ma défense, une pomme;
C'est pourquoi je punis les hommes à jamais.
....
Rien de plus juste. Mais, comme je suis très bon,
Cela m'afflige. Hélas! comment faire? Une idée!
Je vais leur envoyer mon fils dans la Judée;
Ils le tueront. Alors, – c'est pourquoi j'y consens, –
Ayant commis un crime, ils seront innocents.
Leur voyant ainsi faire une faute complète,
Je leur pardonnerai celle qu'ils n'ont pas faite ...[37]

Appropriately, within the context of the Pope's anguish, Swinburne shifts the emphasis from human morality to the feelings of the Father; but the presentation of the Atonement as a logical non sequitur is entirely in Hugo's manner. Caesar's jibes at Christian dogma are in harmony with Swinburne's views at this period.

I am thinking of making public the account of a private mission to the JAH-JAH (pronounced Yah, Yah. 'Praise him in his name JAH') Islands, whose degraded inhabitants worship a three-headed, six-armed ... idol, emblematic of a God consisting of a father and a son of the same age and a tertium quid represented also as a very old pigeon. The identity of age between a father and a son does seem something too unspeakable to be a professed article of faith even among a tribe of inarticulate gorillas. And yet these poor degraded wretches profess to believe it – as also that the 'coeternal son' (as their barbarous jargon goes) once appeared on earth in human form through the disgustingly obscene medium of parthenogenesis (!) in order to be publicly whipped and hanged (!!) in order to gratify the presumably lecherous as well as bloodthirsty appetite of his coeval and amiable parent!!! I can hardly believe that even a talking ape could imagine himself to believe all this unspeakably bestial nonsense. (*L6*:176–7 [1904])

The charge of bestial crudity might also be levelled at Caesar, who for all his cynicism is the product of his religion. He is confidently materialistic, to such a degree that emotion has lost its meaning for him. His mother's pious "Alas, my son!" is icily criticized ("Alas, my mother, sounds no sense for men – / Rings but reverberate folly," *B*10:387), and to his father's query – can Caesar sleep after murdering his brother? – he replies "Flesh must sleep to live" (*B*10:408). In lines made heavy and substantial by numerous *d*'s, he asserts that Christ, the Word, is only bread, to knead and eat; nor can he understand his father's reply, "Bread and wine / Could hardly turn so bitter" (*B*10:408). Nothing, Caesar insists, can alter the nature of the "mortal earth" animated by his calculating mind; "there lurks no God in me" (*B*10:393).

Caesar's universe, without divinity or even feeling, is not the universe that Swinburne evokes in even his most sceptical lyrics. By failing to understand the passions on which his father's superstition is based, Caesar shows the limitations of his materialism; the divine operation of creating meaning or value in the world, for him, is only an illusion. At the end of his career, however, Swinburne values such scepticism as a control upon the potentially deceptive power of the god-making faculty. Still, a genuinely religious language, free of what Swinburne sees as the brutality and nonsense of Christianity, *is* possible; in *Marino Faliero*, Swinburne had tried to demonstrate as much.

The Doge subjects the language of the Church (in the form of two Latin hymns, composed by Swinburne himself) to savage criticism and revision. His own theory of language may be best described as agnostic sacramentalism. Blinded by false hope, he takes the first

Latin chant, sung at dawn, as a "token" that God is with his intended revolution; this song, he says is "a comfortable sign" sent "To match the death indeed of darkness, left / Too long upon the waters." The literal dawn and the great dawn of Creation in Gen. 1.2–3 are both types of the dawn of freedom in Venice; the connection is reminiscent of republican dawns in both Shelley and the earlier Swinburne – "Let there be light! said Liberty; / And ... / Athens arose!" (*Hellas*, 682–4); "Let there be light, O Italy!" ("Siena," *P*2:169). But Faliero immediately follows his expression of republican confidence with a sentence of doubt ("I know not") and an anticipation of failure; and, contemplating the future with eyes momentarily clearer, he stakes his life and faith upon a metaphysical paradox. The incapacities of language, and of all that is mortal, point to an immortal Absolute,

> which if we live or die
> Alike and absolute, unhurt and whole,
> Endures, being proven of our mortalities
> Immortal – yea, being shown by sign of loss
> And token of subdued infirmity,
> And ruin, and all insistence of defeat,
> And laughing lips and trampling heels of men
> That smile and stamp above us buried, shown
> Triumphant. (iv.ii, *T*5:337)

The concept of "God palpable" (*T*5:339–40) provides a crude demonic parody of the tension here between the Absolute and the losses, "Fallings from us, vanishings," which testify to its existence. The typology of the play is similarly hesitant and agnostic. Faliero foresees the resurrection of Italy under Mazzini, the Saviour of liberty:

> This
> The heart of man, buried as dead in sins,
> May feel not nor conceive, and having felt
> Continue in corruption: this alone
> Shall stand a sign on earth from heaven, whose light
> Makes manifest the righteousness of God
> In mortal godhead proven immortal, shown
> Firm by full test of mere infirmity
> And very God by manhood. (*T*5:365)

Merely to imagine Mazzini is redemptive, so far as the individual soul is concerned. Yet salvation for the individual is not enough. Mazzini is Christlike, but his appearance is rather a token that history may become holy and man divine, than the pivotal point of a sacred history designed by Providence. For he is himself a type; in him, his contemporaries may glimpse, "By type and present likeness of a man," that "more perfect manhood, born / Of happier days than his" (T5:363). This evolutionary typology recalls Tennyson's; in the Epilogue of *In Memoriam*, Hallam becomes a "noble type" of the "crowning race" (138, 128), in a union of "evolutionary science and Christian faith" which "holds out the promise both of the Kingdom of Heaven, when all shall 'live in God,' and [of] the Kingdom of Earth, when all shall have evolved into gods."[38] But, apart from Tennyson's emphasis on science and Swinburne's on politics, there is a marked difference in manner between Tennyson's Epilogue and Faliero's vision. The last, 44-line sentence of *In Memoriam*, with its complex, perfectly controlled syntactic structure, its regular iambs, and its use of the imperative and indicative moods exclusively, expresses entire confidence. Faliero's lonely vision of the Italian republic is conveyed to us through a dubious haze of double negatives ("God cannot will that here / Some day shall spring not freedom," T5:374), and he surrounds every assertion of Mazzini's sacred function with conditional clauses: at the patriot's advent, "if God be good / And time approve him righteous," men "shall know / By type and present likeness of a man / What, if truth be, truth is, and what, if God, / God" (T5:363). The metre is jerky, insecure and yet emphatic; the caution of Faliero's conditional clauses and the assurance of his "[they] *shall* know" (italics mine) express the faith of an Old Testament prophet, who knows and does not know – who can answer for religious experience, but not for metaphysics. The Doge can be sure of nothing; but he has envisioned Mazzini, and that vision inspires his hopeless and hopeful faith.

The typology of the play is thus created by the hero – that is, by a fallible mortal; and the great antitype, the "perfect manhood" which gives meaning to the whole typological system, remains at two removes: an hypothesis, a faith, something glimpsed in the flash of a paradox. Instead of a sacramentalist language of analogy, Swinburne offers an agnostic language, complex, unstable, occasionally strained, and always challenging. The development of such a language is in itself a difficult achievement, as we shall see in our subsequent examination of Swinburne's lyrical work. Swinburne does not immediately repudiate sacramentalism for agnosticism when he repudiates Christianity at the beginning of his career; on the contrary, he does his best to salvage at least the image of the eucharistic sacrament to the honour of his new gods. The sacrament of violence, with its implicit criticism of a Christian system of meaning, in fact makes possible the freethinker's sacrament of harmony.

CHAPTER THREE

The Sacrament of Harmony

The sacrament of violence expresses the painful communion of the victim with that cruel energy that organizes a world of pain. In the sacrament of harmony, on the other hand, Swinburne attempts to connect the communicant with a genuinely redemptive force. Eros; the apocalyptic Republic of Man; Apollo – each of the new gods is represented in eucharistic terms. In his late poetry, however, Swinburne abandons the eucharist of harmony as he abandons all attempts to create a stable myth of redemption – a myth, that is, which can be elaborated from poem to poem. The nature lyrics of his last years focus on the immediate experience of a persona who is absorbed by the natural world, instead of being in communion with it.

Thanks, perhaps, to the influence of Dante Gabriel Rossetti, Swinburne early toys with the notion that Eros, or sensual love, might be redemptive – might somehow overcome the power of time. Yet sensuality has all the ambiguity of that material, temporal world within which the sensual man must live and move and have his being. Even "The Triumph of Time," Swinburne's most elaborate attempt to develop the image of an erotic sacrament, implies that we can triumph over time only when we reject that dualism which is basic to a sacramental vision of life, and which is inherent in temporality itself. The hypothetical erotic union could not have transcended that dualism; and, for this reason, the erotic eucharist itself represents an apparent rather than a genuine redemption.

The Swinburne of *Atalanta* and of *Poems and Ballads*, First Series, perceives temporality as essentially divisive. In "The Triumph of Time," the speaker adapts the eucharistic imagery to his own transient moods, and the nature of the sacrament alters as the dramatic monologue proceeds. In the republican verse, where Swinburne chooses to view time as the medium of redemption, the eucharist represents either that political union which will consummate all temporal processes, or the act of self-sacrifice through which the divine and united republic may come into being. In *Songs before Sunrise*, the emphasis is usually on the united republic; in *Erechtheus*, Swinburne stresses the sacrificial act which brings into being a stable political harmony and a "song / That as a bird shall spread and fold its wings ... for ever" (P4:411). The republican eucharist is harmonious indeed; but, by the same token, it is remote from the physical ritual of shared wine and broken bread. The eucharistic metaphor represents an act or relationship conceived in moral terms, and is essentially allegorical rather than sacramental or symbolic.

The Apollonian eucharist developed in *Poems and Ballads*, Second Series, and in *Songs of the Springtides*, is more complex in nature. Swinburne continues to avoid sanctifying the realm of "things"; to him, the world of bread and wine is neither sacred in itself, as it is to Feuerbach, nor sanctified, as in High Church thought, by its analogical relationship to divine truth. Instead, the eucharistic image represents, in a manner increasingly remote, allusive, and difficult as the image develops, the transmission of creative activity. In discussing the Apollonian eucharist, I focus particularly on certain lines from Swinburne's important semi-autobiographical poem, "Thalassius," partly because this text offers one of the last significant eucharists of harmony in the canon of Swinburne's lyrical work, and partly because "Thalassius" shows very well the development of Swinburne's agnostic style. At the same time, this style attempts the transmission of creative activity from writer to reader, so that the poem itself becomes an Apollonian eucharist; within the literary tradition, therefore, the poem participates in the divine action it celebrates, and to that extent fulfils a sacramental function.

From the mid-1870s to the mid-1880s, the nature of artistic creation is the dominant theme in Swinburne's lyrical work. When this theme ceases to be central, however, the last vestiges of a sacramental vision disappear from the lyrics. One might suppose that, when the poet begins to use the distinctively Romantic form of the landscape meditation, and celebrates deities which either subsume or else are immanent in the natural world, he will employ the Romantic metaphor of communion with nature; but not at all. In fact, although Swinburne uses the word "communion" in this Wordsworthian manner earlier in his career, he employs it very little during his most nearly

Wordsworthian phase. The sacrament is now firmly associated with a dualistic vision of the world; and the only vividly developed eucharist in the later lyrics is the eucharist of violence.

"THE TRIUMPH OF TIME" AND THE SACRAMENT OF LOVE

"Je me suis toute ma vie inquiété de la forme du flacon, jamais de la qualité du contenu."[1] D'Albert's maxim seems eminently Pre-Raphaelite, and indeed the poetry of Dante Gabriel Rossetti, for instance, emphasizes the visual image of the cup rather than the wine or blood. The "altar-cup" of the Art-Catholic becomes an "icy crystal cup" when Rossetti moves toward agnosticism, but is "hollow" in both versions of "My Sister's Sleep."[2] In the same way, the eucharist of "Pax Vobis" is sensuous experience without content: the sounds of the "organ," the "chaunt," and the "sacring-bell" serve no sacramental purpose. They provoke vague intuitions of the infinite, "dumb and dim"; but the last line of the poem – "He said: 'There is the world outside'" – makes these "inner things of Faith" seem emptily subjective. Revised as "World's Worth" in 1881, the lyric puts forward an entirely different argument, warranting "The inmost utmost things of faith"; now the priest's final cry ("'O god, my world in Thee!'") conveys the startling paradox of a faith achieved in the face of the blind, deaf, dizzying, and meaningless "world" of sensory detail.[3] In the second draft, the oppressive presence of the physical is ultimately defied, whereas in the first draft the outer "world" gains the victory; in both, however, the power of sensuous experience is the dominating theme.

Swinburne, in his review of the 1870 *Poems*, particularly mentions "Pax Vobis," that study of "an hour made drunken with the wine of worship," as a lyric which Rossetti ought to have included, "if only for the fine touches of outer things passing by as a wind upon the fervent spirit in its dream." The evocation of eucharistic ritual to make an agnostic point, in the early draft, would have been much to Swinburne's taste. Swinburne uses cup-and-wine imagery several times in this review, emphasizing content as much as form; for example, he says of "Troy Town" that "the poet has carved a graven image of song as tangible and lovely as the oblation itself; and this cup he has filled with the wine of love and fire of destruction" (B15:31, 38–39; see also 18, 33). The shape of Helen's cup, in the likeness of her breast, is the central image in the first six stanzas of "Troy Town," but the cup is empty, and the breast is pure form until the image of the cup is displaced by that of the apple "Grown to …

/ Taste and waste to the heart's desire" (59–60), and, eventually, by that of the "nest" containing the flaming heart (80–1).[4] By conflating the images of cup and flame, and adding "the wine of love," Swinburne propels Rossetti's imagery toward the complex of eucharistic, erotic, and destructive images which Swinburne has already developed in his own poetry as the demonic eucharist.

While Rossetti commonly purifies his images "of any possible religious content,"[5] Swinburne is usually more concerned with sacramental content than with ritual form. Contrast his translation of Villon's hymn to the Virgin with Rossetti's. The mediaeval poet's explicit reference to the Eucharist (*Testament*, 890–1) undergoes a startling bowdlerization at the hands of Rossetti, who alludes only to the ritual of the Mass, with a vague hint at its spiritual function: "Oh help me, lest in vain for me should pass / (Sweet Virgin that shall have no loss thereby!) / The blessed Host and sacring of the Mass." Swinburne, on the other hand, translates literally Villon's unequivocal equation of Christ's body with the transubstantiated Host: "O Virgin bearing in a maid's body / The sacrament men worship in the mass."[6]

Even when Rossetti (perhaps under Swinburne's influence) presents a physical sacrament which is the channel of divine grace, liberating the soul and uniting man and God, his nervous tact blurs the theological or anti-theological point of his metaphor. The eucharist in "Love's Redemption" closely resembles the erotic eucharist evoked in *Rosamond* and in "The Triumph of Time," but Swinburne explores and criticizes the mechanics of the erotic sacrament, where Rossetti merely asserts Love's redemptive power:

> O thou who at Love's hour ecstatically
>   Unto my lips dost evermore present
>   The body and blood of Love in sacrament;
> Whom I have neared and felt thy breath to be
> The inmost incense of his sanctuary;
>   Who without speech hast owned him, and intent
>   Upon his will, thy life with mine hast blent,
> And murmured o'er the cup, Remember me! –
>
> O what from thee the grace, for me the prize,
>   And what to Love the glory...!

The first three lines of the sonnet present the lady as the priest, and Love as the Host which she administers to the lover; but in the remainder of the octave the god of love becomes God the Father, and the woman beloved plays the rôle of Christ. The eucharist itself may be a kiss (cp. the lover's apotheosis in "The Kiss," 12–14) or the sexual act; Rossetti here is not concerned with the process of salvation, but with establishing that vision of identity more explicitly celebrated in "Heart's Hope": "Lady, I fain would tell how evermore / Thy soul I know not from thy body, nor / Thee from myself, neither our love from God." So in "Love's Redemption" the reader learns to see the material body and blood of Love as divine, the lady as not merely priest but Christlike priest-sacrifice, and carnal passion as a sacred and redemptive Passion. Through this manoeuvring, the lady herself is also identified with the divine Eros; she is Love incarnate; and the lover partakes of Love through the *condescensio* of the beloved.[7]

This set of equivalences quietly removes the original content of the eucharistic relationship; the sacrament is used not to unite separate realms but to blur their separateness. Swinburne faces the issues involved in the erotic eucharist more directly. As early as *Rosamond* (1858–60), he celebrates

> love
> That makes the daily flesh an altar-cup
> To carry tears and rarest blood within
> And touch pained lips with feast of sacrament –
> So sweet it is, God made it sweet! (*T*1:237)

Here the cup is the body, the sacramental wine the mixture of pain and pleasure felt by each lover; and each lover feeds delightedly on the pain and pleasure of the other. The God who made this process sweet is the God who "wrought so miserably the shapes of men / With such sad cunning" (*T*1: 287), as King Henry perceives later. Rosamond's praise of love, but for its apparently casual references to "tears" and "pained lips," would be in perfect harmony with "Love's Redemption"; but the development of the drama discredits the extravagant claims made in Rossetti's sonnet. Love is delightful, divine – but delight and deity are not simple entities of "ultimate amiability" (*B*15:23). Similarly, the venereal eucharist of "St. Dorothy" (composed in 1861 to "give a pat to the Papist interest," *L*1:38), though painted pleasantly in bright Pre-Raphaelite colours, expresses a strictly materialistic eroticism, at once fatal and delightful. Within the church of Venus, the altars bear "bright cloths and cups to hold / The wine of Venus for the services"; "honey and crushed wood-berries" flavour the wine, shedding "sweet yellow through the thick wet red." By drinking this sacred wine, when it is administered by "Venus' priest," the worshipper may succeed in his love-affairs, since the liquor "that did such grace and good / Was new trans-shaped and mixed with Love's own blood."

> And some said that this wine-shedding should be
> Made of the falling of Adonis' blood,
> That curled upon the thorns and broken wood
> And round the gold silk shoes on Venus' feet;
> The taste thereof was as hot honey sweet
> And in the mouth ran soft and riotous.
> This was the holiness of Venus' house. (P1:239–40)

Christian images of the Passion (thorns, wood) and the Christian concept of transubstantiation are absorbed into a ritual of venereal pain and pleasure. And the hero's martyrdom becomes a sign of Venus's "favour" (P1:241, 251).

At about the time of *Atalanta*'s composition, Swinburne experiments with a somewhat more Rossettian concept of love – but still in a negative context. In "The Triumph of Time," a silent soliloquy in the presence of the speaker's beloved, the persona reverts again and again to eucharistic imagery as he laments the redemption that might have been.[8]

> I have given no man of my fruit to eat;
>   I trod the grapes, I have drunken the wine.
> Had you eaten and drunken and found it sweet,
>   This wild new growth of the corn and vine,
> This wine and bread without lees or leaven,
> We had grown as gods, as the gods in heaven,
> Souls fair to look upon, goodly to greet,
>   One splendid spirit, your soul and mine. (25–32)[9]

The lover who suffers alone is a sad parody of the Messiah. In the Middle Ages, the image of God's treading the winepress of wrath in Isaiah 63.3 had been transformed into that of Christ's fighting and bleeding for our redemption;[10] here, in the first of several ironic references to redemption, Swinburne's speaker imagines himself as a Christ suffering vainly. (In this context, the phrase, "I have drunken the wine," suggests the bitter cup of which Christ drank [Mark 10.38, Matt. 26.39].) The lover might have presented the "wild new growth" of his passion to the beloved, but its saving power would have depended on her acceptance and appreciation of it; only then would she and her Christ-like lover have "grown as gods, ... / One splendid spirit ..." But such a redemption is only a might-have-been; here and in the other eucharistic passages within this lyric, Swinburne uses chiefly the conditional subjunctive, the protasis being always, unhappily, contrary to fact.

"The Triumph of Time" is a dramatic monologue in which the frustrated speaker returns again and again to the same issues, or images, as he eddies all but hopelessly in the circles of his longing. Thus, some sixty lines later, the might-have-been is evoked again – "I had wrung life dry for your lips to drink, / Broken it up for your daily bread: / Body for body and blood for blood" (91–3) – and yet again:

> were you once sealed mine,
>   Mine in the blood's beat, mine in the breath,
> Mixed into me as honey in wine,
>   Not time, that sayeth and gainsayeth,
> Nor all strong things had severed us then;
> Not wrath of gods, nor wisdom of men,
> Nor all things earthly, nor all divine,
> Nor joy nor sorrow, nor life nor death. (145–52)

The *m*-alliteration ("Mine," "mine," "Mixed into me") subdues the beloved to the lover. She is no longer perceived as feeding on him; instead, the united lovers form the oenomel. And for the first time the speaker suggests quite explicitly that a reciprocal love might have overcome the divisions and the self-destructive power of "time, that sayeth and gainsayeth." The redemptive power of love is asserted most strikingly in the echo of Romans 8.38–9: "For I am persuaded, that neither death, nor life, nor angels, nor principalities, nor powers, nor things present, nor things to come, ... shall be able to separate us from the love of God, which is in Christ Jesus our Lord."

The oenomel itself is a vision which in his desperation the speaker pits against the gnomic wisdom of his wretchedness ("Lose life, lose all," 141); "Time has aborted the sacramental promise of the 'corn and the vine',"[11] but the speaker insists that at least his lost hopes had meaning and might have had transcendent power. His compensating hypotheses can go no further, and are followed by a hundred lines of pure rage and grief. The speaker now gives up all hope of redemption (168), and rejects all comfort (174–8); he cannot even wish to change his beloved by giving her some knowledge of his love (187–200). His art is a mourning veil, a mere adornment of his pain (203–20). At this point the persona sinks into a morass of self-pity and self-contradiction (233–48), in which he denies both the redemptive and the destructive power of love: "love lacks might to redeem or undo me" (235). He now turns to a different form of redemption. The alternative which he conceives is of great importance, for it illuminates Swinburne's objections to the sacrament of Eros; it anticipates the poet's later symbolic use of the sea-mother; and it is celebrated in verse of extraordinary beauty and power.

So far, all the imagery has been markedly transient; the Coleridgean moving moon (42), the "little snakes that eat" the persona's heart (112), the "smiles of silver and kisses of gold" (246) – all these images are produced as it were *ad hoc*, casually, and never reappear in the lyric; they are "fugitive" (11, 64). We have seen that even the eucharistic imagery changes its meaning on each appearance. Emphatically, the poem presents (or, rather, is) a process; logic and lack of logic, shifting or vanishing imagery, the pulsation of the speaker's grief, and the hurrying iambic-anapestic metre, all mark the lyric as a dramatic tribute to time. At this point, however, we enter on a passage of singular coherence (257–304): the image of the sea-mother, briefly introduced earlier, is extended and elaborated, together with images of erotic union and of dissolution. And the images in this passage do not dissolve one into another; instead, they are held in solution by the speaker's astonishing ability to combine mythmaking with compensatory fantasy.

> I will go back to the great sweet mother,
>   Mother and lover of men, the sea.
> I will go down to her, I and none other,
>   Close with her, kiss her and mix her with me;
> Cling to her, strive with her, hold her fast:
> O fair white mother, in days long past
> Born without sister, born without brother,
>   Set free my soul as thy soul is free.
>
> O fair green-girdled mother of mine,
>   Sea, that art clothed with the sun and the rain,
> Thy sweet hard kisses are strong like wine,
>   Thy large embraces are keen like pain.
> Save me and hide me with all thy waves,
> Find me one grave of thy thousand graves,
> Those pure cold populous graves of thine
>   Wrought without hand in a world without stain.
>
> I shall sleep, and move with the moving ships,
>   Change as the winds change, veer in the tide;

My lips will feast on the foam of thy lips,
  I shall rise with the rising, with thee subside;
Sleep, and not know if she be, if she were,
Filled full with life to the eyes and hair,
As a rose is fulfilled to the roseleaf tips
With splendid summer and perfume and pride.

This woven raiment of nights and days,
  Were it once cast off and unwound from me,
Naked and glad would I walk in thy ways,
  Alive and aware of thy ways and thee;
Clear of the whole world, hidden at home,
Clothed with the green and crowned with the foam,
A pulse of the life of thy straits and bays,
  A vein in the heart of the streams of the sea. (257–88)

Barbara Charlesworth condemns the entire passage as a decadent, solipsistic fantasy (32); but this is to concentrate on one strand of imagery exclusively. It is true that on one level the speaker is concerned with suicide, drowning, dissolution into an indeterminate purity of non-being among the "pure cold populous graves" (271). This passage, then, can certainly be related to other fantasies of consolation in the poem; and, like other "Sick dreams," the dream of suicide is later repudiated ("We shall live," 307). Yet the chief characteristic of the sea-passage is its triumphant exuberance; the future tense dominates the syntax, for the first time in the poem; the verbs are largely active and heavily stressed ("Close," "kiss," "mix," "Cling," "strive," and "hold" all appear in the two lines 260–1); and the caesuras are richly varied. Why should a decadent fantasy have cadences of such memorable vigour?

Images of oral and erotic satisfaction are mingled with the images of death in this passage. Union with the sea is substituted for union with the beloved; the speaker uses the metaphor of "mixing" to describe both unions (147, 260), and the sexual parallel is evoked in 275–6: "My lips will feast on the foam of thy lips, / I shall rise with thy rising, with thee subside ..." Alliterative assonance suggests that the projected oceanic union and the impossible love-union would satisfy the same impulse: the speaker will "rise" with the sea's "rising," and a few lines later the beloved (wedded to the speaker's rival) will be filled with life "As a rose is fulfilled to the roseleaf tips" (279); each of the [r-z] syllables carries a metrical stress. Separately, both lover and beloved will experience intense joy; the lover will "feast on the foam" as "The strong sea-daisies feast on the sun" (56); the beloved too is "Filled," in a happy pun that connects eating and fulfilment (contrast *Atalanta*, 1169: "With pain thou hast filled us full to the eyes and ears"). All of the recurrent images in the poem here reach their height and perfection of felicity; even the bloodlike, broken, severed blossom of 22, 88, and 103–4 is "fulfilled … / With splendid summer and perfume and pride" (279–80). Above all, the sea herself is transfigured. Earlier, she was a "barren mother" of "mutable winds and hours" and loves, a cold "mother-maid" (65–9) like the Virgin in the "Hymn to Proserpine" (75–81, P1:71–2); within her were only "faint sounds" and "wan beams" breaking (71–2). Her "coil and chafe" were scarcely distinguishable from "the change of years, … the coil of things" (182, 33). But now the sea is not barren, but "fruitful of birth" (302); no maid, but "lover of men" (258); "sure" (301), not a figure of "fugitive pain" (64). And within her is nothing "wan" or "faint," but rather "the life of [her] straits and bays" (287), the green, the foam, the organic motion.

She is a personal deity, partially anthropomorphized, the first person other than the beloved to be addressed; and to her alone the speaker uses the reverential "thou." "From the first thou wert; in the end thou art" (304). Eternal, giving death and birth, concealing and revealing (302–3), she has, to some extent, the sinister ambivalence of the high gods and of time itself; yet she may also promise a redemption from time, a life beyond it. "Set free my soul as thy soul is free," he implores her (264); the antimetabole realizes verbally the happy balance it requests. The sea is only "clothed" with the cyclical sun and rain that ruin the speaker's love and sicken the "pulseless" stream early in the poem (266, 18, 58–60); the Carlylean metaphor is elaborated in 281–8. If the speaker will "Close with" his deity, "strive with her, hold her fast" like Jacob wrestling with the angel, the grave-clothes of time will be "unwound," and the speaker, "Naked and glad, … / Alive and aware," will attain full consciousness of the goddess and her ways. The physical sea becomes a kind of "Time-annihilating Hat" – or crown (286) – which can "Sweep away the Illusion of Time," the "woven … warp and woof" of the phenomenal. Like Teufelsdröckh (who also lost his "Flower-goddess" to another man), Swinburne's persona struggles at last to an apprehension of transcendent reality; but, unlike Teufelsdröckh, he falls away from transcendentalism all too quickly.[12] The Carlylean hypothesis offers a possible triumph over time – but only for a stanza at most; almost at once, the speaker begins to sink back toward the concept of a deity who embodies an eternal duality, who is "strong for death" as well as "fruitful of birth" (302).

It may be that this transition constitutes an implicit criticism of Carlyle's Romantic confidence. Yet the sea-passage is a triumph, however transient. Under the disguise of a suicidal fantasy, the lover has expressed the possibility of a real redemption; he has indicated the only conditions under which redemption would be possible – and thereby suggests the weakness, or perhaps I should say the evil power, of a sacramental linguistics. In the oenomelic passage, the Pauline biblical cadences presented union with the beloved in terms of the very dualities which that union was supposed to transcend (earthly/divine, joy/sorrow, life/death); at the height of the sea-vision, on the other hand, language escapes these oppositions. For the moment, Swinburne's pairings are complementary rather than contrasting:

> This woven raiment *of nights and days,*
>   Were it once *cast off and unwound* from me,
> *Naked and glad* would I walk in thy ways,
>   Alive and aware of thy ways and thee ... (281–4; italics mine)

In this passage, the oppositions of the first line disappear in the next; but they are revived at the end of the sea-vision: "Thy lips are bitter, and sweet thine heart ... / Thou art strong for death and fruitful of birth; / Thy depths conceal and thy gulfs discover" (298–303).

The last line quoted is crucial. To Newman, the "exterior world," the sacraments, and "the veil of the letter" are all partial manifestations of "realities greater," of glorious "truths to which the human mind is unequal"; to Tennyson, "words, like Nature, half reveal / And half conceal" a spiritual power. But Swinburne associates the conceal-and-reveal topos with a sinister deity of division.[13] The sea-goddess is still a figure less negative than positive ("birth" and "discover" are each placed emphatically at the end of a line). But she has dwindled from a transcendent redeemer to the representative of temporal continuity. In the same way, the last hundred lines of the poem sink gradually from the ecstatic power of the sea-vision. From the mythic presentation of the sea, through the legend of Rudel (321–44), to the icon of the "armed archangel" (365); from the triumph of 281–8, through the stoicism of 305–12, to the melancholy meditation on Rudel's *Liebestod*, and the passionate despair of the close; imaginatively and emotionally, the poem seems to descend steadily. The speaker's verbal attempt to transcend time becomes an involuntary celebration of change. So art, like nature, fails us in the end; its synthesis of contraries is momentary at best. Thus, "The music burning at heart like wine" (364) is

> An armed archangel whose hands raise up
> All senses mixed in the spirit's cup
> Till flesh and spirit are molten in sunder ... (365–7)

Greenberg interprets this passage as a vision of "the perfect spiritual hermaphrodite": "Soul and body interpenetrate" ("Gosse's *Swinburne*," 104). But in fact they interpenetrate only to fall apart, "molten *in sunder*" (italics mine). The synaesthetic experience, like the union with the sea, might perhaps have helped the speaker to transcend the phenomenal (the intensity of sensuous delight enkindling the spirit and enabling it to surmount the sensory). But he has lost all hope of such transcendence, for "time has done with his one sweet word, / The wine and leaven of lovely life" (375–6). The internal rhyme *done*/*one*, like the syntactic structure of the "archangel" stanza (a list of glorious joys, followed by the main clause: "These things are over, and no more mine"), underlines the pathos of the speaker's loss; the cup of synaesthesia and the "wine and leaven" are excluded from his future, over and done with.

The eucharist, once constituted by the speaker's (hypothetically) reciprocated love, is now utterly divided from him. Even the substitution of "leaven" for "bread" separates the "lovely life" from the speaker's "wine and bread *without* lees or leaven" (29; my italics). The bread without leaven suggests the "unleavened bread of sincerity and truth" (1 Cor. 5.8), thus emphasizing the speaker's truth in love; "leaven" in 1 Corinthians is emblematic of the old faults that should be put by ("Purge out therefore the old leaven," 5.7), so Swinburne's speaker is also indicating that his "wild new" love is genuinely new and pure. (This point is reinforced by the image of wine without lees, for to "settle on the lees" is a Biblical image of spiritual stagnation; cp. Jer. 48.11, Zeph. 1.12.) The "leaven of lovely life" which appears at the end of the poem is not the converse of the speaker's "unleavened" love, but the image of paradise lost; Christ likens "the kingdom of God" to "leaven, which a woman took and hid in three measures of meal, till the whole was leavened" (Luke 13.20–1; this passage is closely followed by Christ's reference to the "strait gate," verse 24, to which Swinburne alludes at l.168).

Like Arnold's forsaken merman, Swinburne's lover addresses an unhearing woman who is imagined enjoying her salvation while her lover – longing for her, shut out from salvation – may call her in vain: "in heaven, / If I cry to you then, will you hear or know?" (391–2; cp. 161–8). There is perhaps an undercurrent of bitter triumph in the conclusion of Swinburne's lyric. The lady's ignorance sharpens the lover's grief, but it also contrasts with his knowledge, as the silence between them contrasts with his secret music. Unlike all the characters in *Atalanta*, he can conceive and verbally evoke the mixing and even the transcendence of dualities; or, at least, he has done so. Yet he cannot sustain that imaginative fervour; and this is time's real triumph.

One may say that the sacramental and biblical imagery of the lyric enforce the triumph of time, although they are employed in several of the speaker's attempts to reverse that triumph. Thais Morgan suggests that in 91–6 the "metaphorization of the lover's body does not bring off the desired Eucharistic redemption because of the very sensuality of the consummation."[14] Certainly, the first and second eucharistic passages, and the oenomelic stanza, are intensely sensuous (perhaps sensual), and evoke a material world of corn and vine, honey and wine, body and blood. The passage on the "spirit's cup" is more complex, and points toward a transcendence of the sensuous world through sensuous experience of special richness and intensity. But the speaker can contemplate transcendence as a real possibility for himself only when he drops the sacramental metaphor that conceals and reveals, the vesture of the eternal. At the same time, he cannot free himself from the language of shadow and vesture for more than a moment; he unwinds the "woven raiment of nights and days," walks "Naked and glad" in the presence of his goddess – in thought, at least – and then reclothes himself, *sartor resartus*, "Clothed with the green and crowned with the foam." So in 2 Corinthians 5.2–4 Paul insists that, when our earthly tabernacle is done away, we should have a spiritual clothing, "If so be that being clothed we shall not be found naked ...: not for that we would be unclothed, but clothed upon, that mortality might be swallowed up of life." But in "The Triumph of Time" the moment at which the speaker is once more to be "clothed upon" represents the beginning of the descent from a brief vision of perfect life to a hopeless consciousness of mortality; three lines later, the sea begins again to resemble the devouring earth-goddess "fed with the lives of men" (289).

To Gabriel Rossetti, the ritual and artistic form have the enduring toughness of Gautier's enamel; the sonnet, notoriously, is "a moment's monument." To Swinburne, as to Blake and Shelley, eternity is not artifice, but energy: the burning of a star, the huge motion of the sea. Later, eternity will become, for Swinburne, imaginative energy, specifically; but in "The Triumph of Time" imagination is consistently betrayed by the symbols it must employ, most of which smell of mortality. The eucharist itself is firmly rooted in the natural and agricultural cycles of earth. Only the sea, as an image of indeterminacy and spontaneity, can suggest a possible triumph over the cycles of time; and this tension between earth as representative of the temporal, natural cycle, and the sea as a representative of transcendent energy, is central to such later poems as "Ex-Voto," "Thalassius," and "Pan and Thalassius." It would have been easy for Swinburne to relate the freedom offered by the sea to the regeneration offered in baptism; but, as we shall see, he carefully avoids making such a connection. For his justification for the blasphemous transference of eucharistic imagery which occurs so often in his poetry is simply this: that he views the whole sacramental system as concealing and revealing the cruel deity of time. The redemption through the erotic eucharist, hypothesized by the speaker in "The Triumph of Time," is a Rossettian fantasy that merely aggravates the speaker's grief; the redemption through the sea-vision conveys at least a flickering consolation, and redeems the lyric from the entire hopelessness of *Atalanta*. In the remainder of this chapter, we shall see that, wherever Swinburne evokes the sacrament of communion in a positive context, he refines that sacrament so thoroughly that its very nature constitutes an implicit reproach to the sacramental system of Christianity.

SACRIFICE AND REDEMPTION IN THE POLITICAL VERSE

In the republican eucharist, the sacrament is dissociated from the sensuous plane partly by the use of such simple locutions as "the cup of my heart" and "soul's wine," and partly by the essentially didactic context within which the eucharist is presented. The negative eucharist of political oppression, as employed in "Siena," for example, condemns tyranny by associating it with the concrete and barbaric image of cannibalism. But the sacrament of communion also serves Swinburne as an image of political union, or of the sacrifice through which Man may achieve political redemption in the shape of the united Republic, the heavenly Jerusalem upon earth. Generally, the positive political eucharist is more abstract than the negative; "the feast is spread" with "that sweet food which makes all new," but apparently there will be little of the sensuous in our enjoyment of the Republic, on that great day when freedom will be our common food.[15] Only in "Christmas Antiphones" (1869), Parts II and III, does the eucharist of freedom involve the consumption of food in the material sense.

Part I of "Christmas Antiphones" is a devotional lyric composed to please the poet's mother; Parts II and III respectively criticize and reinterpret the terms employed in Part I. In Part II, the poor complain that from their bodies are made the bread and wine of the rich (the protest is obviously figurative, but refers to an economic reality), and they ask:

At what shrine what wine,
  At what board what bread,

Salt as blood or brine,
Shall we share in sign
    How we poor were fed? (P2:130-2)

But in the third section, "Beyond Church," Swinburne reverts to
a purely spiritual eucharist, consisting of "soul's wine" and of freedom instead of bread, and administered to "no sect elect" but to all
men. Yet the context seems to suggest that this spiritual communion
may also involve a practical communism:

What of thine and mine,
    What of want and wealth,
When one faith is wine
For my heart and thine ...?
....
Gods refuse and choose,
    Grudge and sell and spare;
None shall man refuse,
None of all men lose,
    None leave out of care. (P2:133-4)

In this exceptional passage, the distribution of material wealth is
smoothly included in the spiritual communion of the Republic. The
emphasis, however, is on spiritual communion, on the love "Mingling me and thee" (P2:134). The positive eucharist in this poem
expresses primarily the entire recognition by each man of others'
rights and needs. In this state of perfect equality, the two senses of
equal – "just, equitable" and "having the same rights" – coalesce, as
in the phrase, "Equal laws and rights" (P2:133): equality, after all,
is only equitable (see OED, "Equal," a. 5, 2). The one true god, the
sun-god, is named "Right"; when we perceive that there is no god
but this sun of righteousness, "All shall see and be / Parcel of the
morn" (P2:136).

The god is merely human morality; Man will save Man as God
will not; Time, not the Spirit of God, will touch faith's Aeolian lyre
into enduring music (P2:133-5). But, in spite of Swinburne's stub-
born endeavours to secularize his Christian and Coleridgean imagery, the form and substance of his myth remain visibly determined
by Christian symbolic patterns. "Christmas Antiphones" follows the
pattern established in A Song of Italy (1866-7), in which Christian
symbols find their true and highest significance in shadowing forth
the Republic, and the self-sacrificing activity which will bring the
Republic into being. So, in A Song of Italy, each political martyr is a
"Priest and burnt-offering and blood-sacrifice ..., / A holier immo-

lation than men wist, / A costlier eucharist, / A sacrament more saving" (P2:272).[16] Their suffering is the medium through which the grace of freedom is communicated; so, in the "Ode on the Insurrection in Candia" (composed January 1867), the priestess Freedom is slowly "cleans[ing] earth of crime," with "the bloodred tears / That fill the chaliced years, / The vessels of the sacrament of time" (P2:208). These early political sacraments show a certain anxiety on Swinburne's part to apply every sanctifying motif that he can think of to Mazzinian activism; thus the martyr in A Song of Italy is priest, sacrifice, and eucharist – is Christ, in short – and "the sacrament of time" in the Ode suggests the Atonement and the baptismal rite as well as the ceremony of Communion. In poems such as "Christmas Antiphones," written two or three years later, the sacramental imagery is more carefully controlled; Swinburne develops the republican eucharist so as to indicate how this "sacrament more saving" saves us, and from what. Thus in "Mater Dolorosa" salvation may come through our act of faith: we partake of the agony of the goddess Freedom, accept her pain as our own, when we drink of her bitter cup.

> We have not served her for guerdon. If any do so,
> That his mouth may be sweet with such honey, we care not to know.
> We have drunk from a wine-unsweetened, a perilous cup,
> A draught very bitter. The kings of the earth stood up,
> And the rulers took counsel together, to smite her and slay;
> And the blood of her wounds is given us to drink today. (P2:141)

The reference to Psalms 2.2 implies that the kings and rulers have set themselves against the reign of the Redeemer, and will be defeated, as the psalmist prophesies in verses 4–12. So the Virgin/ Christ, at once the grieving mother and the slain Son, will "shine as ... the sun" at last (P2:143), and the tyrants will be cast down; and this will come to pass through our self-sacrifice, through our willingness to drink of her cup, and through "the blood of her wounds"; in view of the gracious properties of Christ's blood, the last line of the stanza quoted seems to have at least a hopeful ambiguity. It is, however, in Erechtheus (1876) that the blood of the virgin redeemer is most explicitly and triumphantly redemptive. For Athens' sake, Chthonia goes to her death willingly, singing her Magnificat: her "barren womb" will now bear fruit,

> for the dry wild vine
> Scoffed at and cursed of all men that was I
> Shall shed them wine to make the world's heart warm,

That all eyes seeing may lighten, and all ears
Hear and be kindled; such a draught to drink
Shall be the blood that bids this dust bring forth,
The chaliced life here spilt on this mine earth,
Mine, my great father's mother; whom I pray
Take me now gently, tenderly take home ... (P4:378)

Swinburne here draws on an important symbolic complex, derived partly from the Bible and partly from Christian literary tradition. The idolatrous Israel was described by the prophets as an "empty vine" (Hos. 10.1) to be rooted up and planted in the wilderness (Jer. 2.21, Ezek. 19.10–13); Christ is the true fruitful vine (John 15.1, 5), who, being pressed in the winepress of the Passion, sheds forth blood that becomes "sweet wine" (George Herbert, "The Bunch of Grapes," 26–8). Like Christ, Chthonia is "for all the world ... a saviour" (P4:377); the reversal of her barrenness parallels the reversals in Ezek. 17.24 (the "dry tree" shall flourish), and in Isa. 54.1 (quoted in Gal. 4.27, in relation to the heavenly Jerusalem, "the mother of us all"): "Sing, O barren, ... for more are the children of the desolate than the children of the married wife." All Athenians will be the children of Chthonia, who sums up in herself both the female and the male agents of redemption; she, perhaps, is the perfect hermaphrodite vainly sought in *Atalanta*, since by her "poor girl's blood" the "dust" of the mothering earth is impregnated (P4:376, 378).

In every way, *Erechtheus* avoids the savagery and frustration of *Atalanta*. The earth is no gaping bloody mouth now, but a tender, welcoming mother. The human mother who sends her child to death shares in that child's sacrifice, and indeed suffers more deeply; for in Chthonia Praxithea's own blood is shed "To do this great land good, to give for love / The same lips drink and comfort the same hearts" (P4:407; on the mother's grief see especially 375–85). To be sure, there seems to be an irreducible element of barbarism in the very act of human sacrifice; this point Swinburne does not evade. Indeed, the Chorus makes it several times over; the Athenians, who profit by Chthonia's death, again and again repudiate the concept of vicarious atonement. "But bless us not so as by bloodshed, impute not for grace to us guilt" (P4:346); "the fruit of a sweet life plucked ... / On his hand who plucks is as blood, on his soul is crime" (P4:371). In the eighth chorus, the Athenians transform the image of the eucharist to the image of an ambiguous apocalypse:

From the cup of my heart I pour through my lips along
The mingled wine of a joyful and sorrowful song;

Wine sweeter than honey and bitterer than blood that is
        poured
From the chalice of gold, from the point of the two-edged
        sword.
For the city redeemed should joy flow forth as a flood,
And a dirge make moan for the city polluted with blood.
....
For a taint there cleaves to the people redeemed with blood,
    And a plague to the blood-red hand. (P4:407–8)

For the moment Chthonia's Christ-like sacrifice becomes a "two-edged sword" (Rev. 1.16, Heb. 4.12), dividing the city between joy in redemption and horror at the means of redemption. It is perhaps because the Chorus does refuse to condone the blood-sacrifice that Athena can pronounce the city "Blood-guiltless, though bought back with innocent blood" (P4:409); the Athenians – like the three members of the king's family who make the great sacrifice (Praxithea endures her daughter's death; Chthonia dies; Erechtheus both yields up his daughter, and perishes in battle) – have shown their unselfish love for the city's virtue. They are, therefore, prepared to learn and to express that harmony, that unity which is liberty (the word "one" appears seven times in Athena's speech). "Thy tongue shall first say freedom," the goddess tells them, and Praxithea's answering speech is filled with images of free reciprocation and organic unity:

                              from a heart *made whole*
    Take us thou givest us blessing; never tear
    Shall stain for shame nor groan untune the *song*
    That as a bird shall spread and fold its wings
    Here in thy praise for ever.
    ....
                              ... There is no grief
    Great as the joy to be *made one* in will
    With him that is the *heart* and rule of life
    And thee, God born of God ... (P4:411–12; my italics)

The central figure of *Erechtheus* is not Chthonia, nor Erechtheus, nor Praxithea, but the state as a whole, i.e., the union of individuals who are each freely and entirely devoted to that union. McGann goes further: "The work's realities are not its characters at all, or its gods, or even nature. All these are metaphors to Swinburne ... The most real, most material and visibly present phenomenon in the play is law – a vast, organic order."[17] The importance of self-sacrifice lies partly in the fact that self-sacrifice willingly acknowledges our subordination to this larger order. And in the order of the ideal Republic there is no exploitation; the Athenians do not devour their saviour. It is significant that most of the eucharistic imagery in *Erechtheus* stresses pouring, not drinking. At that, the eucharistic image at the head of the eighth chorus ("From the *cup* of my heart I pour … *wine*") is pointedly replaced in the opening line of the final chorus: "From the depths of the *springs* of my spirit a *fountain* is poured of thanksgiving" (*P*4:412; italics mine). The steady pouring of the fountain is a Romantic image to match the smooth organic motion of Praxithea's song/bird. [18]

Here the theory of language expressed in *Atalanta* (and, less despairingly, in "The Triumph of Time") – the view that language is hopelessly divisive, part of the cruelty of time – is joyously contradicted. Song is, or can be, eternal life; it is the final fulfilment or self-realization of the Republic, which it crowns "As the sun's eye fulfils and crowns with sight / The circling crown of heaven" (*P*4:411–12). The dying Chthonia's "fountain of song," prophesying the triumph of Athens, contrasts with the deadly boasting of Niobe, who, "too great of mind, … / With godless lips and fire of her own breath / Spake all her house to death" (*P*4:388, 385, 390); the selfless harmony of the republican spirit redeems language, which the self-centred arrogance of a Niobe or an Althaea turns to murderous flame.

Despite the Romantic associations of the bird and fountain, Swinburne's republican poetics are characteristically Victorian rather than Romantic; the use of one kind of language rather than another is made possible by a choice which the author presents in exclusively moral terms. As Praxithea's use of "shall" rather than "will" ("never tear / Shall stain … the song / That as a bird shall spread and fold its wings") suggests, the "organic" harmony of the republic is willed rather than spontaneous; the Athenians are *creating* an "organic" state, and this state is something new ("Thy tongue shall first say freedom"). Athens is achieved through painful moral effort. Thus, metaphors of organic life are of secondary importance in this work; Chthonia's "wild vine" is dry and barren until it pours forth its "chaliced life," and it never becomes the "living plant" which "'effectuates,' as Coleridge puts it, 'its own secret growth' – and organizes itself into its proper form."[19] That plant, invaluable to Romantic theorists on the nature of imaginative creation, has no place in the crucial symbolic structures of *Erechtheus*. Nor does the living vine of Christ (for that matter), on whom all true believers must be grafted (John 15.1–6). The biblical type has been moralized; and the moral is Feuerbach's.

"God suffers ... but for men, for others, not for himself. What does that mean in plain speech? Nothing else than this: to suffer for others is divine; he who suffers for others, who lays down his life for them, acts divinely, is a God to men."[20] The religious attitudes developed in Swinburne's political poetry, though established by Swinburne within an anti-Christian context, strongly resemble the bowdlerized versions of "Christianity" supplied by certain liberal thinkers contemporary with the poet. Thus, for Matthew Arnold, the Crucifixion "redeems" through its exemplary function; it conveys "the moral doctrine that we must die into life."[21] Swinburne's manipulation of such images as that of the vine, in *Erechtheus*, suggests that Chthonia's sacrifice might be interpreted very much as Arnold interprets Christ's sacrifice. In spite of Swinburne's implied criticism of the doctrine of Atonement, *Erechtheus* avoids polemic, and leaves the reader with a sense that most elements of Christian tradition can be harmoniously accommodated within a republican faith. In the last few pages, Swinburne uses words like "worship," "grace," "blessing," "thanksgiving," and "God" freely and positively; and Praxithea's important final speech echoes, without irony, that line which was to become Arnold's favourite touchstone: "In la sua voluntade è nostra pace."[22]

"THALASSIUS" AND THE EUCHARISTIC SONG

I observed earlier that the political and aesthetic eucharists in Swinburne's verse have much in common. Both are presented in somewhat abstract terms; and in both the individual receiving the "sacred elements" is thereby connected with a tradition of activity (literary or revolutionary, or both) which affords an exceptional freedom and illumination – a secular redemption. In the political poetry, the emphasis is generally placed on the source of redemption, the self-sacrifice of the political martyr; the aesthetic eucharists, however – up to and including the important sacrament of song and wisdom in "Thalassius" – direct our attention not to the selflessness of the Saviour, but to the effect of the "sacred elements" on the recipient. In "Ave atque Vale," "Thalassius," and the Memorial Verses to Gautier, the "eucharist of Apollo" (*WB* 133) inspires the recipient to poetic creation. After "Thalassius," the structure of the aesthetic eucharist seems to be influenced by the patterns established in the political poetry: the poet is not the recipient, but the saviour-priest who ordains and administers the sacrament to the world at large. Accordingly, Swinburne stresses here the great poet's generous activity; his spirit has "Given all itself as air gives life and light" (Birthday Ode for Victor Hugo, 509, *P3*:358), to sustain the reader. The recipient is comparatively passive; moreover, he (or she) is neither a poet specifically, nor even, as in *William Blake*, part of a peculiarly gifted élite.

Always, however, the aesthetic eucharist communicates the essential elements of Swinburne's poetics. Thus, in *William Blake* (1862–7), Swinburne defends Blake's apparent obscurity on the ground that great art can be appreciated, not by "the corporeal understanding," but only by a rarer "innate and irrational perception"; if all could be nourished by the "high and subtle luxuries of exceptional temperaments,"

all specialties of spiritual office would be abolished, and the whole congregation would communicate in both kinds. All the more, meantime, because this "bread of sweet thought and wine of delight" is not broken or shed for all, but for a few only – because the sacramental elements of art and poetry are in no wise given for the sustenance or the salvation of men in general, but reserved mainly for the sublime profit and intense pleasure of an elect body or church – all the more on that account should the ministering official be careful that the paten and chalice be found wanting in no one possible grace of work or perfection of material. (*WB* 35–6)

Blake's profundity does not excuse his occasional technical lapses and carelessness of construction; for the "elect" who can penetrate to the "'spirit of sense'" in such a work as *Jerusalem* are precisely those who most require and can best appreciate "executive quality" in art. But Swinburne's main point is that Blake administers his eucharist to the small community of "exceptional temperaments" which share with him a kind of visionary power; the recipients not only accede to Blake's (and Swinburne's) conviction that the Poetic Genius is the true God,[23] but also employ their own poetic faculty in the process of appreciating Blake's.

Blake often uses eucharistic imagery, and usually in a reductive manner: commenting on "A Vision of the Last Judgment," he suggests that the eucharist represents the act of "recieving [*sic*] Truth or Wise Men into our Company Continually"; and in the fragment of "My Spectre," he offers the famous formula: "& Throughout all Eternity / I forgive you, you forgive me / As our dear Redeemer said / This the Wine & this the Bread." But the lines, "To my dear Friend Mrs Anna Flaxman," misquoted in the excerpt from *William Blake*, above, form the only eucharistic passage in Blake's work to leave distinct traces in Swinburne's writing. And the context of Blake's poem is particularly important in this respect. Blake does not mention poetic inspiration specifically to Mrs Flaxman, but his letters to Flaxman, Hayley, and Butts at the time make it clear that he was expecting, and did in fact experience, an influx of such energy at Felpham ("My fingers Emit sparks of fire with Expectation of my future labours"); and Swinburne insists on the inspiring force of "this first daily communion with the sea."[24] We should not, therefore, be surprised by the appearance later in *William Blake* of a phrase ("eucharist of Apollo") which foreshadows the eucharist of poetic inspiration, as it appears first in "Ave atque Vale."

"We know that 'Ave atque Vale' was written while the Blake essay was being prepared for publication." The "elect body or church" in "Ave atque Vale" is still narrower than that in *William Blake*: it is the "mystical body" of all artists, all those whose hearts Apollo "feeds ... with fame" as he fed Baudelaire's "hungering heart" (142–3). [25] A kind of eucharist is administered by the dead poet, and links the mourner and the mourned: "not death estranges / My spirit from communion of thy song" (103–4). The main emphasis, however, rests on the genuine quality of Baudelaire's inspiration, and on its painfulness.

> Thy lips indeed he touched with bitter wine,
> And nourished them indeed with bitter bread;
>   Yet surely from his hand thy soul's food came ... (138–40)

As "Ave atque Vale" hails the "lord of light" (134), and is indeed the earliest careful celebration of the art-god's power in Swinburne's poetry, so it also bids farewell to the venereal parodies and "bitterness" of the *Poems and Ballads*, First Series. Apollo nourishes and illuminates, although he torments as well; the light he sheds emanates from the underworld (154; McGann interprets this line as a "simple, yet brilliant" way of saying that "the undying fires of hell" are "the fountainhead of [Baudelaire's] poetic inspiration"). But, like the power addressed in Baudelaire's "Les Litanies de Satan," this "Luciferian Apollo" partially assuages the torments over which he presides, with something like a noble compassion: "grand roi des choses souterraines, / Guérisseur familier des angoisses humaines."[26] Morally, he exists at the halfway point between the "supreme evil" of *Atalanta* and the luminous sun-god celebrated in another elegy for a French poet: "Memorial Verses on the Death of Théophile Gautier," composed soon after Gautier's demise in December 1872.

The "Memorial Verses" evoke an art vaguely sensuous and intensely joyful: the god who "gives us spirit of song," Swinburne tells Gautier, "made thy moist lips fiery with new wine / Pressed from the grapes of song, the sovereign vine" (*P*3:60–1). The poetic tradition is the redemptive vine, upon which Gautier's own works are grafted. Here the violence implicit in the biblical image of the winepress disappears; inspiration becomes a joyous intoxication; Gautier himself becomes one of the "lords of light" who make the loveliest things "more divine." Gautier's art triumphs over time because his songs, for instance, combine the hard enduring quality of marble with the organic motion of the sea: like Memnon's statue, they "meet the sun re-risen with refluent rhyme / – As god to god might answer face to face – / From lips whereon the morning strikes" (*P*3:61; my italics). This combination, not endorsed by Gautier's "L'Art," is characteristic of Swinburne; thus the organic and the artificial coalesce in the "quiet sea-flower moulded by the sea" ("Ave atque Vale," 3), and in the sea-jewel of "Thalassius." In "Thalassius" the implications of such imagery are fully developed.

Yet in one respect "Thalassius" (1879–80) differs profoundly from the elegies of *Poems and Ballads*, Second Series. "Ave atque Vale" and the "Memorial Verses" both celebrate the harmony of the sensuous with the intellectual elements in verse: the eucharist can be (figuratively) tasted or felt. In "Thalassius," the narrator shows no interest in evoking the "creatures of bread and wine"[27] with their material properties. And as in the previous section I mentioned the fact that Swinburne's attitude to ethics, in certain works, closely parallels Feuerbach's, it may be worthwhile to point out that the English poet's view of the sacraments differs radically from Feuerbach's, and that even the most humanistic materialism finds no place in Swinburne's major poetry. By the date of "Thalassius," the elements of bread and wine, to Swinburne, are not parts of a sensuously evocative ritual, as they are to Rossetti; but, from the moment of his deconversion, one might almost say, they were neither sanctified as the visible analogy of Christ's body and blood, nor sacred as the material proof "that Man is the true God and Saviour of man."[28] Swinburne's use of the eucharistic metaphor, therefore, is never either Anglican or Feuerbachian.

We can see at once the difference between Swinburne and a truly Feuerbachian poet like George Meredith. In his early "Madonna Mia," the former asserts that "white and gold and red" are "God's three chief words, man's bread / And oil and wine," and that God has dowered the speaker's lady with these colours (her gown is red, her hood white, and her hair gold). Thus the sacramental connotations of the bread and wine, the sacerdotal connotations of oil, and the material qualities of all three disappear almost completely, leaving only the idea that the lady's physical beauty is physically and spiritually nourishing to mortal men (*P*1:273–5). On the other hand, in Meredith's "The Day of the Daughter of Hades," section 8, Skiágeneia's Apollonian song gives the young mortal singer Callistes "corn, wine, fruit, oil! / ... to eat" – in a figurative sense, to be sure; yet this figure is the instrument whereby "The *grace* of the battle for food" (italics mine) is transmitted.[29]

Here, as with Feuerbach, the material fruits of the earth acquire sanctity from the labour with which man produces them. Meredith's eucharistic song transmits the "pushing, warm" reality of corn and wine, which in itself constitutes their "religious import": the unmysterious grace of physical objects "With the meaning known to men."[30] Skiágeneia's song becomes food, whereas in Swinburne's "Thalassius" (1880) food becomes song, and loses its sensuous properties in the transformation; Swinburne eschews Meredith's "milky kernel" of particular song (8.59), and creates a very different kind of art. A full discussion of "Thalassius" will appear in chapter 5, but here I concentrate on two passages. The first, from stanza iii, describes the old singer who fosters Thalassius and administers the sacrament:

> A singer that in time's and memory's ears
> Should leave such words to sing as all his peers
> Might praise with hallowing heat of rapturous tears.
> ....
> And at his knees his fosterling was fed
> Not with man's wine and bread
> Nor mortal mother-milk of hopes and fears,
> But food of deep memorial days long sped;
> For bread with wisdom and with song for wine
> Clear as the full calm's emerald hyaline. (44–53)[31]

The close relationship between this passage and stanza xx, in which Thalassius renews his intimacy with the sea, has never been fully demonstrated. Thalassius has abandoned his foster-father and his sea-mother, and fallen under the sway of Eros and Erigone, of Love and loveless passion; at length he returns to the sea, and falls asleep.

> And in his sleep the dun green light was shed
> Heavily round his head
> That through the veil of sea falls fathom-deep,
> Blurred like a lamp's that when the night drops dead
> Dies; and his eyes gat grace of sleep to see

The deep divine dark dayshine of the sea,
Dense water-walls and clear dusk water-ways,
Broad-based, or branching as a sea-flower sprays
That side or this dividing; and anew
The glory of all her glories that he knew.
And in sharp rapture of recovering tears
He woke on fire with yearnings of old years,
Pure as one purged of pain that passion bore,
Ill child of bitter mother; for his own
Looked laughing toward him ... (421–35)

These passages are linked in several ways. To begin with, in each case Thalassius is saved from an influence which would restrict or destroy his power of divine song. The poetic sacrament of stanza iii is distinguished from "mortal mother-milk of hopes and fears"; when Thalassius is reunited with his true mother, he is "Pure as one purged of pain that passion bore" – the labial assonance in both these lines should be noticed – and passion may readily be seen as the "bitter mother" feeding her "Ill child," pain, with the milk of mortal hopes and fears (50, 433–4). The little allegory is quite consistent.

Verbal echoes, as well, connect the singer with the sea. The "glories" of the foster-father are matched by the "glories" of the sea-mother (41, 430); the foster-father himself is "Free-born as ... waves are free" (40), and the use of the word "deep" in conjunction with the simile in 53 suggests the oceanic depth and lucidity of the eucharistic song, matched in 426–7 by the "*deep* divine dark dayshine" and "*clear* dusk" of the sea (italics mine). Even the rhymes on *dead* and *years*, the most significant and most often reiterated rhymes in stanza iii, appear also in stanza xx. The *years/tears* rhyme (41, 46, 431–2) is most important: the hot "rapturous tears" of singers who praise a singer are matched with Thalassius' "rapture of recovering tears" as he awakes from his sea-dream, "on fire with yearnings of old years." As the bread and wine of poetry are "food of deep memorial days," so the process of union with nature appears, in true Wordsworthian fashion, as the process of recovering one's childhood. Thus, in composing poetry and in experiencing nature, the crucial process must be the celebration of the past – of that profound luminous sea on which Thalassius, the "sea-flower" (37, 428), finds it natural to live.

Despite the immaterialism of these communions (Thalassius enters the sea only in a dream, and is fed, emphatically, "*Not* with

man's wine and bread"; italics mine), Swinburne here softens, appropriately, toward the religion of his boyhood. There are definite
parallels between the communion in "Thalassius" and the ritual of
the Holy Communion, as presented in the Book of Common Prayer.
To begin with, the Prayer of Consecration, immediately preceding
the administration of the sacrament, asks "that we receiving these
thy creatures of bread and wine ... in *remembrance* of [Christ's] death
and passion, may be partakers of his most blessed Body and Blood"
(italics mine). Swinburne of course omits all reference to deicide, as
he does to "the remission of sins" thereby achieved;[32] but Thalassius'
communion, like that of the Church of England, is essentially commemorative, a celebration and recovery of "memorial days long
sped." The word *memorial* is used primarily in its obsolete sense of
"remembered" or "memorable"; *deep* I suspect is used in the sense
of "difficult to fathom or understand" (*OED*). Perhaps Swinburne is
suggesting that, through poems (the "creatures" of the sun-god
Apollo), Thalassius comes into contact with the Real Presence of the
past, as in his dream of stanza xx he perceives directly the holy
mystery of the sea, and "The glory of all her glories that he knew"
(430). As the use of identical rhymes in stanza xx (*see/sea, anew/knew*)
implies, Thalassius recovers his own past with a precision and completeness Wordsworth would hardly have credited. Memory, as an
essential element in poetic creation (cp. "On the Cliffs," 424) and in
mature experience of nature, thus triumphs over time instead of
redeeming it.

When "we spiritually eat the flesh of Christ, and drink his blood,"
"then we dwell in Christ, and Christ in us; we are one with Christ,
and Christ with us."[33] And this concept of union with God is all-
important with regard to Thalassius' communion. When he receives
wisdom for bread, and song for wine, he is at once united with
wisdom and song; after his fall into an unhappy alienation from
nature, when he recovers the joy of his childhood and is reunited
with the sea, he becomes "no more a singer, but a song" (474). At
this point the sun-god claims him as a son, and Thalassius undergoes
a kind of limited apotheosis. Song, which in the first half of the
poem commemorates such deeds and words as help men (see especially 129–82), has now become the "manchild" (486) whose very
life is a commemoration of his early joys among suns and winds
and waters. In "Memorial Verses," song is a living god; in "Thalassius," the godlike manchild is a song. As William Wilson has
declared, "Swinburne's poet, like Milton before him, has triumphantly made a poem of his own life ... Surely, a significant part of

the achievement of 'Thalassius' lies in Swinburne's defense of subjectivity and visionary themes as the proper, indeed the necessary, ground for a true poetry of consolation."[34]

Although I cannot agree with Wilson that "a eucharistic covenant is struck between Milton," specifically, "and Swinburne" (385) I accept in principle the statements quoted in my previous paragraph; and I would further point out that here, precisely, Swinburne limits the implications of his eucharistic metaphor. On the one hand, Thalassius is incorporated with "song," and thereby with the blessed company of all faithful poets, of all to whom the "song" reveals divine and mortal love (129–65); but "song, God's living gold" (490) is probably not identical with the god of song himself. On the other hand – and this is more important for our purpose – Swinburne's view of the poetic eucharist is at once "idolatrous"[35] and reductive. The language is that of substitution rather than analogy ("For bread with wisdom and with song for wine"); the wisdom and song are directly communicated to Thalassius, and all that the "high song" reveals to him in 67–243 is also communicated as directly as one flame kindles another (119–24, 146–53).

Even the syntax of the eucharistic passage supports this view. In Swinburne's usual style, the main clause of the sentence appears complete in the first line, and is followed by a series of adjectival phrases in which the nature of the eucharist is progressively defined: first negatively – it is not mortal, nor material – then positively: it is not a eucharist at all, but the transmission of traditional wisdom and the impulse of song. The last adjectival phrase, "Clear as the full calm's emerald hyaline," draws the reader's attention away from the eucharistic metaphor to a sea which becomes a great jewel, a crystalline emerald recalling the "glimmering jewellery" of the shore on which Thalassius is cast in line 4.

Whereas Carlyle cannot use the phrase "skyey Tent" without implying a Maker (or at least an Inhabitant), Swinburne perceives "glimmering jewellery" in pebbles, perceives the sea first as a jewel itself and later as an architecture of "Dense water-walls and clear dusk water-ways" (427), without suggesting a jeweller or builder; as the sea's child makes himself a poem, so the sea, expressing (to employ Vivante's terms) a self-originating and self-purposive value, is at once a living goddess (18–31, 401–8, 434–6) and a work of art.[36] Accordingly, the eucharist administered by the foster-father does not bless Thalassius with an eternal life by joining him to the invisible body of a Saviour above him; nor is it a ritual performed by men but used by a transcendent deity as an instrument or channel of grace. Rather, it is a process of education (or the first part of Thalassius' education) leading ultimately to the realization that the poet, like nature herself, has the power to create himself as a work of art – not in Wilde's sense, but Romantically, by making his whole life a celebration of the divine power within him, the Coleridgean creative "joy ... / Of child that made him man" (437–8). At the same time, of course, Thalassius is restored to no divinely ordained sacramental economy. The sacramental aspect of the eucharistic metaphor, and of the natural world, has been carefully undercut by the flow of Swinburne's shifting and dissolving metaphors: by the images of architecture and sea-flower in the sea-dream; by the allegory of the false and the true mothers; above all, by the metamorphoses of the eucharistic image itself in 48–53. For the foster-father's eucharistic song is presented in the same "Turnerian" style, with the same deliberate mixture of metaphors, that Rosenberg and, earlier, Empson have analysed as characteristic of Swinburne's descriptive poetry.[37]

Lines 48–53 provide us with images of an eucharist, of suckling, of ordinary food, and of a clear gemlike sea. The second and third of these images suggest that the process being described is one of growth, and indicate Thalassius' early dependence on the elder singer; the eucharistic imagery indicates the religious value of this process, which – unlike the religious value of Skiágeneia's song – has nothing to do with the battle for concrete food. Whereas Feuerbach asserts that "in bread and wine we adore the supernatural power of mind, of consciousness, of man," and urges us at the same time not to forget "the gratitude which [we owe] to the natural qualities of bread and wine" (277–8), Swinburne directly addresses the "supernatural" power of an *artistically* creative consciousness, and removes from the sacramental bread and wine all their "natural qualities." The process of Thalassius' growth has a religious value because it unites Thalassius with wisdom and song, with the divine realities.

Finally, the sea-simile at once propels the reader away from metaphors, the implications of which the poet desires to limit, and suggests that the process of growth is inspired by contemplation of the completeness ("*full* calm"), richness, and lucidity of a work of art, just as Thalassius' redemptive dream is, in itself, a contemplation of the multeity and lucidity of the sea apprehended as a work of art – apprehended, that is to say, as the fulfilment of the very creative impulse which was activated in Thalassius by the foster-father's "eucharist."

Read in this way, stanzas iii and xx describe very well the basic assumptions underlying Swinburne's mature style. Empson declares that Swinburne often uses ambiguity of the "fifth type" for "a sort of mutual comparison" in which the author "is not interested in either of the things compared" (193); this is clearly an agnostic use of language rather than a sacramental or an idolatrous one. And this style is useful not merely for impressionistic scenic effects (as in Althaea's "sun-dazed" view of the hunters in *Atalanta*) or the synesthetic effects which Swinburne learned from Shelley and Keats, but also for the subtle intellectual argument of "Thalassius."[38] Swinburne wishes to sum up the poet's relationship to poetic tradition in a few lines; but that is so rich and complex a reality that it cannot be conveyed directly. It is presented in language which demands an action of synthesis and discrimination among the relevant and the irrelevant connotations of each metaphor, within the reader's mind; and as Swinburne's impressionistic passages imply the presence of a spectator, so this language demands the presence of an *imaginative* reader, a reader capable of reenacting within himself Thalassius' process of growth. As such a reader contemplates the "clear dusk," the "one clear hueless haze of glimmering hues" (427, 100) which is "Thalassius," the obscurity of Swinburne's language – private, "[s]ecret and eccentric" as it seems – is transformed. Instead of the meaningless musical superficies which so many critics have deplored, it becomes, like Carlyle's Nature, an "open secret" – to the "elect body or church" of those in whose minds analysis and synthesis occur so quickly as to become a kind of intuition, an "innate and irrational perception."[39] The contemplation of the complete work of art should illuminate the creative impulse which dominates one's own inner life, and also should force it into action.

T halassius, then, is redeemed through the operation of his Wordsworthian memories, which reawaken his power to create and order; the sea represents not only the natural cycle, with which Thalassius is once more in harmony, but also, and more importantly, the manchild's ability to recover and celebrate his own joy, and so to become a living jewel. *Songs of the Springtides* opens with this triumph, since "Thalassius" is the first major poem in the volume (its only predecessor is the dedicatory sonnet to Trelawny); the Birthday Ode for Hugo is the last such poem, and it endeavours to place this triumph within a wider context. In other words, where "Thalassius" presents the development of a poet, or (to be more precise) the archetypal pattern of a poet's progress, the Birthday Ode considers the poet's public function. Hugo receives the genuine inspiration accorded to Baudelaire, Gautier, and Thalassius; yet in Hugo's case the operative agent is not Apollo, but the French poet's own love of humanity: "And love made soft his lips with spiritual wine, / And left them fired, and fed / With sacramental bread" (184–6). And the emphasis is not on this process of inspiration, but on the fact that Hugo in turn gives himself in two kinds (prose and verse): the "bread of [Hugo's] deathless word and the wine of his immortal song" (B13:14) constitute "one sacrament of Love's great giving / To feed the spirit and sense of all souls living" (492–6). As the priest, or rather pope, of this republican Love, Hugo best perceives and celebrates the moral imperative expounded in *Songs before Sunrise* and *Erechtheus*, and his sacrament is appropriately described in smooth and abstract terms.[40]

After 1886 the sacrament of art disappears altogether from Swinburne's work. For one thing, as his scepticism grows on him, even a reductive sacramentalism becomes insufficiently abstract; for another, the idiosyncratic activity of creating art ceases to engage him as a theme. And at this point the eucharist of harmony loses its importance, suddenly and finally, in Swinburne's lyrics. In the final section of this chapter, I shall demonstrate briefly how even the topos of communion with nature fades from his lyrical verse, as the god of his worship becomes too evasive to be represented by sacrament or analogy.

THE DISAPPEARANCE OF THE EUCHARISTIC METAPHOR

The phrase, "to commune with nature," had been established by Wordsworth, and especially by the vogue of his *Excursion*. As early as *The Pilgrimage of Pleasure* (1864) we find Swinburne using "commune" in this sense (Discretion cries, "I commune with the most high stars").[41] The same trick of diction appears a few years later in "Hertha," the "Hymn of Man," and the Prelude to *Songs before Sunrise* (1869–71). In the Hymn, man is at once "Equal with life" and "in communion with death"; "He hath sent forth his soul for the stars to comply with and suns to conspire" (126–8, P2:100). The three words containing the prefix *con-* bind man to the sacred laws of nature; in the same way, the free soul of the Prelude "communes and takes cheer / With the actual earth's equalities, / Air, light, and night, hills, winds, and streams" (37–9, P2:4).

Wordsworth uses "commune" and "communion" to hint that through a sense of all creatures' life we may rise above "animal being" and connect ourselves with "the Uncreated" (*Excursion* 1.205–18, *Prelude* 2.409–18; of course I am oversimplifying Wordsworth's thought, but the association of the communion-motif with a sense of religious adoration and distinctively visionary experience is marked in both of these passages).[42] Swinburne, on the other hand, in his Prelude, resists the notion of a divine consolation or beatitude beyond "hills, winds, and streams"; communion with nature implies rejection of "doubt and faith and fear" and an entire acceptance of time (32, 75–8, P2:4–5). In "Hertha," the communion is equally revisionist, but expresses a more cheerful confidence. Hertha's questions, "Hast thou communed in spirit with night? ... / Have ye spoken as brethren together, the sun and the mountains and thou?" (55–60, P2:74), at once echo and reverse Job 38–41. The questions which in the Book of Job, according to the heading of Job 38, convict man "of ignorance ... and of imbecility," and exalt Jehovah, in "Hertha" disparage theology and urge man to that harmony with nature through which real understanding may be attained.

In *Songs before Sunrise*, "Nature needs man, as man needs Nature";[43] nature is perfected in man, whose conscious freedom is Hertha's self-realization (see chap. 4 below). And man is the child of nature, who should look to his mother to learn what he is, should commune with "the actual earth's equalities" rather than with "strengthless dreams" (Prelude, 38, 40). Yet, a few years later (1878), the speaker in "Ex-Voto" turns from the nourishing earth-goddess precisely because she supplies a Feuerbachian sacrament, a symbol of the mind's power to use and control nature. Those who drink the earth's "blood" in "Fresh wine's foam streaming" seem to make earth their servant. The sea, on the other hand, will not serve "even in seeming": one who "hath drunken of the sea," from the "chalice" in which Fate serves death, will thirst no more (P3:82–4). And the speaker longs for this death by water, for dissolution in an element which represents pure freedom, being uncontrollable. This dissolution alone is an adequate image of entire satisfaction.

Tristram of Lyonesse (1882) combines this fatal eucharist with one more positive and more closely related to the communion with nature in *Songs before Sunrise*. In Canto III, when the hero is grieving for his separation from Iseult, he makes an effort toward stoicism, in the manner of the Prelude: "'O strong sun! O sea! / I bid you not, divine things! comfort me ...'." His suggestion of an amoral nature is contradicted by the narrator, who assures us that nature did console Tristram: "The winds took counsel with him, and the sun / Spake comfort," since "with the live earth and the living sea / He was as one that communed mutually / With naked heart to heart of friend to friend" (P4:57, 61–2). As in the Prelude, to commune with nature involves the rejection of "faith and fear"; but now it also involves abandoning the hope of absolute redemption through politics or love. Even to Tristram and Iseult, those heroic lovers, love is a deadly blessing; "some honey" love has mixed "with life's most bitter wine," but, in the *Liebestod* of which the lovers do literally drink, erotic fulfilment is inseparable from annihilation (*P*4:92, 37, 150). Nature can offer them only a transient delight or comfort – or the peace of dissolution, celebrated in "Ex-Voto"; at the end, the lovers, swallowed up by the sea, enjoy a rest beyond love or life (*P*4:151).

The most markedly eucharistic image in *Tristram* is the image of Fear's bloody chalice – a chalice shattered in the final canto. The associations of the sacrament are essentially negative in Swinburne's late lyrics and tragedies; and the Wordsworthian concept of harmonious communion with the natural world is fatally undermined by the Victorian poet's rejection of an analogical model for the universe. The effect of this alteration can be seen in the late hawthorn poems (1904), where Swinburne very carefully avoids suggesting that the sight of the bloom places us in sacramental communion with the god. The god is immanent within the hawthorn blossom, a Real Presence, and yet "fugitive," unseizable as the immediate and passing moment:

> ... a god that abides for a season, mysterious
> And merciful, fervent and fugitive, seen and unknown
>   and adored:
> His presence is felt in the light and the fragrance,
>   elate and imperious,
> His laugh and his breath in the blossom are love's,
>   the beloved soul's lord.
> For surely the soul if it loves is beloved of the god
>   as a lover ... ("Hawthorn Tide," *P*6:293)

A eucharistic communion with this Bridegroom is suggested only to be denied: "the cup of delight and of worship" is "unpledged and unfilled." The god's presence in the springtime bloom might be taken as an earnest of his eternal being; but no, Swinburne's emphasis is all on the splendour of a transient experience which has no meaning that will survive its passage. The god's presence is "briefer than joys most brief," and disappears "as song subsides into silence" (*P*6:291, 294). The "heaven" he brings on earth does not exist on another plane; it shines here and goes out, leaving a world that collapses into meaningless disunity.

> The passing of the hawthorn takes away
>   Heaven: all the spring falls dumb, and all the soul

Sinks down in man for sorrow. Night and day
  Forego the joy that made them one and whole.
                    ("The Passing of the Hawthorn," P6:296)

We have seen how Swinburne exploits the eucharist in the service of strange gods, from Eros, to the Republic of Man, to Apollo himself. Yet, while he uses sacramental imagery to cast an odour of sanctity around his new deities, he has also contrived to undermine sacramentalism so thoroughly that he must now dismiss it as a sanctifying agent. The divinity present in the may-blossom, and the "unknown spirit" of "A Nympholept," express themselves in no sacrament; they flash out in the present moment, or remain hopelessly inaccessible, mysterious, fugitive. In the end, therefore, all stable systems of meaning disintegrate; and we are left with a cult of the transient moment, as the only defence we can have against the cruelty of transience. Swinburne has at last transcended the patterns of thought (and imagery) which were the result of his High Church training.

PART TWO

The New Gods

CHAPTER FOUR

Songs before Sunrise:
Man and God

Thou art judged, O judge, and the sentence is gone
   forth against thee, O God.
Thy slave that slept is awake; thy slave but slept for
   a span;
Yea, man thy slave shall unmake thee, who made
   thee lord over man.
....
He hath stirred him, and found out the flaw in his
   fetters, and cast them behind;
His soul to his soul is a law, and his mind is a light
   to his mind. ("Hymn of Man," 118–20, 149–50)

So far we have seen Swinburne exploiting and undermining the
language of the Bible and the Prayer Book, together with the symbolism and the theology of the eucharist. His manipulations express
a distinctively modern attitude. Not only does he reveal the violence
that was hidden in religious language, but also, in *Atalanta, Chastelard*, and *Poem and Ballads*, First Series, he presents this violence
as the irreducible basis of our experience. In *Songs before Sunrise*,
however, the violence of religion is depicted as gratuitous and unnatural; we can and should make an end of it. In *Atalanta*, the savage
earth "made man and unmade," and man disappeared in the working of that divine creative and destructive power; in *Songs before
Sunrise*, Swinburne's antimetabole emphasizes the creative and destructive power of humanity: "*man* thy slave shall *unmake* thee, who
made thee lord over *man*" (italics mine).

But how to "unmake" God? In "Before a Crucifix," Swinburne
declares that it is necessary to jettison the whole symbolic system
provided by Christianity; yet we have seen that much of his own
work depends for its effect on manipulation of the typology, the
forms, and the cadences of the Judaeo-Christian literary tradition.

In the Prelude to *Songs before Sunrise*, Swinburne implicitly claims to have abandoned the language that embodies violence, the "iron cadences" of *Atalanta* and the first *Poems and Ballads*. Clearly, then, it is incumbent upon him to develop a new poetic language, and an alternative symbolic system; and it is equally clear that he will need to experiment with new forms which will accommodate his new ambitions.

The Prelude, with its echoes of Epictetus and Bruno, points toward didactic allegory as the mode which best expresses a vision centred on the moral imperative of "self-sufficiency." In the "Hymn of Man," however, Swinburne attempts to justify this imperative in terms not strictly or narrowly ethical; and, although the Hymn is didactic in part, the poet finds that the didactic mode by itself is insufficient to convey his complex vision of the man-god. Accordingly, in the Hymn, and (more successfully) in "Hertha," Swinburne draws on the radical tradition of Romantic prophecy to develop a mode which mingles didactic allegory and "creative myth" in a "manner at once violent and intricate" (*WB* 250, 241). And this prophetic mode in turn will help to develop a new theory of poetry, and a new poetic language, which will come to fruition a decade later in *Songs of the Springtides*.

SWINBURNE'S PRELUDE:
A FAREWELL TO BACCHUS

The reformation that Swinburne desires must entail the repudiation of his own earlier style, for two reasons. First, the style of *Atalanta* embodies an oppressive violence which Swinburne now thinks both evil and unnecessary. Second, as a matter of practical politics, it is necessary for this poet to repudiate his earlier work in order to be taken seriously, as a prophet in his own country. To the Victorian public – as Swinburne knew too well – he was only "the libidinous laureate of a pack of satyrs"; Morley's placard had stuck to his back.[1] In the Prelude to *Songs before Sunrise*, Swinburne implies that the label was once valid, in order that he may ceremoniously discard it. To be sure, he speaks of the youthful singer's development in the third person, and in the most abstract terms; but the prominence given to the Bacchic revel is strongly reminiscent of "The laurel, the palms and the paean, the breasts of the nymphs in the brake" ("Hymn to Proserpine," *P*1:68), as also of the first chorus in *Atalanta*, the worship of Bacchus and Cotytto in "Dolores" (*P*1:164–7) – and Morley's placard.

At the very beginning of the Prelude, Youth's song is presented as a transient dream of self-contradiction and impotence:

Youth talked with joy and grief an hour,
  With footless joy and wingless grief
  And twin-born faith and disbelief
Who share the seasons to devour ... (12–15)[2]

The agnostic pessimism of *Atalanta* is here the complementary "twin" of Christian faith: both feed on time and waste it. When Youth treads down such dualities as "Fear and desire, mistrust and trust, / And dreams of bitter sleep and sweet" (22–3), he moves into the world of "equalities" (38), of liberty, righteousness, and "due proportion." He does not escape time; indeed, he has "given himself to time" and to "the equal year's alternatives" (75–8). In short, he accepts time's "alternatives," knows and endures "the heat / And cold of years that rot and rust / And alter" (26–8), and by this submission paradoxically transcends the variations of time, since he sees them all as part of a single process of incessant flux.

Yet how does this acceptance of time make liberty and righteousness possible? To explain this, Swinburne describes the alternative – Youth's first revel under "The rose-red and the blood-red leaf" (18) – in more detail. The spokesmen of a hedonistic philosophy urge that poetry depends on pleasure, and acclaim the Muse of love, for what other Muse can give "'More joy to sing and be less sad, / More heart to play and grow more glad?'" But the speaker of the Prelude replies that love is both transient and actively cruel. The songs of love are no delicate entertainments, but "iron cadences" that affright the wolf and "Outroar the lion-throated seas" (81–90, 105–7). And these "iron cadences" are as transient as they are violent. The "singing tongues of fire" – a wonderful phrase, at once parodying the Pentecostal inspiration of the Holy Spirit (Acts 2.3) and suggesting the destructive power of Swinburne's earlier Muse – now are "numb" (116). Change, which weaves, rends, and re-weaves "the robes of life" (128–30), silences the songs of love, or turns them to "a wearier wail" (127). To seize the day is to snatch at violence and loss; to recognize and accept time's alternations is to see that there is no stability except that which the "soul" creates for and in itself (131ff).

As Saturn explained in Swinburne's early "Hyperion," we conquer by "yielding[,] in our inward power made strong, / And smiling down the restless rule of Change" (131–2). Terrestrial songs and flowers, "Passions and pleasures," "Actions and agonies," all pass away, but time can neither defeat nor control luminous stars and souls (131–40). This contrast is commonplace, of course; but Swinburne develops its implications with care. The word "soul" occurs fifteen times in the Prelude, ten times in the last six stanzas. For "man's soul is man's God" and guiding star (141, 158). As when paraphrasing Arnold's *Empedocles* in 1867, Swinburne preaches "the gospel of αὐτάρκεια, the creed of self-sufficiency."[3]

This reliance upon self, together with the dignified fatalism of lines 21–80 of the Prelude, and the sense that passions hamper the soul's exercise of its proper freedom, all suggest the influence of the Stoic Epictetus, whose work Swinburne admired. Some fifteen years later, Sidgwick observed that in Epictetus' time the Stoic self-reliance of the rational soul, "looking down on man's natural life as a mere field for its exercise, seems to have shrunk and dwindled, making room for a positive aversion to the flesh as an alien element imprisoning and hampering the spirit." (Swinburne's favourite tag from the Stoic was ψυχάριον εἶ βαστάζον νεκρόν, which he translated in the "Hymn to Proserpine" as "A little soul for a little bears up this corpse which is man.") Yet this contempt for the flesh long antedated Epictetus. In Plato's *Phaedo*, for instance, soul and body are at enmity: the soul, immortal, the rightful governor of the body, tends to be "dragged by the body into the region of the changeable ...; the world spins round her, and she is like a drunkard, when she touches change" (79c), or, as Swinburne ironically puts it, "The soul squats down in the flesh, like a tinker drunk in a ditch." Epictetus' ethic is based on a similar view, but the interests of the Stoic are moral and practical rather than metaphysical; this, perhaps, explains why Swinburne expresses a greater veneration for Epictetus than for Plato.[4]

To put the contrast in simple, or, rather, simplistic terms: Plato in the *Phaedo* urges the philosopher to distrust the senses, and transcend the phenomenal world; the soul must seek wisdom through her own intellectual activity. Epictetus urges us to overcome the world by accepting it; he recommends that the philosopher should seek to control, not events, but his own reaction to events. "The ... characteristic of a philosopher is, that he looks to himself for all help or harm ... He restrains desire; he transfers his aversion to those things only which thwart the proper use of our own will." "Demand not that events should happen as you wish; but wish them to happen as they do happen."[5] The substance of these passages is repeated in Swinburne's Prelude, 151ff, and 31–50. It seems likely, therefore, that Epictetus has influenced the Prelude directly, although, in the absence of sufficient data on Swinburne's philosophical reading, it would be rash to state this as a certainty.

In the same way, Swinburne's allusion to the "soul's light" as the power which makes Stoic "self-sufficiency" possible (151) may be derived from another (and later) philosopher whom the poet also held in high respect. For the "soul's light" here is not the intellect which, in Plato, is "the pilot of the soul" (*Phaedrus* 247c), but a faculty more narrowly moral.[6]

> Because man's soul is man's God still,
> What wind soever waft his will
>   Across the waves of day and night
>   To port or shipwreck, left or right,
> By shores and shoals of good and ill;
>   And still *its flame at mainmast height*
> Through the rent air that foam-flakes fill
>   *Sustains the indomitable light*
> *Whence only man hath strength to steer*
> Or helm to handle without fear. (141–50; italics mine)

In the epistle to Sidney which introduces *Lo spaccio de la bestia trionfante*, Giordano Bruno observes that moral decisions are directed "by a certain light that resides in the crow's nest, topsail, or stern of our soul, which light is called synderesis by some." St Jerome defines synderesis as *scintilla conscientiae*, and the scholastic philosophers agree that this "spark of conscience" is "the spark ... from which the light of conscience arises"; it is that unerring faculty within the soul which directs each of us toward right judgment and right action. This spark, therefore, "set in the highest part" of the soul, and struggling "back towards the source from which it came," connects the soul with God; the mystic Eckhart goes so far as to declare, "Diess Fünkelein, dass ist Gott."[7]

To Swinburne, in the Prelude, there is no other god than this divine flame, this spark which "Sustains the indomitable light," distinguishing shores of good from shoals of ill. And it is suggestive that Swinburne's "flame at mainmast height" is closer to Bruno's "light ... in the crow's nest" than to any other image of synderesis; for *Lo spaccio de la bestia trionfante* is an allegorical attack on anthropomorphic religion. The gods reject those constellations which embody the memory of divine wrongdoing, and replace them with such moral virtues as Truth and Law. And Bruno's overt attack on classical mythology disguises a formidable arraignment of Christian myth.[8]

Like Bruno's *Lo spaccio*, Swinburne's Prelude is a didactic anti-Christian allegory of some complexity; there is a marked difference between the stanzas which refer to the "faith and unfaith" that Swinburne's speaker rejects, and the stanzas which expound the creed of the liberated soul. The allegory of the first two stanzas, for example, is predominantly visual and decorative – with red and green buds, white hair and golden, "The rose-red and the blood-red leaf" – and relies heavily on personification; whereas the allegory of the stanza following is more frankly abstract: "his spirit's meat / Was freedom, and his staff was wrought / Of strength, and his cloak woven of thought" (28–30). "Youth," the languid piece of personification central to the opening stanzas, has become an unnamed pilgrim, a labelled diagram of virtue. Moreover, his nature is conveyed in metaphors soothingly Stoical in tendency. Such adjectives as "equal," "level," "even," and "calm" (34, 36, 41, 48) establish the mood of the philosopher who contemplates "the calm rule of might and right / That bids men be and bear and do, / And die beneath blind skies or blue" (48–50). Swinburne's frequent use of monosyllables in the positive sections of this poem further contributes to the sense of a stark "pure cold purity of pluck."[9]

Like Bruno, Swinburne evokes classical mythology only to dismiss it. In the Prelude, the echoes of Aeschylus' *Edonoi* decisively associate the past of his speaker, and of European civilization, with lust and rage. The sonorous onomatopoeia of Aeschylus' fragment is echoed in the [ai] and [or] assonances of 105–9, the clash of *cymbal/ timbrels* (112–13), and the clatter of the "clamorous kettledrum" (112); this aural imagery evokes the "barbarous dissonance" of Comus's dangerous revels, while it also complements the primarily visual imagery of Swinburne's opening stanzas.[10] The figures of Cotys and the Maenads are joined by more abstract personifications in the very manner of the opening ("Pleasure slumberless and pale, / And Passion with rejected veil," 121–2). But when Swinburne turns from the transient pains and pleasures of the past to the steadfast light of present freedom, he moves once more to a different kind of metaphor. For abstractions like Passion and Pleasure, he substitutes freedom, strength, good and ill; for abstractions pictorially personified – "slumberless and pale" or "gold-haired" (121, 7) – he substitutes abstractions which clothe or environ the free soul. Thus, in the opening stanza, Youth and Time are two visible entities which exist in a somewhat ambivalent relationship (9–10); but in 153–7, youth, age, and time itself have formed a dim seascape through which the free soul moves — invisible but for the "indomitable light" of the sense of duty –

Across birth's hidden harbour-bar,
  Past youth where shoreward shallows are,
Through age that drives on toward the red
  Vast void of sunset hailed from far,
To the equal waters of the dead ...

The sensuous imagery of youth involved in lust and violence yields to a moralistic diagram of the soul's self-illumined progress through time. Like Bruno, Swinburne substitutes moral for pictorial allegory; and the substitution involves an implicit criticism of Christian myth. For the essence of the Prelude's morality is that "self-sufficience" which Trench found incompatible with Christianity. And the sensuous materiality of classical mythology in this poem hints at the materialism of a religion whose votaries sell themselves "To God for heaven or man for gold" (72). Anthropomorphic deities, the "Fancies and passions miscreate / By man in things dispassionate" (53–4), are as cruel and transient as the passions of the Thyiades. Cautiously, delicately, Swinburne intimates that in *Songs before Sunrise* he will turn from the "blood-feasts" of the Christian and the Bassarid (104) to a higher – and drier – morality.

"BEFORE A CRUCIFIX" AND THE SPEECHLESS CHRIST

"Positivism flaunted before a startled world a loftier morality than Christianity; and the entire act of the blessed Passion seemed to be reproduced before us, while Rénan with his treacherous praise, said 'Master, Master' and kissed him; Swinburne insulted Him as He hung on the bitter Cross; and the secret though mournful conviction of many educated people was that Christianity had had its day and was dead." – Oh! monsieur – vous me dites là des choses qui mènent à tout. (Swinburne to William Rossetti, 23 October 1871)[11]

The Prelude, as we have seen, is rigidly programmatic; "Before a Crucifix" (*P*2:81–7) is equally didactic, and more frankly polemical. Yet the latter poem begins modestly enough: a dramatic monologue, apparently, the "I" addressing the carved figure on a crucifix (13–18). But after the third stanza the "I" all but disappears; the speaker is granted an impersonal authority, as he confronts in turn the icon, the unknown historical Jesus, the hypothetical deity who ascended into heaven, the "'bon sans culotte'" who typifies the People (*L*2:160), and the mystic Bridegroom of the Church. In the end, the speaker rejects every one of these Christs; for in every shape Christ embodies the power and subtlety of the exploiter, or, at best, the impotence of the exploited.

To begin with, the image carved upon the crucifix is presented in quasi-Feuerbachian terms as the anthropomorphic "likeness" (14) of the poor who worship it. "God," says Feuerbach, "is the mirror of man" (63). Of course, Swinburne's frame of reference here is more narrowly political than Feuerbach's; but the antimetabole in 9–10 does suggest a mirror image: "The face is full of prayers and pains, / To which they bring their pains and prayers ..." But these prayers are the vain outcries of "helpless" victims (16); the carved Saviour's "ghastly mouth ... gapes and groans" (12). By contrast, the speaker, who has "nor tongue nor knee / For prayer," has a distinct "word" to speak: a word of reproach and condemnation (17–18). The inspiring "flame" of the historical Christ's speech, and the "word" he "passed to set men free," have destroyed and enslaved men; the very "name" of Christ is now a fetter; his "words" are "whips" and "brands" (19–20, 35–6, 32, 51–2). (Some months before the composition of "Before a Crucifix" in November 1869, Swinburne was insisting that the "foul gordian word" execrated in Shelley's "Ode to Liberty" must be "Christ," rather than "King" [L2:7–9, B15:353–4].)

As the speaker challenges the hypothetical deity to "Look down, turn usward ... and see" the Church (43–8), we begin to understand how Christ's language has been so cruelly perverted. On one hand, the Church has exploited the sufferings of the historical Jesus, so that the Crucifix is now, in part, significant of the wealth and wanton power of the priesthood.

> Thy nakedness enrobes thy spouse
> With the soft sanguine stuff she wears
> Whose old limbs use for ointment yet
> Thine agony and bloody sweat. (57–60)[12]

On the other hand, Christ's agony mirrors that of the poor, whose suffering also enriches the Church. As the dead Christ lay bound in linen bands, so the Church binds the People in the iron bands of Christian dogma (64–70); and the People, like the living Christ, "have not where to lay their head" (78; cp. Matt. 8.20).[13] Yet their miseries are greater than Jesus'; they have not even "the rich man's grave / To sleep in" (73–4; ctr. Matt. 27.57–60). Therefore they, and not Jesus, endure the true Passion: "So still, for all man's tears and creeds, / The sacred body hangs and bleeds" (83–4). The ambiguity of "still" points toward Hugo's eternal sufferer in "A un Martyr" – the "Dieu pensif et pâle" whom priests sell to tyrants, and who, "debout sur la terre et sous le firmament, / ... / Sur le noir Golgotha saigne éternellement" (105–11).[14] But Swinburne's martyr is more explicitly assimilated to the class struggle.

O sacred head, O desecrate,
   O labour-wounded feet and hands,
O blood poured forth in pledge to fate
   Of nameless lives in divers lands,
O slain and spent and sacrificed
People, the grey-grown speechless Christ!

Is there a gospel in the red
   Old witness of thy wide-mouthed wounds?
From thy blind stricken tongueless head
   What desolate evangel sounds
A hopeless note of hope deferred?
What word, if there be any word? (97–108)

The paradox in line 97 sets a tone of reverence mingled with indignant compassion; but Swinburne emphasizes less the People's pain than their impotent silence, "nameless," "tongueless," "speechless." The faint echo of Shakespeare's *Julius Caesar* (3.2.225) is appropriate enough: Swinburne, like Antony, would wish the "poor, poor, dumb mouths" of the victim's wounds to stir his audience to mutiny. But the figure whose dumb agony proclaims the gospel of suffering is doubly a "desolate evangel," a messenger with no word of hope.

And we seek yet if God or man
   Can loosen thee as Lazarus,
Bid thee rise up republican
   And save thyself and all of us;
But no disciple's tongue can say
When thou shalt take our sins away. (127–32)

The allusion to Lazarus heightens our sense of the People's passivity: they await a saviour. So Gerald Massey wrote, "They have bound thee in the grave-clothes, but we watch with tears and sighs, / Till Freedom come like Christ, and thou like Lazarus shalt rise."[15] Swinburne revises Massey's republican doggerel: where Massey does not question the implications of his imagery, Swinburne uses one biblical image to undermine another. The resurrection of Lazarus, which traditionally foreshadows Christ's, ironically highlights Christ's failure to redeem humanity, and the failure of the People to "rise up republican." At this point in the poem Swinburne's hostility to Christianity in every form becomes explicit. When the People do arise, the priests who "made songs" of their victims' shame will "hail and hymn" the labourers; but the latter should not permit any admixture of Christianity to taint either their liberalism or their liberty (145–51).

> Let not thy tree of freedom be
> Regrafted from that rotting tree.
> ....
> The tree of faith ingraffed by priests
>   Puts its foul foliage out above thee,
> And round it feed man-eating beasts
>   Because of whom we dare not love thee;
> Though hearts reach back and memories ache,
> We cannot praise thee for their sake. (165–8)

The priests have grafted the "tree of faith" upon the Cross, and the Cross has been corrupted. If the Cross in turn is grafted on the "tree of freedom," the rotting tree will contaminate the healthy plant. Swinburne's "tree of freedom" suggests the iron "trees of liberty" set up in Revolutionary France; Hugo's "arbre saint du Progrès," the republican organism which will grow "Sur le passé détruit"; and Hertha herself, the "life-tree" whose "topmost blossom" is human freedom (99, 198). (In *Songs before Sunrise*, "Hertha" immediately precedes "Before a Crucifix.") Of course, the "tree of faith" is a demonic parody of the life-tree, just as the "dead God" on the crucifix is a mockery of that "communist and stump-orator of Nazareth" whose "live lips" spoke of liberty.[16]

As for that "revolutionnaire transcendant," Renan's "historical Jesus,"[17] he has passed beyond our knowledge. Swinburne's agnosticism extends to Renan's "history": the human Christ is "hidden" behind the "viewless veil" woven by centuries of Christianity (167–8, 170, 181–6). We can see only the "carrion crucified" (192) which the Church presents as its deity. Throughout the poem, oral imagery and the imagery of corruption have predominated; now they combine in the image of the Church as a leprous and syphilitic bride, whose Judas-kiss betrays at once Christ's teaching and the symbolic value of his martyrdom.

So when our souls look back to thee
   They sicken, seeing against thy side,
Too foul to speak of or to see,
   The leprous likeness of a bride,
Whose kissing lips through his lips grown
Leave their God rotten to the bone. (175–80)

The Bridegroom of the Church, the "bon sans culotte," the carved image, and the supposed god – all are disgraced beyond redemption by their own impotence to protest against this exploitation and corruption. "What manhood in that God can be / Who sees their worship, and is dumb?" This "god" has produced a starved world of "haggard" wood and sun; he neither is, nor utters, a saving "word"; he can save neither himself nor others (189–90, 2, 196, 157–8). At the close of the poem, therefore, in a series of monosyllabic imperatives, Christ is dismissed: "Come down, be done with, cease, give o'er; / Hide ..., strive not, be no more" (197–8). To the liberal speaker, as to the People, the symbol of the crucifix is worse than useless.

D.G. Charlton remarks that, "whereas in England the story of the nineteenth-century 'honest doubters' is above all one of attempts to *adapt and revise* Protestant Christianity, the comparable story in France is chiefly concerned with men's attempts to *replace* Catholic Christianity."[18] We have seen that "Before a Crucifix" owes something to Hugo; and the poem's conclusion recalls the *Histoire de la révolution française* (1846–53) by Hugo's friend, that "old lion" (L2:37), Jules Michelet. Michelet pits "Christianity and the Revolution" against one another as the two antagonists – "two grand facts, two principles, two actors and two persons" – who play out the Manichean drama of modern history.[19] But Michelet's (and Swinburne's) intensely dramatic, urgent, and emotive vision of a radical opposition between the Republic and Christianity (in every form) goes beyond Hugo, as it goes beyond the English radicals – Landor, Shelley, Massey – who also influenced "Before a Crucifix" and its rhetorical strategies.

Swinburne's deployment of these strategies is strinkingly original. It is indeed the structure of the lyric, or, as we may say, the strategy of the poem as a whole, that makes "Before a Crucifix" peculiarly successful. The first two-thirds of the poem (1–132) are composed in a tone of "mild and modified hostility" (L2:57), and develop the parallelism between Christ and the People. This political attack upon the Church is marked by "the strong bitterness of pity" ("Apologia," P2:316), rather than by the vituperative frenzy of the "Hymn of

Man"; Swinburne is exploiting the emotive value of the crucifixion. By a strategy dear to Western heretics at least since Lessing's day, Christ is pitted against Christianity: "Change not the gold of faith for dross / Of Christian creeds that spit on Christ" (153–4).[20] The most famous use of this motif in English literature is Shelley's in *Prometheus Unbound* (1.546–59, 597–615), echoed in Swinburne's "Siena" (1868), and, later, in his sonnet "On the Russian Persecution of the Jews" (1882). In both of these poems, Swinburne, like Shelley, insists that Christ's worst suffering must have sprung from his prophetic vision of Christianity – his foreknowledge that "the word of Christian should / Mean to men evil and not good." In "Siena," he goes further, suggesting that Christ's eternal crucifixion is entirely the work of his worshippers. "Still your God, spat upon and sold, / Bleeds at your hands": the lines echo "A un Martyr" and anticipate "Before a Crucifix" (P2:165, 5:245). But "Siena" does not consider how this crucifixion by creed invalidates the traditional significance of Christian symbolism.

"Siena," composed a year earlier than "Before a Crucifix," is thus less radical than its successor. But to appreciate the full audacity of the later poem, we should compare it with a lyric by another free-thinker, equally concerned with the collapse of Christian symbolism. Like "Before a Crucifix," Clough's "Easter Day: Naples, 1849" buries a Christ long dead and rotten: "Long ere to-day / Corruption that sad perfect work hath done ... / Ashes to ashes, dust to dust" (15–24).[21] "Easter Day" also opposes the reality of Christ's life and death to the falsifications of "an after-Gospel and late Creed" (33). And that reality is not merely "speechless," but absent, irrecoverable: "Where they have laid Him is there none to say! / No sound, nor in, nor out; no word / Of where to seek the dead or meet the living Lord" (147–9).

It is not without passionate regret that Clough dismisses Christianity. "We are most wretched that had most believed" (75); "we are souls bereaved" (86). Swinburne had a virulent contempt for this rhetorical strategy. "Nothing ... is more wearisome than the delivery of reluctant doubt, of half-hearted hope and half-incredulous faith." The "melodious whine of retrospective and regretful scepticism" may advertise a Tennyson or a Clough as a responsible, moderate thinker with an instinct for reverence and a proper respect for the feelings of churchmen; but whining, Swinburne insists, is not singing.[22] Yet he himself, for once, exploits this strategy of regret with dignified brevity in "Before a Crucifix," when we are compelled to reject Christ "Though hearts reach back and memories ache" (167).

Clearly, then, "Before a Crucifix" and "Easter Day" share certain attitudes and motifs from the common stock of the literature of free thought. Yet these lyrics differ strikingly in other respects. To Clough, the myth of Christ's resurrection is an "'idle tale'" (124); like Strauss, Clough perceives myth as an unconscious, rather than artful, fiction created by a community rather than by an individual, class, or institution.[23]

> As circulates in some great city crowd
> A rumour changeful, vague, importunate, and loud,
> From no determined centre, or of fact,
>   Or authorship exact,
>   Which no man can deny
>   Nor verify;
>   So spread the wondrous fame ...
>   ("Easter Day," 48–54)

Clough's language divests the "wondrous fame" (his Latinate pun identifies fame with rumour) of all exact form or significance. Swinburne, on the other hand, perceives religious language and symbolism as heavy with precise and oppressive meaning. Even Meleager's nonsense embodies a passionate self-torment exactly formulated, not a "vague" doubt or aspiration; and the prayers of priests in "Before a Crucifix" have a function as concrete as that of eating (183–4). While Clough ascribes blind folly to the "ministers and stewards of a word / Which [they] would preach, because another heard," Swinburne attacks them for their craft in turning the Word to their account: "They scourge us with [Christ's] words for whips" ("ED," 139–40; "BC," 51). Christianity would be an impotent weapon in republican hands only because it is so potent as an instrument of oppression. Swinburne himself has tried his hand at relabelling the elements of the Passion: Christ is the People; the nails that fix him to the Cross are fear, faith, and falsehood; the seamless coat is the natural soul's freedom, and so on (85–90, 118–19). But these parallels have at best only a temporary value. In the last dozen stanzas of "Before a Crucifix," Swinburne deliberately shatters the expectations which his earlier moderation may have encouraged.

What he does is in a way the reverse of what Clough does in the "Easter Day" poems; for Clough, in "Easter Day II," hears a "graver word" (16), which assures him that Christ still lives "In the great Gospel and true Creed" (49–51). The meaning of this is far from clear in "Easter Day II," an unconvincing hotchpotch of tautology and paradox; but Clough's shorter (and better) "Epi-Strauss-ion" suggests that, when the mythical nature of the gospels is clearly understood, the "religious conception" which they embody will also be more firmly grasped. Like Strauss, Clough tries to "re-establish dogmatically that which has been destroyed critically," or, in Charlton's terms, to "adapt and revise Protestant Christianity."[24]

Whereas Clough denies Christianity and then reaffirms it, in a novel but constructive sense, Swinburne attempts to affirm the worship of Christ in a new sense, and then finds that any kind of Christian affirmation is impossible. To revise Christianity is not enough; Swinburne must replace it. But with what? What symbolic system can adequately present the People, their suffering and their self-regeneration? What can replace the Christian myth of sacrifice and redemption? Above all, what can replace that mode of religious parody which has hitherto been central to Swinburne's art? For is not demonic parody itself a graft from the tree of faith?

In the "Hymn of Man" and "Hertha," Swinburne begins to answer these questions. But they continue to haunt him throughout the next decade; and it is not until *Songs of the Springtides* (1879–80) that his answers gain confidence and consistency. For only then does he find a lyrical sub-genre which enables him to handle such issues effectively. In *Songs before Sunrise* he relies on a mixture of allegory and didacticism to see him through his difficulties; and the success of this mixture is questionable.

"Before a Crucifix" itself, like "Easter Day," is undoubtedly a didactic lyric. Both poems open deceptively as dramatic monologues ("ED," 1–4; "BC," 1–18), but drop the first person for the greater part of the poem. Each proceeds to a series of four rhetorical questions emphasized by anaphora ("What though ... What if ... Or what if ... What if ...," "ED," 9–38; "It was for this ...?" four times, "BC," 19–35). Both lyrics use a series of dogmatic statements ("ED," 11–26, 29–35, 42–63; "BC," 49–96) to lead up to an emotional outburst of interjection and apostrophe ("ED," 65–71; "BC," 97–102, 109–14). Both climax in commands: from "Eat, drink, and play" to "Let us go hence" ("ED," 76–152); from the imperatives addressed to the People ("BC," 149–56) to those addressed to Christ ("Come down, ... be no more," 197–8). Each of these works not only recommends a specific course of action (the repudiation of Christianity), but, also, is so constructed as to make that recommendation seem the crucial impulse of the poem.

In the "Hymn of Man," Swinburne will retain some of this didacticism; yet the Hymn's structure is modelled, not on the pattern just outlined, but on the structure of a "song" within a French Romantic prophecy. The dialectical plan of the Hymn, and many of its crucial themes, images, and assumptions, are taken from the satyr's chant in Hugo's "Le Satyre." Indeed, as Swinburne develops his republican alternative – or alternatives – to Christianity, the example of "Le Satyre" is invaluable to him. And, as the Romantic prophecy traditionally mingles explicit didacticism with less direct modes, such as myth, Swinburne's dependence on a Romantic model will eventually lead him in the direction of increasing caution, and increasing complexity.

STYLE AND STRUCTURE IN THE "HYMN OF MAN"

Liberté, vie et foi, sur le dogme détruit!
(Victor Hugo, "Le Satyre")[25]

The "Hymn of Man" is radically derivative in two ways. In the first place, as I have just suggested, its structure is profoundly influenced by the song of Hugo's satyr; I shall elaborate on this point presently. Second, the texture of the Hymn is determined by that impulse to religious parody which was called into question, indirectly, by the rejection of the "rotting tree" in "Before a Crucifix." So long as Swinburne assumed that religious language contains a grain of (cruel) truth, his exploitation of distinctively Christian forms, types, and patterns was logically and aesthetically unexceptionable; but now, when he has told his readers to jettison Christianity altogether, his continuing dependence on these forms and patterns has become a liability. Swinburne is attempting to destroy one symbolic system, and, to give point and power to his destructive activity, he must supply a substitute; for a poet in such a position, parody is a good servant, but a bad master.

Even the history of the Hymn's composition demonstrates the primacy of the impulse toward parody in the poem, and also the primacy of the anti-Catholic impulse. In February 1869 the *Civiltà Cattolica*, a journal then considered to be the organ of the Papacy, announced that the long-awaited Oecumenical Council would "proclaim the doctrines of the Syllabus" (promulgated in 1864 as a sweeping condemnation of "liberalism and modern civilization") as well as "the dogmatic infallibility of the Sovereign Pontiff."[26] Liberal concern found expression in the organization of what William Rossetti called "the Congress of Freethinkers" and Swinburne "the Anti-Catholic council." Swinburne and William sent a letter of approval to the latter council on 10 November 1869; Swinburne insisted on including, as part of the letter, an "'acte de foi' ... appropriate to ... the character and occasion of this protest; an episode in the great suit of Man v. God." This "profession of faith," as toned down by William Rossetti (who apparently felt that Swinburne's draft was too frankly atheistic), is still flatly "anti-Catholic": "The Liberty we believe in is one and indivisible: without free thought there can be no free life. That democracy of the spirit without the body, personal or social, can enjoy but a false freedom, must, by the very law of its being, confront a man-made theocracy to destroy it. Ideal or actual, the Church of priests, and the Republic, are natural and internecine enemies."[27]

As early as 15 October 1869, when he was still drafting this letter, Swinburne had been planning

a sort of Hymn for this Congress – as it were a 'Te Hominem Laudamus,' to sing the human triumph over 'things' – the opposing forces of life and nature – and over the God of his own creation ... It might end somehow thus with a cry of triumph over the decadence of a receding Deity:

'And the love-song of earth as thou diest sounds over the graves of her Kings;
Glory to Man in the highest! for man is the master of things.' (L2:37)

Eleven days later Swinburne had begun "another mystic atheistic democratic anthropologic poem" ("Hertha"), and had drafted those sections of "Hertha" which most closely parody biblical passages (L2:45). Thus he began the composition of both "Hertha" and the "Hymn of Man" in his old vein of religious parody. On 8 January 1870, Swinburne announced that he had "broken the back (not only of God, but) of" "Hertha" by striking a "blow at the very root of Theism"; a month later (12 February) he reported the composition of certain violently "anti-Christian" lines in the "Hymn of Man." "I read not long since something of the Catholic propositions put forth by Mastai and his galley slaves, and ... was moved by honest horror and disgust and scorn to ease myself on them and their God even as did Blake on Klopstock" (L2:79–80, 89).

What Swinburne had read was perhaps the translation of the Canones de Ecclesia – the Curia's restatement of the principles embodied in the Syllabus – published in the Times on 10 February 1870. This expressly condemned agnosticism and religious tolerance (articles 5, 6, 13), and anathematized those who upheld "the natural liberty of man" against "the power which is necessary for the government of civil society" (article 18). Such language seemed fully to justify Mozley's earlier claim that "The council itself is for the very purpose of laying down laws and limits to thought."[28]

In a sense, then, the Hymn is a piece of occasional polemic; but it is also a carefully structured and deliberate statement of Swinburne's views during the period at which his finest political lyrics were composed. It is, however, an oblique and difficult statement. Unlike the "Hymn to Proserpine," its "companion-in-arms-and-metre" (L2:87), the "Hymn of Man" uses three very different styles or modes: the mythopoeic questioning which dominates the first section (1–38); the comparatively direct and didactic assertions of the second and fourth sections (39–92, 119–56), which describe and celebrate the religion of humanity; and the prophetic denunciation of Christianity in the third and fifth segments (93–118, 157–200). The variation and alternation of modes may suggest an evolutionary process – the "rhythmic anguish of growth" (13) – but also they help to define the intellectual and emotional structures which are central to the poem.

Every section of the Hymn shows how closely Swinburne is still clinging to parody as his chief mode of attack. The opening segment, with its echoes of Aristophanes' *The Birds* and its unanswerable questions, subtly ridicules Genesis and other inventions of the blind fools who "feel for the track where highway is none to be had" (40).[29] But, as Eric Wexler shrewdly remarks, the metaphorical language of this passage implies that earth in some sense lives and speaks: "The word of the earth in the ears of the world, was it God? was it man?" Like the queries posed in Tennyson's "The Higher Pantheism," these are leading questions; Swinburne begins to answer them in the second section, but with a direct didacticism which continues to discredit myths of origin. His sudden transition from the interrogative to the declarative implies that he is turning from idle speculation to mere matter of fact:

But what was seed of the sower? and the grain of him, whence was it grown?

....

Therefore the God that ye make you is grievous, and gives not aid,
Because it is but for your sake that the God of your making is made.
Thou and I and he are not gods made men for a span,
But God, if a God there be, is the substance of men which is man. (38–44)

There are obvious difficulties in the way of a religion of humanity. In the first section, Swinburne creates a delightful image of the earth-maiden's rejoicing as her lovely "firstborn passion, and impulse of firstborn things" breaks forth like a bird (21–35). But he also hints that the earth-maiden's joy may be naive; had she foreseen "The rhythmic anguish of growth" and the meaningless crippled efforts of humanity (11–18), she might not have rejoiced. Similarly, the proclamation of a religion of humanity in 41–64 is called into question by a passage which anticipates T.H. Huxley's attack on "Comtist Anthropolatry" by twenty years. "I know no study," says Huxley, "which is so unutterably saddening as that of the evolution of humanity ... [T]he worship of a God who needs forgiveness and help, and deserves pity every hour of his existence, is no better than that of any other voluntarily selected fetish."[30] Swinburne too cries,

O God sore stricken of things! they have wrought him a raiment of pain;
Can a God shut eyelids and wings at a touch on the nerves of the brain?
O shamed and sorrowful God, whose force goes out at a blow! (75–7)

Yet, although man may be a "God fast-bound as with iron of adverse things" (54), he is still a god, because "his own soul only constrains him, his own mouth only denies" (92). That is to say, man constrains himself by denying his own power, by accepting the notion that he is the victim of his world, and that "Tout le trahit; ... / Toutes les surdités s'entendent contre lui."[31] Hence God's "power upon men for a season" is "made out of the malice of things" (108). The concept of a God external to man expresses and sanctifies the "dread wherewith life was astounded and shamed out of sense of its trust" (116); man's innate trust in the power of his own spirit is undermined by the fear that the "malice of things" might overwhelm him, that he needs a Saviour other than himself. In whoring after these fears, man "makes love to disaster, and woos desolation with love" (90), forgetting his true bride, the "truth" of his own spirit's power (cp. 151, "the truth and his spirit are wed").

The Church of fear is the demonic parody of the true Bride, as the Christian God – with his "wings" of "torture and terror and treason" (107), and his "gibbets and stakes" which bear the "fruit" of death (106) – is the demonic parody of the true god, man. It is man whose "wings of the mind" must ultimately take flight for the centre from which he alone can contemplate "the roots of the years and the fruits" (66, 129, 153). The third section of the Hymn arraigns God as a criminal partly in order to explain away the seeming inconsistency in the religion of humanity, as expounded in the second section; most of man's sufferings are inflicted by organized religion; destroy that, and the god apparently "sore stricken of things" will be seen truly as "the master of things." Then it will be possible to celebrate Man Triumphant, as Swinburne does in the fourth section. But the accusations brought against God in the third segment also help to define the nature of the new god more clearly, by contrast, just as Babylon contributes to the definition of Jerusalem.

For instance, God is made out of the *malice* of things, whereas man is "at one with the *reason* of things that is sap to the roots. / He can hear in their changes a sound as the *conscience* of consonant spheres; / He can see through the years flowing round him the *law* lying under the years" (154–6; italics mine). Not only is there an order and "law" in "things," but there is also a "con-science," a shared knowledge or consciousness, and hence a living harmony among them. This harmony is the true "word of the earth," earth's "love-song" (2–4, 199); but it can only be realized, can only be uttered, through the activity of the human spirit. "By the spirit are things overcome; ... / It hath speech, and their forces are dumb" (87–8). Just as the *confounded/astounded* cross rhyme in 115–16 emphasizes the bewilderment which Christian doctrines have imposed upon the spirit, so in 87–8 the *overcome/dumb* cross rhyme underlines the power of the spirit over mute "things."

> Sous l'arbre qui bruit, près du monstre qui brame,
> Quelqu'un parle. C'est l'Âme. Elle sort du chaos.
> Sans elle, pas de vents, le miasme; pas de flots,
> L'étang; l'âme, en sortant du chaos, le dissipe;
> Car il n'est que l'ébauche et l'âme est le principe.
> ....
> Et sans l'homme pourtant les horizons sont morts;
> ....
> Seul il parle; et sans lui tout est décapité.
> ("Le Satyre," ii, 424–8; iii, 530–4)[32]

At this point we should remember that Swinburne's poem is the "Hymn of Man," although its "companion-in-arms-and-metre" is the "Hymn *to* Proserpine" (italics mine). Proserpine's worshipper is distinct from his goddess; but in the later Hymn man celebrates himself. "From the flame that [his] own mouth gives reillumed" (56). His own holy spirit rekindles, perpetuates, and illuminates itself: "His soul to his soul is a law, and his mind is a light to his mind" (150). By virtue of this reflexive activity, man takes his place at the "centre" of the universe; the world of time, space, and "things" is his kingdom (129, 51).

> Space is the soul's to inherit; the night is hers as the day;
> Lo, saith man, this is my spirit; how shall not the worlds make way?

This is not Wordsworthian pantheism, in which, through contact with landscape and non-human life, a man discovers his part in a larger spiritual reality. For Swinburne, it is only through the examination of his own nature that man apprehends his true position in the seemingly hostile world of "things."

Does this mean that evil is an illusion? Not at all; for so long as the many minds which constitute the human soul live in disharmony – so long as these minds are corrupted by lawless tyrannies and false religions – the "reason of things" is not yet. The "law" and the "reason" that give meaning to the flowing years will exist only in the republic of love, in spontaneous political harmony between man and man, since "reason is the sunlight shed from love the sun" ("The Eve of Revolution," P2:11). It is in this world that the union of men in Man must be realized, as Mazzini insisted; but it can only be realized when we assert "the superiority of mind over matter, of the *idea* over the *fact*, ... the search after moral perfection over that of material good."[33] "By the spirit are things overcome." What Swinburne means by man's mastery over "things" is not the ability to manipulate, exploit, or destroy at will, but the ability to maintain the predominant status of the spirit. A spiritual and intellectual reformation is of primary importance, since political revolution should follow as a matter of course.

Swinburne's presentation of spiritual (and, implicitly, political) revolution in the fourth section of the Hymn is, of course, prophetic; it describes what might be rather than what is. Like all Romantic prophecies, it strives to enact its own fulfilment within the mind of the reader. Part of the poem's notorious shrillness derives from the fact that it is an intensely passionate poem without a persona; but against this we might plead that there can be no persona here but man himself. Besides, the unstable mixture of exultation, anxiety, and bitterness in the first two sections finds its catharsis in the hysterical fury of the third, which in turn makes possible the calmer, more dignified exposition of Idealistic humanism in the fourth segment, as well as the sardonic triumph of the fifth. Swinburne's polemical violence thus follows a logical development, controlled by the ideas which he expresses.

To the reader who has followed the fluctuations of the Hymn's thought and passion, and who has enacted within himself, or herself, the rejection of God and the triumph of man, God has ceased to seem a powerful criminal; the furious condemnation of God by God's own principles and in God's own words ("Thou art judged, O Judge," 118; cp. Matt. 7.1) should no longer be necessary. The larger part of the fifth section mocks not God but God's deluded worshippers, even as Elijah mocked the priests of Baal in 1 Kings 18.27. It is here that Swinburne turns to the members of the Oecumenical Council who "would blind [man] with curses and blind him with vapour of prayer" (157). Their language of "chains and clouds" will lose its iron power at last, and become merely vaporous.

> Cry aloud; for your God is a God and a Saviour; cry, make yourselves lean;
> Is he drunk or asleep, that the rod of his wrath is unfelt and unseen?
> ....
> Cry aloud till his godhead awaken; what doth he to sleep and to dream?
> Cry, cut yourselves, gash you with knives and with scourges, heap on to you dust;
> ....
> Yea, weep to him, lift up your hands; be your eyes as a fountain of tears;
> Where he stood there is nothing that stands; if he call, there is no man that hears.
> He hath doffed his king's raiment of lies now the wane of his kingdom is come;
> Ears hath he, and hears not; and eyes, and he sees not; and mouth, and is dumb.
> His red king's raiment is ripped from him naked, his staff broken down;
> And the signs of his empire are stripped from him shuddering; and where is his crown? (167–86)

The first lines quoted follow Elijah's words to the "prophets of Baal" very closely: "Cry aloud: for he is a god; ... peradventure he sleepeth, and must be awaked." Swinburne introduces into these words, however, a phrase from Jeremiah ("the rod of his wrath," Lam. 3.1); the action of cutting oneself with knives is ascribed to Baal's prophets (1 Kings 18.28), but that of heaping dust on one's head is also performed by Jehovah's worshippers (Lam. 2.10). The very texture of Swinburne's biblical allusions artfully confuses Jehovah with Baal. Echoes of biblical prophecy continue through the passage. Thus the phrases *lift up your hands* and *fountain of tears* are borrowed from Jeremiah's expressions of despair at the desolation of Israel (Lam. 2.19, Jer. 9.1), and Swinburne's assertion that none will hear God's cry sardonically reverses God's promise in Zechariah 13.9: "they shall call on my name, and I will hear them."

The raiment of the militant Messiah in Isaiah 63.2–3 is red – sprinkled with the blood of his enemies – but Swinburne, as in "Before a Crucifix," connects this scarlet with the blood of the oppressed, the purple of the emperors, and the glories which are to be stripped from the tyrants of the earth in the day of punishment (cp. Ezek. 23.26). So God's "red king's raiment is ripped from him," and his staff broken: "How hath the oppressor ceased! ... The Lord hath broken the staff of the wicked" (Isa. 14.4–5). The divine tyrant loses his crown (cp. Lam. 5.16), and we are reminded that in expanding on Matt. 6.25 Swinburne had asked, as a republican, "Is ... the head not more than the crown?" These political metaphors tend to revive our sense that God is a criminal, a Bonaparte deposed. Yet at the same time an echo of the psalm *Non nobis, Domine,* as it appears in the Book of Common Prayer, underlines Swinburne's equation of God with the idols of the heathen:

They have mouths, and speak not: eyes have they, and see not.
They have ears, and hear not ...
They that make them are like unto them: and so are all such as put their trust in them. (Ps. 115.5–8)[34]

The tension between Swinburne's inclination to arraign God as a criminal, and his insistence that God is only an impotent idol, weakens the final section of the Hymn. To be sure, God's potency for evil and his impotence are not wholly incompatible; the concept of God is powerful and dangerous, but the personal transcendent deity is a powerful shadow. Only the strength of man's creative imagination makes "God" an effective evil. Yet the emotions with which we contemplate the ineffectual deity and the all-too-effective concept of deity, respectively, are very different; and Swinburne makes a tactical error in evoking both concurrently in 183–98. Even a sympathetic reader must suspect that, if God is dead, we need not rage at him; if he still represents that formidable menace so eloquently assailed in the third section of the Hymn, it is too early to despise him. The Old Testament prophets never confounded Baal with Babylon.

It is clear that the style of the Hymn, and especially that of the final and climactic section, is indeed determined by Swinburne's taste for religious parody – so much so, that the effect of the final section is weakened by untimely allusions to the scarlet tyrants of biblical demonic imagery. But the Hymn seems also to mock a philosophico-religious lyric which itself revises orthodox Christianity rather freely. Three weeks before Swinburne first reported the composition of a substantial portion of the Hymn, he had been rereading Tennyson's "The Higher Pantheism" ("not bad verse altogether, but what gabble and babble of half-hatched throughts in half-baked words!" [L2:86]), and had drafted what later became the final couplet of "The Higher Pantheism in a Nutshell." *The Holy Grail and other Poems* had been published in December 1869, after Swinburne had first conceived of a "Te Hominem Laudamus"; the conclusion of the Hymn, with its parody of the angels' nativity song, was already drafted in iambic-anapestic hexameters. But "The Higher Pantheism," in the same metre, may well have spurred on, and even influenced, the growth of the Hymn.

The Hymn's opening section in particular, with its unanswerable questions, certainly recalls lines 1–8 of Tennyson's lyric.[35] Some of Tennyson's imagery, too, reappears in the Hymn, although strangely transformed. "Earth, these solid stars, this weight of body and limb, / Are they not sign and symbol of thy division from Him?" Tennyson asks (5–6). For "solid stars" and earth, Swinburne gives us the earth-maiden hymning the Divine Man to "the starry and sisterly throng" (2–4, 200), while the detaining and deforming weight of "things" presses on the man-god, instead of symbolizing man's alienation from God. (Yet, as this seeming weight alienates man from himself, Swinburne may be following Tennyson more closely than he seems.) Later in the Hymn, Swinburne manages to reverse two of Tennyson's statements on the nature of man's relationship with God. Tennyson cries, "Speak to Him thou for He hears" (11); Swinburne declares that "no man" will hear God's cry. Tennyson (providing a variation on a theme by St. Paul) declares that "the ear of man cannot hear, and the eye of man cannot see" the "Vision of Him who reigns" (17, 2); Swinburne says of God, "Ears hath he, and hears not; and eyes, and he sees not..." Man, on the other hand, has eyes that "take part in the morning," ears that can catch the harmony of the spheres, and a tongue to announce his own power (123, 155, 132). In short, while Tennyson encourages his reader to a leap of faith which is at the same time a confident dependence upon God, Swinburne resists every thought of dependence; his revisions reduce God to mute impotence, and ascribe life and vision to man alone.

A stronger and more positive influence on the Hymn is Victor Hugo's "Le Satyre" (1859), which is also composed in hexameter couplets. If "The Higher Pantheism" suggested the opening section of Swinburne's poem, the structure of the Hymn as a whole can be traced directly to the satyr's song, as a summary of that song will demonstrate. The satyr first "chanta la terre monstrueuse" (ii, 279), with its "palpitation sauvage" (314), as Swinburne opens with "the word of the earth" and its "rhythmic anguish"; then, as Swinburne turns to the promulgation of the great god man, Hugo's satyr – somewhat more modestly – begins to explain man's special position:

"Quelqu'un parle ... [L]'Air veut devenir l'Esprit, l'homme apparaît" (425–30).[36]

Like Blake, the satyr avers that "everything that lives is Holy": "l'arbre est sacré, l'animal est sacré, / L'homme est sacré" (438–9). Swinburne's religion of humanity seems more exclusive than Hugo's pantheism. However, the two poets take a very similar view of history. Both secularize the Christian pattern: the world rises out of chaos; man, embodying the spiritual principle within the world, falls from his primitive freedom into a state of slavery, a submission to priests and kings which is morally ruinous and distorts man's relation to nature.[37] It is thus that "la Chose vient mordre ... l'homme" (566), detaining man's apotheosis. Yet man, when he recognizes himself as his own self-sufficient saviour, may rise to his primitive freedom and learn to master "tout ce qui l'a jadis persécuté" (594).[38]

When man masters "things," "things" will enter into a loving harmony with him: "tout s'entendra, tout étant l'harmonie" (724).[39] For "his soul is at one with the reason of things"; "on verra l'homme devenir loi" (590), as the world's order realizes itself in man. Both Swinburne and Hugo declare that man, by the power of his spirit, will rise through the heavens and join the spheres, "car un esprit se meut comme une sphère" (627).[40] But both are concerned less with the physical exploration of space than with developing an image of infinite expansion – "l'élargissement dans l'infini sans fond" (iv, 710) – and of "la révolte sainte" (iii, 584), "the divine spirit of rebellious redemption" (WB 234), which scales and secularizes the heavens: "if higher than is heaven be the reach of the soul, shall not heaven bow down?"

Both poets begin with a song of earth; indicate man's unique position; deplore the disasters that priesthood has brought on humanity; and celebrate the coming hour of man's liberation. By way of completing the five-part structure of satyr's song and human Hymn, respectively, both end on a polemical note, vigorously condemning God or the gods, and proclaiming his or their fall. Hugo's satyr invokes "ce noir dieu final que l'homme appelle Assez" to end "tous les à peu près," those partial glimpses of the divine which men mistake for the whole (iv, 678, 671); all evil comes from the error of giving gods a form, since by this error man obscures the infinite power within him.

Monde, tout le mal vient de la forme des dieux.

....

Place au rayonnement de l'âme universelle!

Un roi c'est de la guerre, un dieu c'est de la nuit.
Liberté, vie et foi, sur le dogme détruit!
Partout une lumière et partout un génie!
Amour! tout s'entendra, tout étant l'harmonie!
....
Place à Tout! Je suis Pan; Jupiter! à genoux! (713–26)[41]

"I have improved and completed my hymn of Te Hominem Laudamus," Swinburne wrote to William Rossetti on 19 August 1870,
"without treading too much on ground preoccupied by Shelley or
Hugo – on the outworks of Prometheus Unbound or the Légende
des Siècles [*sic*]" (*L*2:120). It should now be clear that Swinburne is
underestimating his debt to the *Légende*, that study of

the agony and passion and triumph of invincible humanity, the protest and
witness of enduring earth against the passing shades of heaven, the struggle
and the plea of eternal manhood against all transient forces of ephemeral
and tyrannous godhead. Within the orbit of this epicycle one poem only of
the first part [of *La Légende des Siècles*] ... can properly be said to revolve;
but the light of that planet has fire enough to animate with its reflex the
whole concourse of stormy stars ... There may be something of Persian or
Indian mysticism, there is more of universal and unimaginative reason, in
the great allegoric myth which sets forth here how the half-brute child of
one poor planet has in him the ... principle of life everlasting, and dilates
in force of it to the very type and likeness of the eternal universal substance
which is spirit or matter of life. ("La Légende des Siècles" [1883], *B*13:124)

It is interesting that Swinburne emphasizes the didacticism of "Le
Satyre." The Hymn, of course, is frankly didactic (although its didacticism, like that of "The Higher Pantheism," is complex and difficult); the satyr's song is also largely didactic, but it functions
dramatically within a mythic frame. The impact of Hugo's poem
depends less on the satyr's "message" than on the way in which,
as he sings, he transforms himself from the half-bestial butt of the
Olympians to the "Démesuré" figure crying, "Place à Tout! Je suis
Pan" (683, 726). The Hymn has nothing to match the superb tau-
tological insolence of this apotheosis. Echoes of Pan's cry ring
through "Pan and Thalassius" and "A Nympholept," but these are
late lyrics in which Swinburne at last turns against the Master, criticizing his too confident pantheism.[42] It is in "Hertha" that the
younger poet most nearly parallels Hugo's achievement, as he provides an "allegoric myth" informed by the intellectual concerns and
polemical intentions dialectically embodied in the Hymn.

MYTH AND ALLEGORY IN "HERTHA"

The finite is the infinite, Man, God.
> (Clough, "As one who shoots an
> arrow overhead")

> Man, in short, will be an unprecedented God –
> neither purely naturalistic nor supernatural, but the
> embodiment of the meaning of the universe. (Wexler,
> 126)

Swinburne's odd phrase, "allegoric myth," is actually a rather good description of the Romantic prophecy as Blake and Hugo employ it. Speaking of Blake's prophecies in general and of *Europe* in particular, the Victorian poet remarks, "Allegory, here as always [in Blake], is interfused with myth in a manner at once violent and intricate" (*WB* 241); and it is clear from Swinburne's *William Blake* (see Appendix) that Swinburne viewed allegory and myth as the two chief and complementary elements of Romantic prophecy. In his view, they spring from the impulse toward control and the impulse toward creation, respectively, within the poet; and either is weak without the other. Yet how can the discipline of allegory interact harmoniously with the creative freedom of myth? In the 1860s, Swinburne fails to find any unifying principle within Romantic prophecy, other than the "one truth" that human freedom is the only "secret and sense of the earth."[43] This "one truth" is the common theme of all the political poems; but no aesthetic is founded on it, as yet. Only in "Hertha" is this discrepancy at least partially resolved.

According to Roppen, "Hertha" is Swinburne's attempt to create "some metaphorical framework" which might give his views a "range and significance beyond direct and doctrinal formulation."[44] "Hertha" is also an attempt to harmonize myth with didactic allegory. In the "Hymn of Man," as we have seen, myth is given short shrift; the cosmogonies of Orphic and Christian tradition are sternly dismissed, and Swinburne's proclamation of the new faith is openly didactic. By contrast with the Hymn, "Hertha" is smooth, seamless; polemic alternates with the proclamation of the new faith in lines 158–90, but the former is carefully subordinated to the latter, and both are coordinated with the two central myths, or mythological metaphors, of the poem.

It is difficult to distinguish between myth and metaphor in "Hertha." For one thing, all myths can only be inadequate metaphors of a deity originally conceived on a very abstract level. "In Hertha," Swinburne told Gabriel Rossetti, "I have tried not to get the mystic elemental side of the poem, its pure and free imaginative part, swamped by the promulgation of the double doctrine, democratic and atheistic, equality of men and abolition of gods" (*L*2:98). But Swinburne's phrasing suggests that the "free imaginative" element of myth is a vulnerable component of the lyric, likely to be "swamped," unless the poet is careful, by the predominant didactic element. It is the primacy of the didactic impulse in "Hertha" that makes such critics as Ridenour uneasy. The myth of the earth-mother "operates," according to Ridenour, in a "rather formal way"; her "always shadowy personality" is further compromised by Swinburne's introduction of the Yggdrasil-myth; the unity of the world-tree itself is "weakly imagined."[45] All this is true; yet perhaps Ridenour is unduly distressed by it. Swinburne's use of myth in this poem should be compared to the use of figurative language in Shelley's "To a Skylark": myths, made by men, evoke Hertha without containing her, as the similes of maiden, poet, rose, and so on evoke the skylark. The difference is that Shelley's lark represents an inaccessible, inexpressible reality ("What thou art we know not"), whereas in "Hertha" abstract formulations of the deity's nature (1–25) compete with the myths which express that deity less directly (61–160).

"Hertha" is not, like the "Hymn of Man," obviously divided into thematically distinct sections; still, we can discern three main stages in the progress of Hertha's argument. In lines 1–40, the goddess proclaims her nature; in 41–145, she condemns dogmatized cosmogonies and creeds, and urges man to turn to her. For man's relation to Hertha is entirely different from the relation between humanity and deity in most organized religions: as Hertha explains in 146–200, she is fully realized only in man – "Man, equal and one with me, man that is made of me, man that is I" (200). The shift from an emphasis on the nature of deity to an emphasis on man as the self-realization of deity enacts the process of evolution which Swinburne evokes in this poem, and exemplifies the kind of intellectual progress which he would like to stimulate in Western literature.

"Hertha" begins in the pantheistic mode which Swinburne's contemporaries had been adapting from Oriental sources. The self-proclamation of a deity may be found in Exodus 3.14, John 8.58, and Job 38–9 – all of which passages Swinburne parodies in "Hertha" (15, 41–60).[46] But these biblical passages are paradoxical, or lyrical; the didacticism of Hertha's self-annunciation has another source. In

January 1869 Swinburne had been studying the Mahabharata with the atheist Bendyshe. The Bhagavad Gita is that book of the Mahabharata which contains the most sophisticated and impressive theology; and, while we cannot be certain that Swinburne read as far as the Gita in Fauche's elegant translation, the evidence of "Hertha" alone suggests that he had some acquaintance with Hindu pantheism. Lines 11–14, 16–17 of "Hertha" roughly paraphrase the opening of Krishna's pantheistic boast ("I am the cause of the production and dissolution of the whole universe. There exists no other thing superior to me"); and the assurance that Hertha, and we in her, have always existed and shall exist (10, 100) further echoes the Gita.[47]

Swinburne had read and admired Emerson's "Brahma" as early as July 1867 (L1:252); and Emerson's influence is discernible in "Hertha." Swinburne insists that Hertha is immanent in all things and all passions ("I am that which unloves me and loves ...," 18–25), and this amorality recalls "Brahma," lines 1–2 and 9–12 ("I am the doubter and the doubt"), rather than the equally pantheistic – but not amoral – passages in chapters 7 and 9 of the Gita.[48] Yet, unlike Krishna or Emerson's Brahma, Hertha is anthropocentric. She takes the Idealist view that man is her own self-objectification, and her description of the Time-bird suggests that he is moving steadily upward (116–20), whereas time in the Gita is cyclic rather than linear and progressive (in "Brahma," too, there is no hint of libertarian progressivism). Moreover, Krishna exacts disinterestedness, and the suppression of the passions, as methods of worship, tributes of devotion toward himself, whereas Hertha explicitly rejects this vision of the proper relationship between man and deity. The maternal image developed in 41–70 implies that man and goddess are of the same stuff; accordingly, Hertha warns man, "Not as servant to lord ... shalt thou give thee to me" (85). Like Hugo's satyr, Hertha attacks cosmogonies and creeds in order to make room for a new ethical and political imperative.

> A creed is a rod,
>   And a crown is of night;
> But this thing is God,
>   To be man with thy might,
> To grow straight in the strength of thy spirit, and live out thy life as the
>   light. (71–5)

The first two lines of this stanza rewrite Hugo's aphorism in "Le Satyre," "Un roi c'est de la guerre, un dieu c'est de la nuit" (721).

Swinburne's next three lines enforce a point which Gerald Massey had made more awkwardly: "Slaves, cry unto God! but be our God reveal'd / In our lives, in our works, in our warfare for man."[49] Hertha is, undoubtedly, firmly rooted in the tradition of radical Romanticism; even her choice of verbs – *be, grow, live* – anticipates that Carlylean emblem of organic life, Yggdrasil, "the Tree of Existence," which appears twenty lines later. "The 'Machine of the Universe,' – alas, do but think of that in contrast!"[50]

> The tree many-rooted
> > That swells to the sky
> With frondage red-fruited,
> > The life-tree am I ... (96–9)

Abrams has discussed the "organismic" implications of Romantic plant-imagery exhaustively in *The Mirror and the Lamp*; his conclusions must be recapitulated here. First, the plant's origin in a seed indicates that, as Coleridge put it, "the whole is prior to the parts." In "Hertha," this principle is so important that it led Tillyard to find an embryo totalitarianism in Swinburne's celebration of the "beloved Republic." Second, the plant's growth enforces a respect for process, for becoming; Hertha says, "Though ... my growth have no guerdon / But only to grow, / Yet I fail not of growing" (136–40). Third, the process of growth involves the assimilation of foreign and disparate elements, which are transformed, being made integral parts of a new unity. Fourth, "The plant evolves spontaneously from an internal source of energy – 'effectuates,' as Coleridge put it, 'its own secret growth' – and organizes itself into its proper form." Hertha, of course, is the one source of energy and of organization for the 'beloved Republic" in which she will realize herself: "In me only the root is / That blooms in your boughs" (163–4). Fifth, the plant exemplifies "organic unity."[51]

In some respects, Hertha-Yggdrasil represents the (literal) apotheosis of the Romantic plant-image. But she falls short in regard to Abrams's third and fifth specifications: she does not really assimilate disparate elements, and her image as Swinburne presents it in 96–145 is not remarkable for organic unity. On the contrary, the "mythic" tree becomes an allegorical emblem, a picture in which the separate elements are carefully labelled. Stars (i.e., man-made "gods") are caught in the tree's branches; the past lies beneath her roots; the sea-sound of her rustling is caused by the clambering of a parrot, "Time"; the winds of war and peace blow through her boughs, but do not disturb them (108–25). Neither stars, nor winds, nor Time-parrot can be part of the tree; although Hertha contains all these things, as an hourglass contains its flowing sands, we are not made to feel that all things are part of her "organic unity" – "All death and all life, and all reigns and all ruins, drop through me as sands" (135).

In fact, Swinburne's imagery implies that only one creature, man, is truly one with Hertha. "In the buds of your lives is the sap of my leaves," she tell us (100); in her springtime, human blossoms "shot out from [her] spirit as rays" (150), and their beauty and fragrance were "strength to [her] roots" (154); and she seeks to produce such blossoms again.

> I bid you but be;
>   I have need not of prayer;
> I have need of you free
>   As your mouths of mine air;
> That my heart may be greater within me, beholding the fruits of me fair.
>   (156–60)

This Swinburne thought a crucial stanza, expressing the "root or master-thought" of the poem. On 8 January 1870, he quoted it as a reasonable explanation of the "All-Mother"'s presumed republicanism: "I have broken the back (not only of God, but) of the poem in question by this time, having perfected the verses necessary to bring out the root or master-thought, and to combine and harmonize the connecting links of the idea: which needed to be done with all distinctness and delicacy at once, as it was not at first evident *why* the principle of growth, whence and by which all evil not less than all good proceeds and acts, should *prefer* liberty to bondage" (L2:79–80; italics Swinburne's).

Morality, in the shape of "love, the beloved Republic" (190), develops naturally from an amoral origin, from a force which "unloves ... and loves" (20). Moral consciousness and republican love form our deliberate fulfilment of that impulse toward spontaneous growth and self-organization which constitutes Hertha. As Coleridge said, "[W]hat the plant *is*, by an act not its own and unconsciously – *that* must thou *make* thyself to *become*!"[52] Once man was "made perfect with freedom of soul" (155), a worthy blossom of the life-tree; but his worship of gods external to himself has diminished him. Now at last, as he recognizes the "living," "whole" truth of his own divinity, man again becomes Hertha's "topmost blossom," the ray shed from her eye (191–2, 197–9).

This vision of history is precisely that found in the "Hymn of Man" and in "Le Satyre." And, as the gods of "Le Satyre" are shown at first radiant with their stolen triumph, and later (at the end of the satyr's song) stricken with awe (i, 76–245; iv, 640–1), so in "Hertha" the Christian God is shown first in thunder and glory (165–70), and then in abject terror before his fall (176–85). The terror of the divine tyrant is, of course, a prominent topos in radical Romantic literature; we remember Shelley's Jupiter, confident and severe until, in Swinburne's phrase, "his hour taketh hold on him stricken" ("Hertha," 185; the "hour" seizes God in Swinburne as Shelley's Demogorgon seizes on Jupiter). Only when the shadowy tyrant is fallen – when thought breaks the idol it has made (186) – can men see that human thought is the sole source of that ineffable value which we call divine. Thus "Hertha" counterbalances and corrects the despairing vision expressed in *Atalanta*, and particularly in the "antiphonal lamentation" for Meleager; for the lament, in the same metre and rhyme-scheme as "Hertha" (anapestic A2B2A2B2B6), ends by proclaiming man to be the slave of the gods.

> The gods guard over us
>   With sword and with rod;
> Weaving shadow to cover us,
>   Heaping the sod,
> That law may fulfil herself wholly, to darken man's face before God.
>   (*Atalanta*, 2177–81)

In *Atalanta* man is ashamed and made dark before God; in "Hertha," God's terror infects the angels with a "grey" pallor (184), as he quails before the divinity of man. God's "law" destroyed man's faith in his own power; but now we see that the "law" and harmony of the universe can only be realized through the mind of man. In a particularly effective continuation of the plant-metaphor, man appears as the fruit of Hertha's body and the seed of her soul (195). Hertha can become an object to herself only through man:

> One birth of my bosom;
>   One beam of mine eye;
> One topmost blossom
>   That scales the sky;
> Man, equal and one with me, man that is made of me, man that is I.
>   (196–200)

The maternal and vegetative images in this stanza refer back to the myths of the All-Mother and the Life-Tree respectively; man, as the crest of a long-gathering wave, "scales the sky," exploring space and storming heaven, as Hugo's satyr commands. Such imagery is in perfect harmony with the secular religion of humanity developed in the Hymn.[53] Less so is the Neoplatonic imagery of man as a "beam" or light-stream emanating from Hertha – imagery which reminds us that together man and Hertha make up a spiritual entity creating time as a mode through which the Divine can discover itself. The Divine recognizes itself in human freedom; this is why the republic is part of the living tree, while historical tyrannies are merely parasitic. Thus, "All death and all life," and all the reigns and ruins of "time-stricken lands," drop "through" Hertha (134–5), whereas man has part in Hertha's enduring life and growth: "In the buds of your lives is the sap of my leaves; ye shall live and not die" (100).

The alternations of imagery in the last stanza, particularly, recall Shelley's "To a Skylark." Like Shelley, Swinburne seizes on diverse metaphors to express the various aspects of a single power (the *b*-alliteration and *m*-assonance in 196–8 help us to see these images as relating to a single entity). This power is in its totality inexpressible. Every image in "Hertha" is at last inadequate to contain that "spirit or matter of life" which was Hugo's satyr, and which is Hertha. Can abstract language do what images cannot? Swinburne seems to imply as much when he writes (for example) that "truth only is living, / Truth only is whole" (191–2). Such abstract didacticism has alienated some; Riede, for instance, declares that Hertha is "an allegorical, not a mythic, giantess," who "stands for certain conceptualized ideas rather than embodying a living perception."[54] Certainly, those who believe that a "living perception" must embody itself in a myth or symbol of essentially mysterious force and implication will resist the "palpable design upon us"[55] so evident in *Songs before Sunrise* generally; yet in "Hertha," at least, there is a certain mystery, a fruitful ambiguity. In "Hertha," the goddess exists in the space – or, rather, in the tension – between the radiant eye and the growing tree, two incompatible images of divinity; moreover, the relationship between man and goddess, blossom and tree, is by no means a simple or transparent one. The smooth intermingling of Hertha's didactic self-descriptions with the allegorical presentation of the tree-hourglass, and the "imaginative vision" of the tree that flowers into man, conveys a complex perception of man as "an unprecedented God – neither purely naturalistic nor supernatural, but the embodiment of the meaning of the universe."[56]

In "The Triumph of Time" and "The Garden of Proserpine," metaphors and images evolved, or dissolved, one into another; but this shifting surface was itself the focus of attention. It embodied an acute sense of transience; it evoked no unifying principle within the process of change. "Hertha" provides a new way of using that flow of metaphors in continuous metamorphosis which is characteristic of Swinburne's best poetry. In "Hertha," this flow of metaphors is used to hint at a godhead that contains time and is, in part, beyond it. Whereas in the "Hymn of Man" time itself "lives, thinks, and hath substance in man" (140), history passes through Hertha without changing her, as Time clambers up through her boughs (116–35).

Later, as Swinburne's interest in the possibility of transcendence increases, he will manage the flow and variation of his imagery in such a way as to evoke an unknowable deity. Moreover, the identification of "freedom and man" as "earth-god" and "sun-god"[57] – the concept of nature's self-realization through man – will be at the centre of Swinburne's aesthetics within ten years. In *Songs before Sunrise*, however, the poet is as little concerned with poetics as a poet or an "Italian stump-orator" can well be. "Hertha" succeeds largely because its persona happens to be the sole and self-sufficient principle of unity in the world; her speech is part of her growth and fulfilment in man, her self-realization. Elsewhere in *Songs before Sunrise*, the author must define his own position as Hertha's prophet; and he defines it as that of a loyal, but clumsy, servant.

The bard is the All-Mother's lyre, her trumpet and storm-thrush ("Mater Triumphalis," *P*2:147–9); these are Romantic commonplaces. But Swinburne's extravagant use of the modesty topos is scarcely reminiscent of Blake; throughout *Songs before Sunrise*, "formulas of submission and protestations of incapacity stand side by side."[58] Many of the poems announce themselves, not as inspired prophecies, but as the "weak word-offerings" of an incompetent to a greater spirit (Epilogue, *P*2:227). It is remarkable that, even in the Prelude, where Swinburne repudiates his earlier style and adopts the dignity of a prophet, he has nothing to say about a prophet's function. Youth, Time, and the Bacchae sing (2, 8–10, 105–18, 124); the pilgrim, the voyager, and the racer (161–7) do not. Only nature utters enduring speech or music – the sun's "morning song," the stars' "ageless rhyme" (188, 135; see also 34–8, 51–4).

It is not surprising, then, that it is once more the earth spirit herself who prepares the way for the elaborate poetics of 1880. Of course, Hertha criticizes religious language sharply, condemning prayer, cosmogony, and even the "I/Thou" distinction in devotional speech (68–70, 41–65, 31–5); but she also drops a few hints which will be developed later into a constructive poetic theory. Nature "Makes utterance of me," she says (114); she speaks of the "wind's tongue and language of storm-clouds" (130); and she seems to suggest that man may commune with nature (see chap. 3 above). But she herself also speaks directly within man's soul: "I am in thee to save thee,

/ As my soul in thee saith; / Give thou as I gave thee" (76–8). And man's free action is like "sweet singing" that magically strengthens Hertha's own roots (151–4); the pattern of mutual strengthening here anticipates the paradox of "The Last Oracle," "Song should bring thee back to heal us with thy song" (P3:10). Each of Hertha's hints bears fruit. The "soul" that speaks in man anticipates, not only Apollo in "The Last Oracle," but also the "soul behind the soul" in "On the Cliffs" (P3:315); and the presence of the speaking soul in nature is established in "Thalassius," "By the North Sea," and the later landscape poetry.

CHAPTER FIVE

Songs of the Springtides: *The Sun-God and the Sea*

In 1876, Swinburne began to replace the scrappy, stump-orator's poetics of *Songs before Sunrise* with a poetics at once more complex and more genuinely Romantic. His lyric, "The Last Oracle" (1876), set forth the basis of the new poetics; in the important volume *Songs of the Springtides* (1880), Swinburne attempted to explore and apply his new vision, and established the major forms and themes which were to dominate his later work.

"The Last Oracle" proclaimed the primacy of Apollonian song, the sanctity of the Word. This is in one sense a continuation of the concerns of *Songs before Sunrise*: the concept of the Apollonian Logos explains and justifies the worship of man, and also explains man's tragic tendency to whore after false gods, since the god-making faculty itself is the power that makes humanity divine. In another sense, however, the new worship of Apollo radically challenges the visionary confidence of *Songs before Sunrise*. Apollo is both healer and destroyer, and therefore Swinburne must once more wrestle with "the problem to solve in expression," the problem which "Hertha" had supposedly resolved. If humanity is the true God, can humanity be in any way morally superior to "The supreme evil"? Is not making inextricably linked to unmaking? Does not the Word "divide and rend" as often as it creates?

Again and again the images and aperçus of *Atalanta* return to haunt the later poetry, whether we contemplate the potentially deadly Logos or that fecund and cruel mother, Nature. As Swinburne increasingly explores his neo-romantic concept of the Apollonian imagination, he begins also to explore the Romantic landscape; but, more and more, that landscape is encroached upon and subordinated by the sea. As such lyrics as "Ex-Voto" and "By the North Sea" vividly demonstrate, the sea for Swinburne embodies untamable freedom, even the wanton liberty of a Mary Stuart. ("By the North Sea" presents a violently amorous embrace between male death and the female ocean.) In his seascapes, Swinburne can examine not only the interaction between the sunlike Apollonian power and the natural world of tidal rhythm, but also the apparent amorality of the creative power. Rapidly, both sun and sea become symbols for human creation and for the godhead therein; as in "Hertha," each successive image helps us to apprehend a part of the complex deity that the poems celebrate.

The same may be said of the three main poems which make up *Songs of the Springtides*. Each presents one aspect of Apollonian action. "Thalassius" sets up a program for the development of the poet, who must learn to synthesize the art which expresses pain and passion with the art which provides visions of redemption. He must also learn to fuse artifice, aesthetic control, with the creative freedom of myth. Appropriately, "Thalassius" is another of Swinburne's attempts to combine myth and allegory. The story of Thalassius' birth (which begins the poem) and of his reconciliation with his parents (which begins the poem) and of his reconciliation with his parents (which ends the poem) is couched in a mythic and visionary mode. The tale of Thalassius' education, however, with its schematized account of his guardian's teachings, its decorative allegorical personification of "Love," and its Bacchic revel (so much like the revel of the Prelude), is essentially a programmatic allegory. Swinburne attempts to combine the mixed, public mode of Romantic prophecy with the equally Romantic mode of the fictionalized autobiography; the result is certainly not an unmixed success, but, together with "The Last Oracle," "Thalassius" provides a useful introduction to the poet's late work.

"On the Cliffs" is a more private, apparently less ambitious lyric, depending for its success on a delicate evocation of psychological processes; its model is the Romantic meditation on a landscape, which may also be entitled the descriptive ode, or "Greater Romantic Lyric." In my view, this is one of Swinburne's finest lyrics, and I shall accordingly discuss it in some detail. In "On the Cliffs," we see how the principle of harmonious song incorporates memory and love, and transforms the natural world, within the work of two poets (Sappho and her admirer). Sappho worships Apollo, and leaps into the Leucadian sea for love; she achieves the death by water of which the protagonist in "The Triumph of Time" only dreamed, and she achieves, too, the transcendent triumph over time of which he conceived only fleetingly. By contemplating, celebrating, defining her triumph, Swinburne's persona reproduces it; both poets infuse "a deep sea like death" ("On the Cliffs," 82) with Apollonian light.

In "The Garden of Cymodoce," Swinburne carries further the interfusion of Apollonian light and violent sea. In fact, both sea and sun-god in this poem are cryptic, double-natured as Hugo's abysses. Art and nature confront each other as two formidable infinities, each strong to curse or bless, and each uttering "Praise, and response applausive" of and to the other (247). Yet this system of echoes and responses can only attempt to express the inexpressible power which creates them, even as the series of images which constitutes the "landscape" in this lyric can only attempt to evoke the power that works within nature, and that is adored in the person of the mythical Cymodoce.

"On the Cliffs" is Swinburne's first experiment in the genre, or sub-genre, of the Greater Romantic Lyric; "The Garden of Cymodoce" is the earliest example of a peculiarly Swinburnean form, which we might call the Symbolist landscape poem, or, more humbly, the "topographical poem" (this was Swinburne's term [L6:153]). In the Birthday Ode to Hugo which concludes *Songs of the Springtides*, Swinburne initiates a series of odes which celebrate poets by alluding to their works in riddling terms; the topographical poem has an affinity with this form. In "The Garden of Cymodoce" Swinburne refers to all the features of Sark and its waters which would be mentioned in a handbook (Murray, for example) and visited by a tourist – the tunnel from Creux Harbour, Les Autelets, the Coupée, the Gouliot caves – but he mentions none of them by these names. He does not try to give a visual impression of the landscape as a whole; nor do we feel that we are moving through a solid landscape. Instead, Swinburne focuses on a single landmark at a time, and expands it until it becomes a vast and complex symbol, conveying its own vision of universal order – or disorder. It is the succession of these symbols, the fluid variation of vision, which constitutes the "meaning" of the poem. And this Romantic emphasis on temporality is at once the source, and the corrective, of apocalyptic hope; the power that shapes our redemption also constitutes the darkness in which we are lost.

THE APOLLONIAN LOGOS:
A PRELUDE TO *SONGS OF THE
SPRINGTIDES*

I am the eye with which the Universe
Beholds itself and knows itself divine.
(Shelley, "Hymn of Apollo")[1]

"The Last Oracle" marks the beginning of a crucial period in Swinburne's development as a poet; for now he addresses himself explicitly to the creation of a new poetics. In 1870 his most pressing problem was to justify a libertarian religion of humanity, or (more precisely) to construct a pattern of metaphors which might give depth and persuasive force to the republican humanism of *Songs before Sunrise*. The Idealist "metaphysical speculations" of that volume constitute just such a pattern of metaphors. But these experiments in Idealism, as Swinburne gradually perceives, have certain aesthetic implications: the "generative and destructive world-spirit" that creates "law" must also create meaning.[2] Thus in *Bothwell* (1871–4) Mary Stuart's "will and present force" imparts a fluid meaning and order to the world about her (see chap. 1 above); and in "The Last Oracle" (1876) Swinburne begins "the construction of a definitive semantic system."[3]

Swinburne's own letters show that he ascribed a peculiar value and originality to "The Last Oracle," and that the source of that value lay in the conception of the Apollonian Logos, "the Light and Word incarnate in man,"

the spirit or influence informing the thought or the soul of man with inner light (of which the sun's is the physical type) and thence with song or articulate speech which is the creator of all Gods imagined by man to love or fear or honour, who all are born and die as surely as they are born at the bidding of the same spirit. Thus Apollo-Paian, destroyer and healer, and not the Galilean, is established as the Logos which was not *with* but *before* God in the beginning.[4]

In most strains of Neoplatonism, the Logos (an active principle of rationality, accounting for cosmic order as well as for the human power of reason and the articulation of reason) is combined with the light-stream by which the One radiates its own beauty into the human soul. As we begin to apprehend and love this beauty, it inspires in us spiritual passions (from the *furor poeticus* to the *furor amatorius*) through which we ascend to the One.[5] Bypassing the mechanisms and hierarchies postulated by the Neoplatonists of the Renaissance, Swinburne presents a principle of creativity, lucid and radiant, enkindling and enlightening both the "soul of earth" ("The Last Oracle," 124) and the souls of men (128). This Logos "older than Time" may be the source of all creation in two senses.[6] First, it is apparently the author of "the world's whole story" (75); all life is brought into being as a flame is kindled, by the fiery power of Paian Apollo, "father of all of us" (28). But Swinburne is far less interested in the cosmogony than in the poet's act of creation; and the Logos celebrated in "The Last Oracle" is presented chiefly as that which kindles creative potency within us, making it possible for us to make gods and poems.

According to Greenberg, "The Last Oracle" is "best read as a companion piece" to the "Hymn to Proserpine" and the "Hymn of Man." "Its mixed, antiphonal voices assimilate those" which speak in the Hymns,[7] and, I might add, in the Prelude to *Songs before Sunrise*. Years have passed, says Swinburne, "While the world sought light by night" (3) – in contrast with the self-sufficient pilgrim of the Prelude, "Who seeks not ... light / And heavy heat of day by night" (43–4). To seek a "light" separable from the sun-god incarnate in human speech, as Christianity does, is to look for "light by night"; such an attitude must necessarily silence "the fount of song," or, at best, leave us only with "words more sad than tears of blood" ("The Last Oracle," 5, 6). Such words violently pierced and clove the heart of Julian the Apostate, and his own words became a part of the violence that killed him: "*Thou hast conquered*, he said, / *Galilean*; he said it, and died" (15–16; italics Swinburne's). The emperor's dying speech, which Swinburne had quoted sympathetically in the "Hymn to Proserpine," seems now to have the self-destructive force of Althaea's last speeches: "I say this and I die."[8] Since Julian's defeat, Christianity has "Made the whole world moan with hymns of wrath and wrong" (32).

Christianity was radically vitiated by its failure to locate its own source in the "God-positing potencies" of man.[9] By the "light of thought" (a Shelleyan phrase which Swinburne borrows in his letter to Morley concerning "The Last Oracle"), we can now grasp the nature of these potencies theoretically, just as in the "Hymn of Man" man finds that his mind is now "a light to his mind" (150). But to this "light of thought" Swinburne adds the "spirit of speech," which "makes [the soul] vocal and articulate" (*L*3:130), and which is also called "song." From this "song" (to which Swinburne seems to refer in lines 58, 86–7, and 136 of "The Last Oracle") spring the vatic "song" of line 5, the high poetry which derives from man's perception of and reverence for the power of language (27), and poetry in the most ordinary sense (30). The Apollonian Logos sums up all light and song (27–8); it is the light of thought, the capacity for speech, and, also, each verbal artefact. The Logos can realize itself within the temporal world only if we give it a body of words – only if "the word" is "clothed with speech by lips of man" (60).

As in *Songs before Sunrise*, we are on the verge of the apocalypse: the deity is about to fulfil itself upon earth, and man to recover the radiant freedom and power which he lost in the era of dogmatic religion. "Lo, the Gods that ruled by grace of sin and death! / They are conquered, they break, they are stricken" (108–9). The triumphant inversion of Julian's despairing cry, and the echo of the "Hymn of Man" ("Thou art smitten, thou God," 198), reaffirm the polemical confidence of *Songs before Sunrise*. "For how, my beloved brethren, without the destruction of God, can Man be healed?" (*L*3:144). For the first time, however, Swinburne has granted the dark era of Christianity a clear-cut and positive function in the progressive self-realization of the sun-god. The poets and prophets of classical Greece degraded the god-making, god-breaking faculty to the status of a mere god (53–4); only by destroying the Christian deity can we recognize our own Apollonian power over heaven.

Swinburne's myth of history now approximates more closely than in *Songs before Sunrise* to the Romantic "spiral" pattern: we proceed from a simple harmony with Apollo, in which we worship and celebrate without fully understanding the god, to a state of division from his light, a state of darkness; but we return to him at last, recognizing our unity with him in more complex terms than before. Our alienation from him was therefore a "fortunate fall": *O felix culpa!*[10] But how is our comprehension of Apollo superior to the Greeks'? First, we have seen "that orthodox religion is the externalizing and petrifaction of fluid inner process," and we now know by experience the lethal results of such "petrifaction"; second, Christianity, though based upon a radically false premise, has developed certain concepts and images relating to the one God which are genuinely illuminating when rightly understood.[11] The last three stanzas of "The Last Oracle" move beyond parody to takeover, in a Romantic adaptation and revision of Christianity more sweeping and audacious than anything in Swinburne's earlier work.

Here we need only consider the strikingly inclusive lists of Apollo's titles: "the word, the light, the life, the breath, the glory" (73), heaven's "one / Light, life, word, witness" (91–2), "God, king, priest, poet" (131). Obviously, Swinburne is drawing on the Gospel of John (1.1–14), where Christ is described first as the Logos, then as the life and the light (verse 4: "In him was life; and the life was the light of men"), and is said to have or to express divine "glory" (verse 14). In the Gospel, John the Baptist as "witness" (verses 7–8) is carefully distinguished from the light to which he bears witness; but Swinburne's Apollo appropriates the function of bearing witness to himself, just as he appropriates the character of the Holy Spirit (literally "the breath"). Here Swinburne makes explicit what the echo of Shelley's "Ode to the West Wind" in the refrain of "The Last Oracle" ("Destroyer and healer, hear!") had already implied: "The Last Oracle," like the Ode, invokes inspiration, the in-breathing of vatic power. It is by inspiring human poets that the Apollonian Logos bears witness to itself.

Besides all this, the sun-god is in the fullest sense the "glory," the "Shechinah, or visible divine presence" (as George Eliot names the sunlight; cp. Ex. 40.34, Zech. 2.5); it is also the "glory" that Coleridge celebrates in "Dejection" as "Joy" and as "Life, and Life's effluence." "This beautiful and beauty-making power" is the quasi-secular Romantic adaptation of the Shekinah as Shelley's wind is of the Holy Spirit.[12] As this luminous power emanates from the individual soul it becomes part of "a ceaseless and circular interchange," a brilliant "eddying."[13] In "Dejection," this interchange connects man with nature; in "The Last Oracle," it connects man with man: "By thy light and heat incarnate and impassioned, / Soul to soul of man gives light for light and takes" (127–8; the chiasmus in the last six words helps to suggest this perpetual eddying).

Finally, Apollo, like Christ, is "God, king, priest" – a priest, that is, after the order of King Melchizedek, and therefore an unfathered and eternal mediator between God and man (Heb. 2.17–18, 5.1–10, and especially 7.1–3 and 15–28). But, just as Apollo is his own witness, so he is also his own mediator, conveying his salvation to men through "song"; his last and proudest title is "poet." These titles are all-important, because in "The Last Oracle" naming has become equivalent to invocation, as Swinburne suggests in the punning line, "Healer *called* of sickness, slayer *invoked* of wrong" (130; my italics). To forget the name of the god is to lose the power he dispenses ("Song forsook their tongues that held thy name forbidden," 27); to know his name is to be capable of invoking him: "As they knew thy name of old time could we know it, ... / Song should bring thee back to heal us with thy song" (129–32).

This emphasis on the magical power of the word is strikingly Hugolian. Indeed, several of the themes of "The Last Oracle" are anticipated in *Les Contemplations*, i.viii ("Suite," 1855), a lyric which Swinburne described as "at once profound and sublime enough to grapple easily and thoroughly with so high and deep a subject" as "the divine and creative power of speech" (*B*13:67). "Suite" insists that "les mots sont des choses," and that words can eat, wound, kill, or revive (Hugo's reference to the vicious potencies of words – "Le mot dévore, et rien ne résiste à sa dent" – may have influenced *Atalanta* and *Lesbia Brandon*). Language has this "pouvoir surprenant" because it embodies the action, within this world, of a transcendent deity: "Le mot, le terme, type on ne sait d'où venu, / Face de l'invisible, aspect de l'inconnu ... / Le mot tient sous ses pieds le globe ..." Thus the word greets the light as "sister," but proclaims her own primacy: "'Sois l'aube; je te vaux, car je suis la raison'."

> Oui, tout-puissant! tel est le mot. Fou qui s'en joue!
> Quand l'erreur fait un noeud dans l'homme, il le dénoue.
> ....
> Il est vie, esprit, germe, ouragan, vertu, feu;
> Car le mot, c'est le Verbe, et le Verbe, c'est Dieu.[14]

Like Swinburne, Hugo identifies human speech with the Logos; like Swinburne, Hugo relates language to light; and both poets list the titles of the Word. But their lists differ. Hugo uses "le mot" as he uses the imagery of storm and fire throughout his work, to draw us toward "l'inconnu"; he is primarily concerned here with the divine rather than the human aspects of the Word. Swinburne tends rather to stress the action of the Word on earth, and the saving power of the Word "clothed in speech." However, he is at one with Hugo in celebrating the power of the word to free us from the bonds of error; we shall see in *Songs of the Springtides* that Apollo, like Hertha, is a good republican. As Hugo said elsewhere, "Du verbe de Dieu est sortie la création des êtres; du verbe de l'homme sortira la société des peuples."[15]

The anti-Logos of *Atalanta* expressed the self-contradicting violence of generation and destruction; but in "The Last Oracle" the generative and destructive powers of language emanate from a central principle which can always create meaning anew – a saving, all-originating spirit which, in the words of the Epilogue to *Songs before Sunrise*, "Sees the world severed, and is whole" (P2:231). "In thy lips the speech of man whence Gods were fashioned, / In thy soul the thought that *makes them and unmakes*" ("The Last Oracle," 125–6; italics mine). Here Swinburne uses precisely the same rhetorical device that he had used in Althaea's frenzied speech of self-apotheosis, but to the opposite effect. Althaea saw that the divinity inherent in the world "made man and unmade"; the speaker in "The Last Oracle" sees that the Logos, through man's act of speech, "makes [gods] and unmakes." The anacoluthon – the omission of the pronoun *them* after *unmakes* – dissipates the gods, leaving man healed of Christianity, that long disease.

So in the "Hymn of Man" Swinburne cried to the Christian God, "man thy slave shall unmake thee, who made thee lord over man" (120); but now he explains how and why man makes and unmakes gods. In "The Last Oracle," Swinburne finally addresses the problem of the poet's status in a potentially harmonious world. The starry "ageless rhyme" must be "clothed with speech"; the Logos incarnates itself in poetry. In this way only can earth "take heaven upon her" (59), for the god is truly known only through the act of song (137–8). Hence, to ask for poetic inspiration is to invoke the Logos itself, or, to put it another way, we can help the Logos to realize itself only by invoking it in words. "Song should bring thee back to heal us with thy song" (132); "The Last Oracle" culminates in this triumphant paradox.

In his development of the aesthetic eucharist, from *William Blake* on, Swinburne has been experimenting with the Blakean view that "the Poetic Genius ... was the first principle, and all the others merely derivative" (qu. *WB* 214). But until "The Last Oracle" Swinburne's Apollo was too slight a figure to support so vast an assertion. The sun-god of "Ave atque Vale" and the "Memorial Verses" to Gautier administered the eucharist of poetic inspiration to a very select congregation, and with limited effect; for "not all our songs ... / Will make death clear or make life durable" (*P*3:56). Baudelaire and Gautier at the end are "silent" souls (*P*3:57, 65), and swallowed up by silence; there is "Nor sight nor sound to war against [them] more, / For whom all winds are quiet as the sun, / All waters as the shore" (*P*3:57). In "The Last Oracle," for the first time, the act of making poetry is endowed with a cosmic and "durable" significance.

"THALASSIUS": PRINCIPLE AND PASSION

Poets, like their works, may be art and part of the sun-god. But it is not easy to advance from the concept – the essential principle – of the Apollonian Logos, to the demonstration of Apollonian power. *Songs of the Springtides* shows Swinburne turning Apollo from an abstraction to a vivid passion: we see how the poet prepares himself – or herself – to become an incarnation of the god.

Both its admirers and its detractors agree that *Songs of the Springtides* is a profoundly Romantic text.[16] The Romantics supply Swinburne with the forms, the structure, the techniques, which enable him to turn Apollo from a principle into a living passion; Swinburne's reliance upon his models at this stage is unusually strong, though not uncritical. From the beginning, the book is an act of homage to Shelley and Victor Hugo, two great Romantic presences; the opening sonnet dedicates the text to Edward John Trelawny, the friend of Shelley and Byron, and presents Shelley as the guiding spirit of Swinburne's verse.[17]

Like the language in "Thalassius" (see chap. 3 above), the poetry of this volume, in general, evokes both the rhythmic life of the natural world and the deliberate, "shaped" quality of an aesthetic object. The sea-mew of the dedicatory sonnet (we should remember that "sea-mew" is almost a code-name for Swinburne himself)[18] has "wings imbrued with brine, with foam impearled," and, being thus steeped in the sea, and decorated by it, the impearled sea-mew is an image at once organic and artificial. Similarly, the sea-mew's songs arise spontaneously, but are then carefully developed. They were "born" (that is, presumably, conceived and perhaps sketched out in the poet's mind) "lightly," "between the foam and sand"; so far they were the spontaneous result of his physical experience of nature, and specifically of the seacoast. The songs were then "reared" (brought to perfection, made complete) "by hope and memory and desire / Of lives that were and life that is to be, / Even such as filled his heavenlier song with fire ..." Hope, memory and desire, and the perfect life to which they should all refer, were present in Shelley and "filled his heavenlier song with fire"; the hope, memory, and desire of such a life as his has motivated Swinburne's poetic work.

Appropriately, then, the first major poem in the book – "Thalassius" – is a "symbolical quasi-autobiographical" sketch of the poet as such, "after the fashion of Shelley or of Hugo" (L4:106). Like "The Last Oracle," "Thalassius" puts forward a program of spiral development. Thalassius' progress follows the pattern established in *Sartor Resartus*, Wordsworth's *Prelude*, and other major Romantic texts: a pattern of alienation from a primitive state of bliss, and eventual return to a condition which contains that primitive state, but is superior to it in glory and complexity. Like Teufelsdröckh, Thalassius is a fosterling whose experience of Love paralyzes him, silences the world around him, and places him in a universe of dead or withered "things." Like the speaker in Wordsworth's *Prelude*, Thalassius escapes this death-in-life by a return to the complex harmony of the natural world, and by deliberately recalling and celebrating the creative passions of his childhood.[19]

He is reared by a foster-father, who clearly represents the poetic tradition;[20] from him Thalassius learns the "high song," which teaches him the value and necessity of Liberty (90–4), as well as the passions of love, hate, hope, and fear, each springing from and having reference to the central passion for freedom. (As Hazlitt remarked in his *Lectures on English Poets*, "Fear is poetry, hope is poetry, love is poetry, hatred is poetry.")[21] Thalassius must learn to hate (utterly to reject and actively to oppose) the opponents of political freedom, but he must also hate "all / That brings or holds in thrall / Of spirit or flesh ... / The holy body and sacred soul of man." A little later in the poem, the dark god Love enthrals Thalassius, body and soul; and when the Bacchic revel frees Thalassius' body, renewing his physical joy through an escape to a Dionysian group hysteria (373–8), his spirit is still enthralled through Erigone's controlling music (393–5, 415–16). But both forms of slavery are rejected when Thalassius turns from Erigone to the sea. What motivates Thalassius at this point is not clearly stated, but the imagery of lines 401–8 suggests that the sea's appeal may renew his former holy fear "to be / Worthless the dear love of the wind and sea ... / Fear to go crownless of the flower he wore / When the winds loved him and the waters knew" (203–15).

This sacred fear rejects all timidity, and, therefore, all thraldom; and it springs from "the dear love of the wind and sea / That bred him fearless." Sacred hate and fear, then, are the gifts of the sea, the gifts of Thalassius' mother Cymothoe; sacred love and hope are the gifts of his father, the sun-god. For love as defined in the high song is the act of imparting one's inner freedom (137–58), and hope is the vision of outward freedom, the vision of the republic of love. In this vision all "things" are radiant as the sun "That marries morn and even and winter and spring / With one love's golden ring" (185–96). The apocalyptic hopes of Swinburnean republicans marry Apollo to the natural rhythms of "morn and even and winter and spring"; that is, they marry eternity to time. Like free hate, love, and fear, hope in the high song is itself at once a passion and a principle. It is revealed as a principle in the relatively abstract formulations of the high song; it is also part of the "manlike passion of a godlike man" (126). As a principle, it is embraced by the free light of reason, and directs Thalassius' energies; as a passion, it arouses his emotional energies spontaneously, as concentrated light kindling a fire.

The dark Love, and Dionysian passion, are passions but not principles: they seize upon the youth willy-nilly; hence they are surrounded by images of fire and darkness. The erotic Love is blind and blinding (286, 255–7); his eyes shed only the "Hard light" of mockery, and he darkens all but Hell (292–301). The dread lady Erigone also obscures all light but that of her own eyes (388–9). During this period of passion and pain, Thalassius is divorced from love proper; he returns to a loving communion with nature through the trance which reveals to him the sea's "dark dayshine" (426). But not until Thalassius has known and shaken off emotional enslavement can he feel hope and the other passions of Liberty in their full and ideal intensity. Thus when the "strife / Of thought and flesh," principle and passion, has been ended (444–7) – when, as Thalassius communes with his own heart, his "days and dreams" run together (439–42) – he can become a perfect poet, the true son of the sun-god Apollo, lord of light, song, and harmony (450–2).

In "Thalassius" – though not in the Prelude to *Songs before Sunrise* – the passions involved in the allegorically-presented enthralment to Love and Bacchus are subsumed, rather than negated, within the mythic reunion of sun-god, sea-nymph, and semi-divine poet; the Apollonian Logos must realize itself through a marriage with the physical world. Cymothoe herself appears at first as a dumb and passive consciousness receiving the inner sunlight of thought or imagination. She sees the sun-god, "brighter than the sunbright sphere" (19); she feels his fiery kiss; she hears the sounds of song and of soaring flight, and at last she has the synaesthetic perception – appropriately expressed in another of Swinburne's magical anti-metaboles – of "Light heard as music, music seen as light" (25–31). The Apollonian embrace transforms her passive consciousness to a creative perceiving and conceiving, as she makes synaesthetic connections and conceives her "sun-child" (34). So far the tale might well be that of any human soul, the sun-god representing the distinctively human faculty of articulate thought and speech, and the sea – "the world of sunless things / That round the round earth flows and ebbs and flows" (36) – representing the rhythm of natural life prior to conceptual thought. But the transformed consciousness of the sea-nymph is the necessary preliminary to poetic action; Cymothoe is the physical, natural world from which Thalassius springs, but she is also Thalassius' own true nature, his best self, to which he must return before he can become an Apollonian poet.

The poems of 1880, from "Thalassius" to "By the North Sea," tend to produce Apollo at the close, to pronounce the benediction and confirm the creative triumph achieved by human demigods. So in the last lines of "Thalassius" Apollo blesses his child with song – the song (says the god) of "all the winds that sing of me" – and with "the sense of all the sea" (499–500). For the spontaneous, self-ordering power that makes a song out of Thalassius' experience also produces the living architecture of the sea. Indeed, by the end of the *Songs of the Springtides*, the sea has superseded the sun-god as an adequate expression of the creative principle. Even at the close of "Thalassius," the architecture of the sea-dream is a more persuasive symbol than the solar radiance that enfolds and blesses the hero.[22] The synaesthetic vision conferred by Apollo's "resonant radiance" (29) is only one aspect of the complex synthesis toward which Swinburne is working. "Thalassius" examines three different kinds of art: the republican "high song," associated with the "laurel-laden" foster-father (59–62); the "music that makes mad," associated with the vine and rose of the Bacchic revel (383–4, 393); and the nature poetry in which "land's laurel" glistens with sea-flowers and "sea-dew" (402–7). The true Apollonian song must be of the last kind. Yet it must also contain and transfigure the republican and the Bacchic songs, uniting principle and passion, deliberation and spontaneity, the artificial and the organic, in one music as large, fluid, and inclusive as the sea.

"ON THE CLIFFS": THE ART OF CELEBRATION

"Thalassius" celebrates the process of poetic growth; "On the Cliffs" is less a revelation of the creative process in any general sense than a celebration of "the greatest poet who ever was at all" (*L*4:124). It is Sappho whose power transcends the force of the oceanic natural rhythm; it is she who combines the worship of Aphrodite and Apollo, the amorous rage and the poetic. As "soul triune, woman and god and bird" (352), Sappho attains transfiguration and apotheosis; she creates the "song above all songs" (302); and for lesser poets she provides endless inspiration and revelation. To celebrate her is to reenact her triumph.

At the same time, this triumph is less simple and complete than Thalassius' restoration. Like "Thalassius," "On the Cliffs" begins by the sea and ends in fire and sunlight. In "Thalassius," these elements cooperate in a recurrent beneficial synthesis: this is the source of the poet's life, his creative (or "singing") power, and his mental health. In "On the Cliffs" too there is a synthesis, but it is not easy, nor is it very explicit; the antitheses are much more strongly marked. The thematic structure of "On the Cliffs" is largely a matter of contrasting antitheses and parallel contrasts: pain and joy, time and eternity, barren peace and fruitful struggle. Most important of all is the opposition between the temperament which either evades or submits to the contraries of a temporal world, and the temperament which recognizes, expresses, and masters these contraries, through that process of cognition and expression which is art. Like Althaea, Sappho is tormented to the point of insanity by the contraries of life; this "woman and god" is also "Song's priestess, mad with joy and pain of love, / Love's priestess, mad with pain and joy of song"

(213–14). In her art, however, contraries are mastered and harmonized: "pain makes peace with pleasure in thy song" (432). In her soul, too, contraries are mastered, but in a different way: she sustains the "strife" of "love and song" – keeps two opposing forces explosively, savagely alive within her heart, in tormenting equipoise – and from their friction springs the "Fire everlasting of eternal life" (433–4), which constitutes Sappho's godhead.

Althaea in her madness cried, "I am fire, and burn myself; keep clear of fire" (*Atalanta*, 1805). But the fire imagery in which the figure of Sappho is enveloped has a threefold significance: it suggests suffering, but it also represents a spontaneous radiant delight, and both of these are fused in the inspirational fire of Sappho's holy spirit. The "fire eternal" within her (419) makes possible the mastery of contraries in her "ruling song" (394), "A song wherein all earth and heaven and sea / Were molten in one music" (402–3). Through her song, the natural world and time itself are subsumed in the eternal energy of her godhead, and burn with everlasting fire. Similarly, in the soul of her worshipper, the landscape of cliff and sea about him is subordinated to the Sapphic song which he hears in the music of the nightingale, and also to the psychological process by which the speaker learns to celebrate the bird-god and so to conquer time himself.

As Riede has pointed out, "On the Cliffs" is "a meditative-descriptive lyric in which the description of nature is wholly subordinate to the thoughts the landscape inspires" – in other words, an example of the "Greater Romantic Lyric."[23] And the poem both exploits and criticizes an earlier example of the Greater Romantic Lyric, Coleridge's "The Nightingale," which also finds a "venerable," quasi-religious meaning in the song of the bird.[24] Both poems begin by describing the evening, and go on to locate the persona within the natural setting; the nightingale's song then launches the speaker on a complex meditation. Both poems include an image of nightingales singing responsively, in a group: Coleridge's nightingales "answer and provoke each other's song" (58); Swinburne's hear the human persona sing, and applaud him "with answering song" (246–51). And this image, in both cases, precedes a more striking instance of responsive music: a moon, pushing through the clouds, is greeted by song on earth. In both works, therefore, "antiphonal music and reverberating patterns" of song and light are crucial, as creative power is transmitted, through responsive sympathy, from creature to creature.[25] "On the Cliffs" and "The Nightingale" both follow the usual pattern of the Greater Romantic Lyric in moving from the speaker's own experience outward to the experience of others. As Wordsworth in "Tintern Abbey" turns finally to his sister, as Coleridge's thoughts move from his own experience to that of the "gentle maid" and of his child, so in "On the Cliffs" the speaker turns from his own sense of desolation to the fiery joy – and pain – of the god he celebrates.

And yet the differences between "On the Cliffs" and "The Nightingale" are radical. In "The Nightingale," the "balmy night" hints at a fruitful landscape of "verdure" and "green earth" (7–10); this rich joy overflows into the song of the nightingale, and the speaker-poet has only to surrender himself to the ease and fullness of the dark natural world; "so his song / Should make all nature lovelier, and itself / Be loved like Nature" (29–34). In "On the Cliffs," by contrast, the bird's joy is derived, not from its harmony with the natural world, but from the inner sunlight of human thought or imagination. It is "The sun whom all our souls and songs call sire" who grants the bird-god "Life everlasting of eternal fire" (97, 103). The joyous divinity of this nightingale is Apollonian, and is inseparable from the human creative power.

When the nightingale is first heard, its song "Cleaves" the web of darkness and meaningless silence (36–45). This song is illuminating, liberating, and yet piercing, a cry of human pain (61–3) which has "rent apart / Even to the core Night's all-maternal heart" (44–5). As in Matthew Arnold's "Philomela," the pain, passion, and triumph of classical literature is felt to be immediately present within the nightingale's song. But Swinburne goes still further than Arnold; for the bird's song is also apprehended as in some way redemptive, divine. As the speaker turns to that singing god, he attempts to establish some connection between himself and her, to lift himself somehow to her plane – to be saved by her, or through her example to save himself.

> We were not marked for sorrow, thou nor I,
> For joy nor sorrow, sister, were we made,
> To take delight and grief to live and die,
> Assuaged by pleasures or by pains affrayed
> That melt men's hearts and alter; we retain
> A memory mastering pleasure and all pain,
> A spirit within the sense of ear and eye,
> A soul behind the soul, that seeks and sings
> And makes our life move only with its wings
> And feed but from its lips, that in return

Feed of our hearts wherein the old fires that burn
Have strength not to consume
Nor glory enough to exalt us past our doom. (128–40)

The speaker and the nightingale have overcome time, not indeed
by ascetically evading all its joys and loves, but by refusing to find
a delusory comfort in these delights. To feel pleasure and "all pain"
with an unflagging sense of the transience of both is to master both;
in McSweeney's words, the creative "soul behind the soul" "continues to burn only because it continues to be fed by the lacerating
fires of the poet's own being."[26] The pain and complexity of this
situation are beautifully conveyed through the complexities of Swinburne's rhetoric and syntax.

The senseless flux of time was expressed in line 127 by antimetabole: "day sows night and night sows day ..." The pointless alternation of emotions in those who set their hearts upon the things
of time is similarly expressed in 131 by a chiasmus heavily underlined
by alliteration and assonance ("*Assuaged* by *pleasures* or by *pains*
affrayed"). As Swinburne turns from contemplating the self-contradictions of temporality to describing the operation of the poetic spirit
(which seeks and constructs its own meaning), he moves toward a
more and more emphatically alliterative verse. Yet in the last two
and a half lines of the stanza, the emphasis and lyrical authority of
133–7 fail us, as the focus shifts once more to the "doom" of the
burning heart. That sub-clause of a sub-clause of a sub-clause,
"wherein .. doom," is a very minor modification of the main sense
of the stanza; its formal syntactic function is menial indeed. But the
hypotactic structure, which would place the logical emphasis on the
main clause ("we retain / A memory, ... / A spirit") – that expression
of triumph – is disguised by the position of the subordinate clauses,
which suggest a linear, dramatic progression. From the confident
assertion of power in 132–4, the speaker rises to a religious, almost
mystical confession of dependence (135–7), which modulates into
the bleaker perception that this divine energy, this "soul behind the
soul," does after all exact its toll – feeds on the energy and passion
of the human lives which it directs (137–8). The elegiac tone of the
last sub-clause recalls Sappho's bitter comment on her fiery triumph
in "Anactoria": "Alas, that neither moon nor snow nor dew / Nor
all cold things can ... / Assuage me" (295–7).

The syntactic difficulties of the passage under discussion are characteristic of Swinburne's late style. As Peckham has remarked, reading Swinburne involves a double effort: "The mind must always
remain focused intensively on the task of comprehending the syntax,

of grasping how the parallel syntactic sub-units fit into the larger sentence construction; and it must do this as they come along, in the order in which the poem offers them."[27] In *Songs of the Spring-tides*, and to some extent in the works which follow it, this double effort is made more difficult by the fact that the dramatic effect of Swinburne's clause-placement often works against his hypotactic structures; in our endeavour to reconcile the two, we apprehend the contradiction within the speaker's thought, the problem he has yet to solve. He cannot yet grasp, emotionally, that triumph which he longs to proclaim; he is still in the position of Cassandra, who tried to gain Apollo's gift of prophetic immortality without being willing to pay for it by enduring the "lacerating fires" of passion (141–60). So the speaker still longs to escape "the old fires" of his "doom."

But the literary parallel provided by Aeschylus (141–8 echo *Aga-memnon* 1146–9) gives the speaker some illumination; he can now see clearly that Sappho's tormented service to Aphrodite forms the basis of her triumph over time (166–91). What Sappho's worshipper celebrates, therefore, must be not the unshadowed happiness which seemed to him earlier (as it seemed to Cassandra) so far beyond his reach (90–4, 144–8); it is a blessing whose bliss is very hypothetical (the word *if* appears four times in 173–91), an intolerable mingling of pain and joy.[28] In the magnificently symmetrical hymn to Sappho which constitutes the thirteenth stanza, antimetabole, used earlier to convey the meaningless alternations of time, is gloriously trans-figured:

Love's priestess, mad with pain and joy of song,
Song's priestess, mad with joy and pain of love,
Name above all names that are lights above,
We have loved, praised, pitied, crowned and done thee wrong,
O thou past praise and pity; thou the sole
Utterly deathless, perfect only and whole
Immortal, body and soul.
....
All praise, all pity, all dreams have done thee wrong,
All love, with eyes love-blinded from above;
Song's priestess, mad with joy and pain of love,
Love's priestess, mad with pain and joy of song. (192–214)

Yet it is not enough for the speaker merely to contemplate the bird-god's triumph over time; somehow he must make Sappho hear him, somehow he must establish a connection between them, share in her triumph. He begs again for an "answer" (215, 232, 241–2); he implies that his own poetic art has already won a "good word" from the responsive choir of nightingales in Majano (243–7). If he has thus entered into harmony with Sappho's sister birds, surely his gods are as hers, "and their will / Made my song part of thy song – even such part / As man hath of God's heart" (258–65). Yet surely Apollo and Aphrodite have given "much happier things" to Sappho than to him or to any other mortal – and, as the speaker contemplates Sappho's privileged godhead, he begins at last to forget himself, to be wholly absorbed in his worship (in 280–4, indeed, his attention is so entirely focused on the bird-god's "singing soul" that he fails to complete the syntactic structure; he provides only the noun and its modifying subordinate clause). Paradoxically, this devotion effects the connection between the speaker and his god which has been sought for so long. Instead of continuing to seek assurance that his song is a part of hers, the speaker now makes Sappho's poetry a part of his: "*O deathless, O God's daughter subtle-souled! ... I Loved thee ... Atthis, long since in old time overpast*" (307, 326–30; italics Swinburne's).

Child of God, close craftswoman, I beseech thee,
Bid not ache nor agony break nor master,
Lady, my spirit –
O thou her mistress, might her cry not reach thee?
Our Lady of all men's loves, could Love go past her,
Pass, and not hear it ? (334–9; italics Swinburne's)

Swinburne celebrates Sappho's poems as a Roman Catholic priest celebrates a mass, reenacting a redemptive process in a ceremony of religious devotion. The mood of these utterances requires our particular attention. The first line and a half of the Hymn to Aphrodite, in isolation, simply celebrates the goddess; the Atthis-fragment expresses a melancholy acceptance of time and change; the first stanza of the Hymn, in its entirety, is the cry of desperation. Just so "On the Cliffs," as a whole, is a desperate, obstinate appeal to a higher power; but we have seen how the speaker vacillates between the celebration of that higher power and the acknowledgment of time's power over himself. In the verse paragraph quoted above, the speaker's appeal to Love is combined with Sappho's so that together they form a single symmetrical stanza.

The translation of the Hymn will repay scrutiny. To convey the full meaning and emotive content of the Greek, Swinburne relies heavily on reiteration with variation. The effect is that Sappho's formal invocation of the goddess at the opening of the Hymn takes on an almost magical character: as though, by reciting the attributes of the goddess, one could recreate her, bring her living before one's eyes. Swinburne is well acquainted with his text, and provides alternative readings where the Greek word is doubtful (*"of divers-coloured mind, of the divers-coloured seat"*). But he takes considerable liberties with that text. He heightens the tone of urgency by adding interjections (300, 307). The name "Aphrodite" he omits entirely. *"God's daughter"* is a fair translation of παῖ Δίος, but misleading in the context of the whole poem: what Sappho means is "child of Zeus"; "God" elsewhere in "On the Cliffs" means either Sappho herself or the Apollonian sun-god (160, 178). The compound *"subtle-souled"* may possibly be another rendition of ποικίλοφρον ("of divers-coloured mind," "full of various wiles, subtle-minded"),[29] but its position makes it more likely that *"subtle-souled"* and *"close crafts-woman"* three stanzas later are complementary, bringing out different aspects of δολόπλοκα, "wile-weaving" (as *"break nor master"* more accurately brings out the full range of meaning in δάμνα). The net result of these alterations and modifications is that Aphrodite's cunning charm, and indeed her identity as the object of the invocation, are partially suppressed; and the deathless craftswoman, daughter of the shining God, with a mind subtle and rich in variety, resembles Sappho as much as she does the foam-born goddess.

Has Swinburne's Sappho then established her identity with Love? No; but she has established a correspondence between herself and the goddess of Love. Aphrodite did not hear her, or grant her prayer (according to Swinburne, though there is no authority for this in Sappho's Hymn): Sappho was unhappy in love. Similarly, neither Aphrodite nor the bird-god hears or grants any appeal of the speaker's. But Aphrodite's "lyric days" survive only in Sappho's song (348–57), and the true nature and triumph of the Sapphic bird-god are revealed only in "On the Cliffs."

The speaker worships and celebrates the bird-god, who worships and celebrates Apollo and Aphrodite. She does not (like Cassandra) take the power of art for a means of controlling her circumstances; when she appeals to the power of love, she finds that that too is no instrument for gaining temporal joy; but she recognizes the gods for what they are, she utters forth their attributes, and in the act she and her song become symbols, *correspondances*, of the deity they celebrate. In this sense, the mind becomes that which it contemplates. Sappho perceived that love is the expression and offspring of the creative principle, "The sun whom all our souls and songs call sire" (97). Therefore she now combines in her own person love and song; without gaining the least power over her external circumstances, she has gained the attributes of divinity by exactly and perfectly expressing and invoking those attributes; she herself became a deathless craftswoman, a god (352) and a daughter of God – a "parcel[30] of the sun" (208) – and, finally, the bird which above all others is associated at once with love and song.

The concept of love as springing from the principle of harmony, imagination, and song, and realizing that principle in its own illuminating ardour, is one which we have seen in "Thalassius." In "On the Cliffs" the concept is subtler, less schematized, untainted by a prescriptive libertarian philanthropy. It is also more painful. Neither Sappho nor the speaker will be "purged of pain that passion bore"; but as we move on from Sappho's song, we leave behind the speaker's last expression of bitterness or lamentation. He has urged the magnitude of Sappho's poetic achievement, in a kind of passionate sympathy for her sorrows in love, as some compensation; but as he considers her achievement, sympathy gives way to awe, and consolation to celebration.

And as he celebrates her unique song, he creates a myth which radically revises the most striking image in Coleridge's "The Nightingale." In Coleridge, the moon, emerging from a cloud,

> hath awakened earth and sky
> With one sensation, and those wakeful birds
> Have all burst forth in choral minstrelsy,
> As if some sudden gale had swept at once
> A hundred airy harps! (77–82)

In "On the Cliffs," however, during Sappho's life, the whole world is silent – field, wood, lawn, hill, and vale – for the song of all nightingales is absorbed in Sappho's poetry (368ff); at the "deep divine moondawn,"

> clouds gave way
> To the old reconquering ray,
> But no song answering made it more than day;
> No cry of song by night
> Shot fire into the cloud-constraining light.
> One only, one Aeolian island heard
> Thrill, but through no bird's throat,
> In one strange manlike maiden's godlike note,
> The song of all these as a single bird. (373–84)

Coleridge converts the nightingales into Aeolian harps, swept by a moon like an "intellectual breeze, / At once the Soul of each, and God of all" ("The Eolian Harp," 47–8);[31] the emphasis in "The Nightingale" is on a unifying supernatural power of delight, whereas in "On the Cliffs" the moonlight controls only the clouds, and is freely answered by a power equally "divine" – and yet distinctively human, distinctively artistic. The powers of self-expression in art and nature correspond and reciprocate. Through this myth, the speaker manages to conceive of the redemption of the natural world, which, after Sappho's death, will contain and transmit her triumphant song for ever (385–92). What Sappho gives to the nightingales is her own fire as "parcel of the sun": she is (as they were not) human, free with the freedom of *fully* conscious and articulate humanity (unlike the slave Cassandra) and therefore divine. Because of this she was supreme among them, in her human form; but only by her death, her entrance through the "sea's portal" (385), did she achieve complete fusion with the natural world. We think of Adonais, "A portion of the Eternal, which must glow / Through time and change, unquenchably the same ... He is made one with Nature: there is heard / His voice in all her music, from the moan / Of thunder to the song of night's sweet bird ..." (340–1, 370–2).

By the bright fire of the bird-god – which transcends the power of time and space and yet is immanent in nature – the speaker's "inward night" is transfigured, and his old grief and frustration are completely subordinated to his perception of the power of worship, the power of art, of seeing and loving. Through this power, Swinburne has been "able at last to generate his myth from the desperate void."[32] Riede's formulation is exact: it is Sappho's (and the speaker's) intense consciousness of temporality, together with a passionately articulate frustration in the face of an indifferent deity, that permits her (and him) to conquer time at last. Swinburne and his persona will never claim any certain triumph higher than this transformation of perception, but that in itself is an experience of absolute value. In the "treble-natured mystery" of "woman and god and bird" (341, 352) is adumbrated the Christian Trinity of Christ (priest and sacrifice), the Father, and the Spirit whose symbols are the Dove and the Fire; that the woman must die before the birds sing suggests John 16.7; while the hierarchy of illumination (from the gods through the bird-god to the speaker) and worship (from the speaker through the bird-god to the gods) is reminiscent of the Neoplatonic hierarchies. But the metaphysics of "On the Cliffs" are so much subordinated to the emotional experience of the speaker that the poem cannot be taken as a direct metaphysical or theological affirmation. We can say only that the statements and images which are used to realize the speaker's emotions precisely, in "On the Cliffs," do substantially agree with the metaphysical framework provided by Swinburne's more explicitly religious poems from the same period; and that the quality of the speaker's experience is the best justification for the metaphysics which explain it.

T his emphasis on the *process* by which the speaker resolves his difficulties is, of course, characteristic of the Greater Romantic Lyric; and the "varied but integral" quality of this process, which unites thought and feeling, memory and desire, is equally characteristic of the genre. The apparently casual development of the meditation is misleading. Sometimes the speaker hammers out his argument steadily from stanza to stanza, as in 141–214: stanza x describes the alternative "dooms" of the Sapphic nightingale and the bondslave Cassandra; xi accounts for the doom of the latter; xii, for the doom of the former; and xiii develops the real meaning of that "doom" which the nightingale enjoys. Sometimes the speaker contradicts himself, as in 292–3; a single word may be enough to stimulate a new train of thought: "Even thy soul sang itself to sleep at last. / To sleep? Ah, then, what song is this ...?" We may compare Coleridge's reversal: "'Most musical, most melancholy' bird! / A melancholy bird? Oh! idle thought!" Similarly, as both Buckler and Ridenour have pointed out, the word "doom" in 140–1 operates much as the word "forlorn" does in Keats's "Ode to a Nightingale," 70–1, calling the speaker back, from his contemplation of the triumph he shares with Sappho, to a sense of the contrast between them.[33] Finally, Swinburne's speaker may revert to an idea earlier expressed, perhaps to a phrase that appeared five lines before (85–90, 98–104); the recurrence of the phrase, "The singing soul," in 273–80, is roughly paralleled in Coleridge's "Dejection: An Ode," 54–62, where the speaker first declares the importance of projecting "A light, a glory, a fair luminous cloud" upon the world, and – after a few lines – comes back to the phrase, and begins to define it.

No critic has yet done justice to Swinburne's acute observation of mental processes; and yet, as we can see, many of his techniques are drawn from earlier examples of the Greater Romantic Lyric. And, like his predecessors, Swinburne employs these techniques to suggest "the casual movement of a relaxed mind," whereas "retrospect reveals the whole to have been firmly organized around an emotional issue pressing for resolution."[34] To be sure, Swinburne's poem is longer than most of the lyrics in this genre ("On the Cliffs" is almost four times as long as "The Nightingale"); the sinuous development of "On the Cliffs" is more twisted and more complex, and involves more violent alterations of direction, both intellectual and emotional, than we usually find in the Greater Romantic Lyric. This is mainly because, to make his point, Swinburne must provide a double resolution, a double triumph: Sappho's and the speaker's. As Riede says, "Swinburne is doing more than stating a theory of poetic influence – he is demonstrating ... how it works in practice" (158). Hence the poem must double upon itself, in order to become truly antiphonal.

The metre is very well adapted to express this sinuous advance. It is the same metre that is employed in "Thalassius" and in the epodes of "The Garden of Cymodoce": the "irregular Italian metre of Lycidas [sic]" (L4:109), but with fewer lines unrhymed and a greater proportion of trimeters.[35] This metrical fluidity enables Swinburne to signal passages of particular importance, and especially passages of rapture or triumph, by using a large number of pentameters together, as when the bird-god is first heard (37–46), when the speaker makes his assertion of shared Apollonian power (128–38), when he celebrates the priestess of love and song (180–96, 207–14), when he describes the nightingales celebrant (248–57) or the power of the Sapphic nightingale (364–76, 380–96, 414–34; the final stanza of "On the Cliffs," as of "Thalassius," is entirely in pentameter). The flexibility of Swinburne's rhyme scheme allows him to add emphasis to a short line, by making it complete a rhyme (as in 195–97, the solitary triplet of xiii); to repeat a key rhyme at intervals throughout the poem, without making it too obtrusive (as *word/bird* in 36, 46, 59, 61, 233–4, 352, 360, 384); to connect stanzas (as *word* in 360 follows on the rhymes *bird, stirred* of xxiii, or *red-wet* in xii on *yet, net, forget* of xi); to point the theme of a verse-paragraph (as, when Sappho earns the gift of eternal life, the long stanza xii is bound together by rhymes on *give* and *live: forgiven thee/given thee, gives/lives, live/forgive/live/give*); to provide an air of authority, at appropriate moments, by dint of heroic couplets (as in the final stanza of "Thalassius" and in "On the Cliffs" 431–4, 199–202, 207–10); or to shape a stanza of particular symmetry, when Swinburne wishes to show how Sappho transfigures the meaningless alternations of time (192–214), or how the speaker, in translating and celebrating Sappho's poetry, completes it and fulfils its promise (334–9).

In short, the irregularity of Swinburne's metre and rhyme scheme, like the irregularity of the Pindaric ode in "Dejection" or the Intimations Ode, permits that free, apparently casual movement which is so important in the Greater Romantic Lyric, while at the same time it allows for marked emotional emphasis at specific points. Most important, however, for the purpose of "On the Cliffs," Swinburne's manipulation of pentameters and trimeters makes it possible for him to incorporate the cadences of the Sapphic stanza within English verse. The speaker does re-create the bird-god's harmonious song; and he also rediscovers, in his own experience of that song, the tormenting equipoise of Sappho's life. The world of a divinely-ordained and spontaneously joyous reciprocity, the world of Coleridge's nightingales, does not exist. No god will ever answer the speaker's appeal, except for "Our Father which is in Delphi" (L4:106). Rather, it is for the speaker to answer the divine song of another mortal; and, in the effort of answering, he activates his own inner sunlight, which mingles with the bird-god's in an "exchange of gleams,"[36] a difficult and free reciprocity of love.

"THE GARDEN OF CYMODOCE": DOWNWARD TO DARKNESS

Like "On the Cliffs," "The Garden of Cymodoce" centres on a psychological process – on the gradual perception of the world as radically cryptic, and on the attempt to harmonize, within a Neo-Romantic art, the vision of pointless violence developed in *Atalanta* and the vision of significant order developed in "The Last Oracle." Unlike "On the Cliffs," "The Garden of Cymodoce" seems to present a psychological process in a void; except in the proem and epilogue, the persona is invisible. We must assume either that the persona exists only for the sake of the frame, and that the poem is essentially public and impersonal, or that the persona lies concealed in his creation, in the metaphors of 74–105 and the myth of 137–275: "a Poet hidden / In the light of thought."[37]

The latter alternative seems to me the more likely. It is true that "The Garden of Cymodoce" is couched in the form of a classical Pindaric ode, with strophe, antistrophe, and epode, and that Swinburne viewed the classical ode as a public statement.[38] Yet, although there is some reference to public events in this poem (Louis Napoleon's *coup d'état*, Hugo's exile), the main focus is on private experience, on a tourist's delight in the landscape and the myths he weaves around it (L6:153). The absence of the tourist through most of "The Garden of Cymodoce" makes this poem exceptionally difficult to follow. We are forced to relate the Channel waters, the blossoming fields and groves, Les Autelets, the Coupée, and the Gouliot caverns as symbols which are to be contemplated as in a

montage, rather than as stimuli to a persona's psychological progress. Our thought seems to focus upon the images, rather than upon
the process by which these images are made to succeed one another,
because the speaker's psyche cannot easily be distinguished from
that which it contemplates; and only when we have reached this
realization can we perceive the psychological development which
the poem does in fact embody.

The thematic and emotional structure of the poem is almost dia-
metrically opposed to the structure usual in the Greater Romantic
Lyric. In such works as "The Nightingale" or the Intimations Ode,
the speaker begins by evoking a condition of doubt or dejection
which is triumphantly resolved by the end of the poem; and the
persona of "On the Cliffs" reaches his ecstatic apprehension of the
bird-god only through long meditation. In "The Garden of Cymodoce" ecstasy comes first, analysis and understanding later; the
poem begins in rapture and undulates "Downward to darkness,"
like the pigeons of "Sunday Morning."

We are confronted immediately (lines 1–24) with the exultant sim-
plicity of the proem: with intense, pure, positive emotion directly
expressed. In the speaker's confident assertion of intimate relationship with the presiding divinity of the poem, "The Garden of Cymodoce" begins where "On the Cliffs" ends; for the persona's
opening appeal for poetic inspiration is also an ardent expression
of love for and trust in the inspiring deity. This opening passage is,
as well – and this, I think, is a new departure for Swinburne – an
appeal simply for new perception and a new power of feeling (6–
9), for a religious rather than a strictly artistic reawakening. The sea
is invited into the speaker's mind and heart, is desired to become a
dominating "spirit" and a "light" within the speaker's spirit, exactly
like the Holy Paraclete. *Accende lumen sensibus, / Infunde amorem cor-
dibus* ...[39]

> Be with my spirit of song as wings to bear,
> As fire to feel and breathe and brighten; be
> A spirit of sense more deep of deity,
> A light of love, if love may be, more strong
> In me than very song.
> For song I have loved with second love, but thee,
> Thee first, thee, mother ... (5–11)

The power of living song is secondary to the transformation of
the soul – not, as in "On the Cliffs," identified with it. In the epilogue,
too, the speaker in "The Garden of Cymodoce" requires a double

gift. He cries to the goddess, "Take thou my song ... to keep" (336), i.e., he asks her to accept the poem as a work of art and to grant it durability; but he concludes with a somewhat different request: "Take my song's salutation; and on me / Breathe back the benediction of thy sea" (342–3). This expresses a personal religious relationship, or at least a Wordsworthian vision of man and nature in reciprocal intercourse. The *me/sea* rhyme of course echoes lines 2–3 ("O to me / Mother more dear than love's own longing, sea"); but there he greeted the sea as "mother," not (as in 332) as "Goddess." Clearly she has indeed become a dominating "spirit" within his, and he has attained the "sense more deep of deity" for which he begged in the proem.

This is a dubious blessing. As goddess of the seas around Sark, Cymodoce contains a murderous violence comparable to the savagery revealed in *Atalanta*: Sark is enmeshed in conflicting webs of savagery (58–70) that recall both the "intolerant net" of "On the Cliffs" (156) and the "web of night" in "Thalassius" (104–19). But here light does not pierce or cleave the web; light springs up magically within it, "midmost of the murderous water's web" (70–4). The next fifty-three lines (forming the second triadic bloc of the ode) are the most brilliant and joyful in the poem.

> O flower of all wind-flowers and sea-flowers,
>   Made lovelier by love of the sea
> Than thy golden own field-flowers, or tree-flowers
>   Like foam of the sea-facing tree!
> No foot but the seamew's there settles
>   On the spikes of thine anthers like horns,
> With snow-coloured spray for thy petals,
>   Black rocks for thy thorns. (74–81)

The furious waters of the Channel are suddenly transmuted to petals. Here the speaker's imagination begins perceptibly to act – to re-create the island, out of his love for it and for the sea. Here too is a startling reminiscence of Shelley's "To a Skylark." Swinburne might well be asking Sark, "What is most like thee?" for the island resembles successively (89–97) a bride-bed, a flower, a (formerly) anchored ship, a (formerly) fettered prisoner, and – "a lark by the heart in her lifted / To mix with the morn."

Like Shelley's skylark, the island acts as a model for the hidden persona – perhaps even as a surrogate. To the island is given all that the speaker has desired for his "spirit of song" and "spirit of sense." For his "spirit of song," he desires wings (and he imagines

Sark freed from the land by Boreas, and drifting on the wind like a lark) and "fire to feel and breathe and brighten" (and he conceives of Sark's own "desire" as "Self-satiate, centred in its own deep fire"); for his "spirit of sense," he asked a deeper perception of deity, and a light of intense love (5–9, 94–7, 126–7). And now, in 137ff, the Master comes to Sark, the child of God (259–65; cp. "On the Cliffs," 334), the Promethean figure who brings a rarer fire to the island "Than thrills the sun's own shrine" (254, 338, 169–72); and the island trembles with delight and burning love (267).

The love of the sea, as Swinburne explained in the proem, requires and inspires in the sea's adorers a love of freedom, the "one thing more divine" than the sea itself (24); so it should not surprise us to find the exiled Victor Hugo's visit to Sark transformed into the central mythus of the poem – the advent of a Prometheus triumphant through art, and the loving response of Cymodoce's "world aflower against the sun" (219). It is a very simple story: the Master arrives, and is greeted; but it is the expression in mythic terms of a relationship which (like the relationship of Sark and the sea, though in a different manner) parallels the relationship between the speaker and the inspiring and renovating sea.

Yet, at the moment when Hugo lands at Sark, the island and the sea about it – and indeed the lands beyond the sea – darken ominously. Swinburne virulently recalls the "joy more foul than fear" (190) which attended the establishment of the Second Empire in France, and brought about Hugo's exile; while the island and its surrounding waters, even in their welcome to the Master, show that their own luminous glory is inseparable from a kind of darkness.

> Even from the dark deep sea-gate that makes way
> Through channelled darkness for the darkling day
> ....
> To where the keen sea-current grinds and frets
> The black bright sheer twin flameless Altarlets
> That lack no live blood-sacrifice they crave
> Of shipwreck and the shrine-subservient wave,
> Having for priest the storm-wind, and for choir
> Lightnings and clouds whose prayers and praise are fire,
> All the isle acclaimed him coming ... (214–30)

Here sea, wind, storm, and stone (Les Autelets are rocks in the shallows off Sark) all partake in a religion of cruelty and murder; in their dark rites, "prayers and praise" are potentially destructive "fire." The "black bright" Altarlets recall the "brown bright" nightingale of *Atalanta*, with her self-assuaged memories of "all the pain" (69–72). Like her, too, they seem to exist in a world of violent and unresolved conflict.

But, as Swinburne's focus shifts from one feature to another of Sark's landscape, we perceive gradually that each successive image is a new attempt at defining the true nature of divine action and the right relation of man to deity. The tunnel from Creux Harbour and Les Autelets have been made into elaborate symbols of cosmic significance; but now they are replaced by the Coupée,

> that steep strait of rock whose twin-cliffed height
> Links crag with crag reiterate, land with land,
> By one sheer thread of narrowing precipice
> Bifront, that binds and sunders
> Abyss from hollower imminent abyss
> And wilder isle with island, blind for bliss
> Of sea that lightens and of wind that thunders ... (237–43)

Every severance is also a kind of binding: two things defined as separate are, by the very act of definition, placed in relation to one another; two voices can make harmony. The elaborate use of reiteration in this passage suggests that "infinite set of harmonic responses which the world in fact *is* ... Both Shelley and Swinburne are attracted to antiphonal music and reverberating patterns because they agree with Demogorgon: 'The deep truth is imageless'."[40] I might add that Hugo took the same view. Swinburne's image of the two abysses is peculiarly Hugolian; we may compare Hugo's image of the two infinities in *Les Misérables*: "At the same time that there is an Infinite outside us, is there not an Infinite within us? Do not these two Infinities (monstrous plural) lie one over the other? The second Infinite, does it not, so to say, underlie the first? Is it not the mirror, the reflection, the echo of that other; the abyss concentric with the other abyss? ... To place, in thought, the Infinite below in contact with the Infinite above, that is called 'prayer'."[41] His godhead is shown precisely in his unrelenting exploration of the abyss, the meaningless darkness – or the inconceivable radiance – all about us.

"La religion, la société, la nature ... La mystérieuse difficulté de la vie sort de toutes les trois." In *Les Travailleurs de la Mer* (Swinburne's favourite among Hugo's novels), the French writer concentrates on "l'anankè des choses": his Promethean hero from Guernsey does battle with the elements. Yet the practical difficulties and dangers represented by nature are less than the horror of its inexplicbility. "L'obscurité nocturne est pleine d'un vertige." "Nous sentons dans cette obscurité le Mal." The embodiment of the evil sensed in nature's obscurity is in the novel a devil-fish which the hero finds in a sea-cave, and which by its monstrosity propounds "[l]'enigme du mal." Against this, as against sea, storm, and wind, the hero must struggle alone.[42]

It is absolutely necessary that the hero should descend into the sea-cave and confront the abyss. So in "The Garden of Cymodoce" the traveller descends "as one from a citadel crept / That his foemen beleaguer" (279–80); the simile echoes 58–9, and helps to suggest that humanity is indeed surrounded by hostile darkness. The descent brings us to a horrific vision of emptiness ("all is as hollow to hellward," 281). And yet – the sea-cave in "The Garden of Cymodoce," it transpires, refers to the larger of the Gouliot caves, famous for their sea-anemones.

All under the deeps of the darkness are glimmering; all over impends
An immeasurable infinite flower of the dark that dilates and descends,
That exults and expands in its breathless and blind efflorescence of heart
    ... (288–90)

This beautiful and effective symbol can and indeed should be matched with the self-lit flower-illumined trees of 119. Both incarnate a principle of spontaneous life and joy, but the "flower of the dark" expresses also a principle of harmony, of infinite multeity in immeasurable unity ("One infinite blossom of blossoms innumerable," 287), springing out of the darkness itself. Even the power of Love, which paralysed and discrowned Thalassius, partakes in this infinite spontaneous vitality: the flowering roof of the cave is compared to

    a beaker inverse at a feast on Olympus, exhausted of wine,
But inlaid as with rose from the lips of Dione that left it divine:
From the lips everliving of laughter and love everlasting, that leave
In the cleft of his heart who shall kiss them a snake to corrode it and
    cleave.
So glimmers the gloom into glory, the glory recoils into gloom
That the eye of the sun could not kindle, the lip not of Love could relume.
So darkens reverted the cup that the kiss of her mouth set on fire:
So blackens a brand in his eyeshot asmoulder awhile from the pyre.
    (292–9)

"The Last Oracle" attempted to subsume Christianity in the worship of the Apollonian Logos; "The Garden of Cymodoce" attempts to subsume the pessimism of *Atalanta* in the worship of the loving Apollonian sea-mother. The force of language, that reduced Meleager to "a long brand that blackens" (*Atalanta*, 1890), is the sun-god, the radiant eye of the universe; Apollo can kindle or rekindle all but that which he has himself blasted. Similarly, the serpentine tongue of Love (cp. "Thalassius," 261) can wither and cleave or make divine. The flower which is also a cup "inlaid as with rose," like the sea-jewel and sea-architecture of "Thalassius," combines the imagery of nature with that of artifice, and thus prepares us for the final, explicit equation of Hugo's song with the flowers of Cymodoce: "Even like that hollow-bosomed rose, inverse / And infinite, the heaven of thy vast verse, / Our Master, over all our souls impends" (308–10). In Hugo's verse, too, gloom and glory glimmer and recoil into one another: "lightening still and darkling downward, lo / The light and darkness of it" (320–1). But this reciprocity of gloom and glory in itself forms a fluctuant harmony.

There may be – as Hugo insisted – a transcendent, purely luminous harmony beyond this achieved temporal harmony of light and darkness; the night may flower into endless light. There is another cave, "through the side-seen archway aglimmer again from the right" (304); this can be related to the *Tubularia* cave, which Swinburne did not see on his first visit to Sark, because it is accessible only at low spring-tide. Although Swinburne knew very well that the cave could be visited only once a fortnight (*L*3:188), he has turned the *Tubularia* cave into a "mystery of night," sealed by the tide – "And the seal on the seventh day breaks but a little, that man by its mean / May behold what the sun hath not looked on, the stars of the night have not seen" (305–7). The allusion to Rev. 5–8 (especially 8.1) delicately suggests that the "dark sea is not merely a 'murderous web,' but is the 'ghostly reverse' [line 301] of the realm of divine life. Within its phenomenal appearances, the sea conceals and reveals the secret of eternity."[43]

The thematic development of the poem, structured as it is by the succession of symbols drawn from the topography of Sark, can now be summed up. The images of the Channel waters and the flowering isle indicate the nature of the self-kindling, self-illuminating creative principle, and show that this principle can subsist within the net of cruel temporality. The Altarlets, served by the storm whose praise of the Promethean Master is so fiery and savage, testify that the violence of temporality is a part of this creative principle, and the "bifront" precipice of the Coupée suggests that this principle is in fact dualistic, connecting the gulf of light with the hollower gulf of darkness. As the hidden persona struggles to imitate his Master, toiling downward to the knowledge and acceptance of the worst, the dark fire of the infinite void becomes ever more prominent in the speaker's concept of imaginative power. And in the end, when we reach the Gouliot caves, the dark void and the "hollow-bosomed rose" of the Apollonian heaven are alternately presented aspects of a single power: void and heaven glimmer and recoil into one another, in a continual fluctuation like the ebb and flow of the tide.

In the epilogue, the reciprocity of salutation and benediction suggests a final harmony; in the myth of Sark and Hugo, and in the myth of the speaker and his mothering sea, Swinburne has created paired systems of mutually responsive figures who express their loving relationship articulately. Yet each of these figures is radically cryptic and double-natured. Behind the powers of language and of nature is concealed an unseizable, "imageless" force, "Hooded and helmed with mystery, girt and shod / With light and darkness, unapparent God" (Birthday Ode for Hugo, P3:350). This deity manifests itself both in creation and in destruction. The "image anthology technique," the successive tearing and creation of new veils for the deity, itself demonstrates the dual nature of the god.[44]

"The Garden of Cymodoce," therefore, functions as an important transitional poem, a link between the self-consciously triumphant art of "Thalassius" and "On the Cliffs," and the art of the later poems, in which a momentary triumph gleams like a spark in a vast darkness of doubt. "The Garden of Cymodoce" concludes on a note of triumph; but in its plunge downward to darkness it has moved us toward the agnostic world of *Astrophel*, with its more radically sceptical view of the ambiguities that pervade both language and nature. Nevertheless, the atmosphere of joyous reconciliation and union at the close of the poem maintains the sense of high exuberant triumph – of springtide (suggesting both the renovation of the spring and the highest tides of the month, the moment when the sea's tide reaches its peak) – which characterizes *Songs of the Springtides* as a whole.

CHAPTER SIX

Astrophel: *The Unknowable God*

> Wit learnes in thee perfection to expresse,
> Not thou by praise, but praise in thee is raisde:
> It is a praise to praise, when thou art praisde.
> (Sir Philip Sidney, *Astrophil and Stella*)[1]

By celebrating his "demigods" in *Songs of the Springtides*, Swinburne contrives to reproduce their triumphs. In *Astrophel and Other Poems* (1894), he develops this approach further. The demigods of the earlier volume are poets, and in praising them the poet expresses his own confidence, at that period, in the power of song to master and synthesize all dualities. By the 1890s his approach to language is more sceptical; in "A Nympholept," for example, language is identified with an amoral Apollonian Pan, a Logos both violent and meaningless. Lyrics like "A Nympholept" and the Elegy for Burton recall the dualistic vision of *Atalanta* – but only to transcend that vision. By praising Sir Richard Burton, "demigod of daring," explorer and freethinker, Swinburne's persona learns to aspire like Burton toward an "incognisable" reality. And, through the force of his yearning for "that sustaining Love" ("Adonais," 481) which would give value and meaning to Pan, the speaker in "A Nympholept" draws to himself the "Unknown sweet spirit" who embodies that Love, and in praising her finds nature and language transformed to her radiant likeness.

Yet how can we conceive of a condition independent of time and change? How can we be sure that the "Unknown sweet spirit" is more than a delusion of the speaker's? In *Astrophel*, to a greater degree than in any of his earlier volumes, Swinburne dwells upon these epistemological difficulties; but, by concentrating on his speakers' experience, on the activity of praise as it affects the praiser, he can avoid dogmatizing on the subject. Every triumph over time, every Hugolian transformation of the void, is the precarious achievement of an individual mind. His emphasis on this point transforms the elegy and the Romantic landscape meditation, the two forms which dominate *Astrophel*.

In order to show how Swinburne's determination both to raise and to question transcendental possibilities divides the *Astrophel* elegies, in particular, from his earlier elegies, I shall spend some time discussing his revisions of the elegiac tradition from 1867 on; I shall then examine the Elegy for Burton, as the finest example of the genre in *Astrophel*. But in the Elegy, although the epistemological problems mentioned above are raised explicitly, the corresponding problems of expression (can we in any way express or evoke supratemporal reality?) are not discussed. My analysis of these problems in "A Nympholept" will therefore begin with a brief review of Swinburne's anti-sacramentalist poetics, as revealed in his manipulation of the conceal-and-reveal topos from *Atalanta* to *Astrophel*. And the nympholept's precarious triumph will in turn lead to the more radically sceptical resolution of "The Lake of Gaube." The conclusion of this chapter will analyse the resolution of "The Lake of Gaube," as briefly as possible, in order to locate the post-*Astrophel* Swinburne within the symbolist tradition which influenced him so powerfully throughout his career.

GARDENS OF THE DEAD: THE LATE ELEGIES

> If I write any more necrological elegies on deceased poets, I shall be taken for the undertakers' laureate or the forehorse of a funeral car hired out to trot in trappings on all such occasions. (L2:334)

Traditionally, the English pastoral elegy contains an invocation of the Muse, a fairly elaborate formal expression of grief (involving a procession of mourners, a strewing of flowers, or both), and a consolatory conclusion: assurance of the dead man's continued life after death, or eventual resurrection, makes it possible for the mourner to return to his own life with new power. But the three major examples of the genre in the nineteenth century – Shelley's "Adonais," Matthew Arnold's "Thyrsis," and Swinburne's "Ave atque Vale" – were all composed by sceptics. (Tennyson's *In Memoriam*, by virtue of its length and structure, is *sui generis*.) In "Adonais," the speaker is inspired to become "What Adonais is," to follow him to "the abode where the Eternal are" (459, 495), as the spiritual power of "The One" "beams" and "descends" on the persona, destroying the "last

clouds of cold mortality" which enshrouded him (460, 485–8). Instead of returning to the temporal world at the end, we are rapt into
the speaker's contemplation of "the Eternal," understood in a sense
which certainly is not Christian. "Thyrsis," on the other hand, ends
by speaking of a "quest" to be pursued in this world, by the living,
while the lamented friend has disappeared into "morningless and
unawakening sleep" (211–15, 169), or into literary tradition; the "call
celestial …/ And all the marvel of the golden skies," the possibility
of resurrection, can be only a part of the pastoral fiction (181–90).[2]

"Thyrsis" was published in 1866; Swinburne, writing "Ave atque
Vale" a year later, ends, like Shelley, by concentrating on the dead
man's condition, which will eventually be ours (186–7): "Shall death
not bring us all as thee one day / Among the days departed?" But,
like Arnold, he offers no possibility of a transcendental union with
the Eternal; the continuity of literary tradition alone offers a frail
and limited consolation. As in "Thyrsis," an elaborate Keatsian
stanza (ten iambic pentameters and a quiet closing trimeter, as compared with Arnold's nine pentameters and a trimeter in mid-stanza),
emphasizes the importance of artifice and deliberate balance within
the poem. (It is worth remembering that Swinburne was one of the
first to greet "Thyrsis" as "a third with 'Lycidas' and 'Adonais,'" and
that he considered Arnold's elegy "a model of style": "No country-
man of ours since Keats died has made or has found words fall into
such faultless folds and forms of harmonious line" [B15:92–3].) The
structure of thought within "Ave atque Vale" as a whole is also
carefully balanced.

The first half of the poem follows the pattern presented in lines
2–4 of Catullus' *Carmen CI*, from which Swinburne takes his title.

> [A]dvenio has miseras, frater, ad inferias,
> ut te postremo donarem munere mortis
>   et mutam nequiquam alloquerer cinerem …
> [I come, my brother, to these sorrowful obsequies, to present you with
> the last guerdon of death, and speak, though in vain, to your silent
> ashes …][3]

Swinburne offers Baudelaire the flowers which are the guerdon
of death, but these flowers can only take the shape of the elegy
itself: in what style should the poet praise the dead? "Shall I strew
on thee rose or rue," or the laurels of "Lycidas," or the "quiet,"
"simplest growth" celebrated in "Thyrsis"[4] – or the "Half-faded fiery
blossoms" of Baudelaire's own *Fleurs du Mal* (1–8)? What would be
appropriate? What flowers grow in Proserpine's garden (67–77)? In

"The Garden of Proserpine" Swinburne answered the last question with some confidence (24–32), since he was only evoking an image of rest; but now, confronting the reality of death, he is reduced to "ironic, faintly mocking" rhetorical questions.[5]

Does the dim ground grow any seed of ours,
　　The faint field quicken any terrene root,
　　In low lands where the sun and moon are mute
And all the stars keep silence? Are there flowers
　　At all …? (73–77)

Evidently not. The mourner's "flowery" speech, with its ornate imagery and wide range of decorative mythological reference, confronts the barren silence of death. At the centre of the elegy (indeed, precisely at the half-way point, at the beginning of the tenth stanza), the speaker turns from this confrontation to the literary tradition, the "mourning musical" (109), of which he feels himself a part.

Not thee, O never thee, in all time's changes,
　　Not thee, but this the sound of thy sad soul,
　　The shadow of thy swift spirit, this shut scroll
I lay my hand on, and not death estranges
　　My spirit from communion of thy song … (100–4)

In chapter 3 above, I discussed the implications of this "communion," and of the eucharist of poetic inspiration which the "Luciferian Apollo" administered to Baudelaire in life. "Baudelaire's sanctification rests upon the continuance of a humanity which can bless and sanctify him by showing the influence which [his] … works have had, and continue to have, on the … works of the living."[6] Apollo himself is the chief mourner at Baudelaire's funeral rites, as Urania was "Most musical of mourners" at the rites of Adonais (28); but, while paying this high tribute to the French poet, Swinburne is careful not to exaggerate Apollo's power. The "God of all suns and songs" can only hallow the "unmelodious mouth and sunless eyes" of the dead; he cannot call them back (151–4). The consolations of art will not "make death clear or make life durable" (171-2). We can only return once more to the Catullan model, as Swinburne's persona offers the dead poet his flowers – now identified as "rose and ivy and wild vine" (173) – and confronts the silence of the dead.

For thee, O now a silent soul, my brother,
　　Take at my hands this garland, and farewell.

Thin is the leaf, and chill the wintry smell,
And chill the solemn earth, a fatal mother,
  With sadder than the Niobean womb,
  And in the hollow of her breasts a tomb.
Content thee, howsoe'er, whose days are done;
  There lies not any troublous thing before,
  Nor sight nor sound to war against thee more,
For whom all winds are quiet as the sun,
  All waters as the shore. (188–98)

By choosing to wreathe the tomb with "rose and ivy and wild vine," Swinburne is in effect choosing to celebrate the dead in his own way, in the style of *Atalanta* and *Poems and Ballads*, First Series; for ivy and "wild vine" are the emblems of the Bacchic revel, and are employed as such in the final stanza of *Atalanta*'s first chorus (113–20), while the rose dominates *Poems and Ballads*, First Series, from the vampire-roses of "Ilicet" to the vital rose of "The Triumph of Time," 279–80, and from the "rose-garden" of "The Two Dreams," with its delicate eroticism, to the blatant "raptures and roses" of "Dolores," 68. It is as the Dionysian poet of life's beauty and brevity that Swinburne bids farewell to Baudelaire. The last stanza of "Ave atque Vale" echoes both *Atalanta* (where Althaea, the "fatal seed-land," identifies herself with earth, the mother-Chronos who eats her children) and *Poems and Ballads*: as in "The Garden of Proserpine," 92, the dead experience no "sound or sight," but lie in unawakening sleep. Earlier in the elegy, Swinburne had described the dead man's "quiet eyes wherein the light saith nought, / Whereto the day is dumb" (51–2); the sun-god's final silence is the proof of his bleak compassion as "Guérisseur familier des angoisses humaines." Swinburne can now find a grim consolation in the self-negating powers of language and nature, the sun-god and the earth-mother; and, as he lays down his thin-leaved, wintry "garland, which is the poem," he provides a "climactic testament" to that "early faith" in the "diabolic" which he was about to discard.[7]

McSweeney has suggested that Apollo's limitations in "Ave atque Vale" qualify "the claims made for poetry's power in 'The Last Oracle'."[8] But "The Last Oracle" was written nine years after "Ave atque Vale." In the same year (1876), Swinburne had pursued the concept of a self-negating deity to its extreme, ironic conclusion: change has forsaken the garden where it has "left nought living to ravage and rend," and until the "loveless," meaningless sea overwhelms the garden, the dualities of time are suspended, cancelled out.

Here now in his triumph where all things falter,
  Stretched out on the spoils that his own hand spread,
As a god self-slain on his own strange altar,
  Death lies dead. (*"A Forsaken Garden," P3*:24–5)

But, long before Swinburne had invented this demonic parody of the *mors mortis* topos, he had begun to develop alternatives to his early "diabolic" faith. I have already traced these developments, and it will be necessary here only to show how the elegy's evolution through the seventies reflects the growth of Swinburne's Apollonian myth. In the "Memorial Verses" for Gautier (1872), the sun-god has already achieved a definitive triumph over time: his "House of Fame" is still purely a matter of literary tradition, but literary tradition is no longer a melancholy communion, a frail artificial barrier against time's destructive power; it is now the joyful creation of a new mode of experience, within which all divisions are temporarily overcome.

Within the graven lintels of the gate
That here divides our vision and our fate,
  The dreams we walk in and the truths of sleep,
All sense and spirit have life inseparate. (*P3*:60,63)

By virtue of his synaesthetic song, which has shown us "All form, all sound, all colour, and all thought ... as one body and soul," Gautier has illuminated this House of Fame for our "spirit of sense," and we can strew the flowers of the "sleep eternal" (lotus and poppies) upon his bier without regret (*P3*:62, 65). Similarly, "In Memory of Barry Cornwall" (1874) suggests that the "fame" of the poet's life and work will grow forever in "the garden of time," "For with us shall the music and perfume that die not dwell, / Though the dead to our dead bid welcome, and we farewell." The man lamented goes to a "soft long sleep," and not to the fictitious "garden of death" projected in the first stanza; there is no place where dead singers "One with another make music unheard of men"; but their song will continue to affect the living – subconsciously perhaps, "As a thought in the heart shall increase when the heart's self knows not" (*P3*:69-71).

These elegies of the mid-seventies are as rigidly humanistic and secular as "Ave atque Vale," but they place less emphasis on the bleak finality of death and more on the enduring power of works of art. They prepare the way for the development of the Apollonian Logos in "The Last Oracle." After "The Last Oracle," Swinburne begins to experiment with a new approach: to suggest the possibility of (another's) life after death as real, if still very remote. This shift may reflect Swinburne's tentative but hopeful attitude in regard to the question of immortality, during the period between his father's death in 1877 and his mother's in 1896: "... who knows after all?" "I do hope and trust and believe ..." "In spite of all the creeds and all the clergy on earth, I am not convinced" that there is no "revival and reunion after death." Tentative, sentimental, or ironically anti-clerical, all of the letters which mention the topic at all in these years take the survival of the soul seriously as a possibility.[9]

On the other hand, the shift in Swinburne's approach to the elegy seems to be part of a larger alteration in his poetic stance and technique. As his lyrics grow more personal, they become more experimental and *ad hoc*; he is willing to entertain transcendental possibilities, but he is very unwilling to dogmatize, and he is particularly careful to avoid the imputation of Christianity – especially in the fifteen elegies of *Astrophel*. "Via Dolorosa" (1887), the sonnet-sequence in memory of the blind poet, Philip Marston, begins in the quiet confidence of a determinedly hopeful agnosticism: "We know not at all: we hope, and do not fear." This hope seems so firm that Swinburne can use the *mors mortis* topos without irony, and attempt to thank Death for illuminating Marston's darkness. Yet the last half of the sequence increasingly stresses the ambiguity and the dark silence of death; the speaker can know nothing of the state of the dead. He must try to be "content with failure," since "Wild words or mild, disastrous or divine, / Blind prayer, blind imprecation," are all too much a part of this "blind" temporal world to grant us any vision of the dead. The "last word" of the sequence "seals up sorrow, darkens day, / And bids fare forth the soul it bids farewell" (*P*6:230–7).

Words become mere gestures of love and hope, and the power of literary tradition is no longer the chief source of consolation, as it was earlier. To some extent this change may have been determined by considerations of tact; after all, several of the late elegies commemorate very minor *littérateurs*, like Marston or William Bell Scott, or people who had no artistic pretensions whatever, like Swinburne's own relatives. Yet, even in "A Sequence of Sonnets on the Death of Robert Browning" (1889), the consolation of a *monumentum aere perennius* is subordinated to the expression of a faith which is not aestheticism. At the beginning of the sequence, to be sure, Swinburne does celebrate Browning's "works of words ... moulded of unconquerable thought, / And quickened with imperishable flame"; but as the sequence progresses Browning becomes less a creator of aesthetic objects than an explorer, whose "strong and sunlike sense invade[s]" time and eternity. As in "Inferiae," the sun becomes the symbol of a spiritual energy which endures even when it disappears from our knowledge; as in "Lycidas," 167–72, the sun sinks into the waves, and yet is "subdued not of the sea." Those who feel that nothing of Browning survives but our memories and his work "trust not in his truth"; Swinburne passes beyond his own agnosticism in an effort to celebrate the "faith superb" of another man (cp. "On the Death of Richard Burton," *P*6:199). This act of sympathy is in two senses an act of faith. Personal loyalty demands respect for the basis of a friend's life, for the way in which that friend exercises his own freedom as his own Deus; by repeating and celebrating the "faith" of one whom he loved and admired, the elegist doubly transcends solipsism.[10] His experience (in this case, his experience of another man's ardent soul) points to a value beyond the limits of the self; but his faith in that value is a leap in the dark, in a world where we can only "dream of what [Browning] knows and sees, being dead" (*P*6:208–11).

In the sonnets to Browning, as in the "Memorial Verses on the Death of William Bell Scott" (1891), Swinburne celebrates a "faith that leapt from its own quenched pyre / Alive and strong as the sun, and caught / From darkness iight" (*P*6:249). By a magic very like that which transforms the abyss in "The Garden of Cymodoce," the darkness of our ignorance becomes the light of our hope. But this consolation is a difficult and fragile achievement, as the best of the *Astrophel* elegies make clear. For example, none of these elegies is more brilliantly triumphant than the elegy for Burton ("Auvergne, Auvergne," 1891–2); but few poems of comparable length are so riddled with ifs and buts. Like "Via Dolorosa," the Elegy opens in a mood of confidence, using the *mors mortis* topos without qualification (Richard Burton is "A spirit now whose body of death has died / And left it mightier yet," 15–16).[11] Later in the poem, however, Swinburne stresses the melancholy fact that we cannot express, or even conceive of, Burton's hypothetical triumph over the dualities of the temporal world. Indeed, the Elegy itself has a dual nature: lines 1–88 form a topographical poem, in which Burton's triumph is rendered allegorically; lines 89–140 praise the dead in more direct and explicit terms. I propose to begin by studying these two sections separately. We shall see how the landscape is transformed into a complex allegory of human attitudes in a world of change, and how this allegory is discarded as the speaker tries to define the condition of the dead more clearly. But in the process of this attempt he discovers that all definition of the transcendent is all but impossible; his explicit account of the dead becomes increasingly melancholy and frustrated, but by the creation of a full, unstable symbol – the "garden of the Sun" (125) – he finds a way in which loss and ignorance can be tempered with exultant hope.

L ike "Thyrsis," the elegy for Burton opens with an evocation of the landscape through which the mourner and the mourned once wandered together; and in both elegies this landscape embodies, or represents, the elements both of transience and of permanence within the speaker's experience. But Arnold presents altered villages and enduring tree naturalistically, through the persona's eyes and memory, interweaving past and present in the manner of "Tintern Abbey"; whereas Swinburne's speaker schematizes the topography of Auvergne as he recalls it, and that to such an extent that the concrete Auvergne disappears. It is instructive to contrast lines 1–88 of the Elegy with the description of the countryside in Swinburne's letter to his mother, during his tour with Burton in 1869:

There is between Le Puy and Polignac one great cliff front of towering columns which faces the valley of the Borne river – columns broken off at a great height, and as regular as if designed for a cathedral: then a lower, more abrupt and irregular range; and then, further west, and covering a whole hillside, an immense heap of the same basaltic columns crushed sideways and slanting out of the accumulated weight ... above it ... Don't believe one word that the wretch Murray says about the cathedral of Le Puy; it is one of the grandest as well as one of the strangest churches ever built, and adapted with almost a miraculous instinct of art to the tone of the landscape and character of the country about, where, except the deep fields and lawns of grass that spread about and slope up from the narrow valleys ... there is nothing but alternately brown and grey mountain-land ending in a long and beautifully undulating circle of various heights and ranges. These mountain colours are most delicately repeated in the alternate stripes of the cathedral front; the effect, like that of the whole town, reminded me as well as Burton ... of my beloved Siena. Indeed Le Puy is a smaller Siena – the highest praise *I* can give. (*L*2:26–7, italics Swinburne's)

In the Elegy the "brown and grey mountain-land" disappears altogether. Everything in the Auvergne of the poem is black and white: "Crags dark as midnight, columns bright as snow" (20), "vapour white as snow" around "The grim black herbless heights" (61–2); most significantly, the land itself, as a whole, is "white as gleam / The stairs of heaven, black as a flameless brand" (2–3). As in "The

Garden of Cymodoce," Meleager's "long brand that blackens" supplies an emblem for one extreme: sterile death. The other extreme, of course, is that death which is transfiguration and aspiration, the stairway to "heaven".

The individual topographical features mentioned as the poem proceeds establish a further set of oppositions. In life, the daring Burton "Hailed once ... the crowns that load [Auvergne's] brow" (19) just as "The fearless town," Le Puy, "hails and braves / The heights" (27–8). In "the dawn of death," however, Burton surpasses his living self even as at dawn the "pillared mountain-side" between Le Puy and Polignac surpasses Le Puy itself in beauty (21–44). But the area around Le Puy also represents the opposition of certain human attitudes in a more general sense. On one hand is the "fearless town" described in 21–8, set in a land "more fierce and fluctuant than the sea" (we have seen that the sea in Swinburne's work frequently symbolizes – among other things – extreme peril, and the freedom which comes of embracing peril); on the other hand, "The huddled churches" are described in similes which suggest terror and timidity (29–32). There is an invitation here to associate religious orthodoxy with "perilous refuge," and to reduce the poetry to the rigidly moralistic terms of popular "freethinking" polemic. Yet the town and the churches are all less beautiful than the dawn-lit mountain-side; so the world revealed by death dims the world of opposition and the human antagonisms which it contains.

By a development at once logical and natural, Swinburne begins to recount the ascent of this mountain-side, and makes his description a fable of the soul's confrontation with death. Here one would expect a Pisgah-vision in the manner of Browning's "La Saisiaz," where the mourner comes "face to face with – Nature? rather with Infinitude" (11), seeing in the beauty around La Salève "heaven's own god in evidence" (6).[12] But when Burton and Swinburne reached the summit of the Puy de Dôme in 1869, they found it "wrapt in a rolling and rushing sea of mist – very favourable of course to the chance of a prospect" (*L*2:22); the climbers in the Elegy are "Blind ... / And shrouded as a corpse with storm's grey shroud" (47–8). As in "The Lake of Gaube," a few years later, the tourist is "girdled about with the darkness and coldness and strangeness of death" (*P*6:285), and through this experience of the dark attains to a sense of his own power and freedom (53–66). Swinburne's agnostic revision of the Pisgah-sight makes it clear in the following stanza (57–60) that the shadows of Christian materialism are what blind us to the "wondrous world" of death. "The might of raging mist and wind ... made our path / Like theirs who take the shadow of death for

God." The wild weather which has already been associated with the "viewless" world of time is now linked to the God created by those who fear and deify the darkness.

The fear of death stems from a form of materialism, from an over-emphasis on the existence – or non-existence – of the physical body. Certainly nothing could have been better calculated to reinforce and enrich the concept in this way than the obsessive repetition of funeral rites with which Isabel Burton, after her fashion, had honoured her dead husband. According to Eliza Lynn Linton, in her attack on Lady Burton (which Swinburne had encouraged), Burton "was no sooner dead than his widow surrounded him with the emblems and rites of her own faith – which was not his."[13] She was not merely commemorating the dead; she was attempting to reconstruct her husband in the image of a closet Catholic. This is what Swinburne means by "vulturous acclamation, loud in lies" (90); in his letters he refers to her "popish mendacities" and "treacherous profanation of [Burton's] name and fame" (L6:45).

Fear is the mother of God (94), and it is only the shadow of fear that makes death seem like darkness: "on the soundless and the viewless river" that carries the dead "through night perchance again to day," "No shadow save of falsehood and of fear ... / Hovers" to darken their new life (77–84). Here Swinburne drops his topograph-ical allegory, since he wishes to transcend all the dualities of his black-and-white landscape, and to evoke a shadowless reality "That turns our light to darkness deep as death" (88). Yet how can he express that light beyond light except in terms of the oppositions he has already established, between Christian dread and freethink-ing valour, between that death which leaves the corpse a "flameless brand" and that death which is aspiration and triumph, between darkness and light? Swinburne's answer to this problem is the rad-ically ambiguous, supremely interesting and evocative image of "the old garden of the Sun" which contains the "unwithering root ... of all growths that thought brings forth" (125–8). This principle is very much like the Apollonian Logos, "of whom comes the inner sunlight of human thought or imagination" – and from whom all deities take their being. But the approach to that concept in the Elegy is utterly unlike the approach taken in "The Last Oracle" or in any of its Apollonian successors. In the late seventies, Apollo's presence can be as immediate as a song, since the god incarnates himself in the poetry of human singers; in the Elegy, the divine "unwithering root" is scarcely conceivable, and the "garden of the Sun" may never be attained. Burton on earth moved "sunward" (121),

Still toward the old garden of the Sun, whose fruit
  The honey-heavy lips of Sophocles
Desired and sang, wherein the unwithering root
  Sprang of all growths that thought brings forth and sees

Incarnate, bright with bloom or dense with leaf
  Far-shadowing, deep as depth of dawn or night:
And all were parcel of the garnered sheaf
  His strenuous spirit bound and stored aright. (125–32)

These very difficult lines, the heart of the poem, deserve close analysis. The reference is to Sophocles, Fragment 655:

Ὑπέρ τε πόντον ταντ' ἐπ' ἔσχατα χθονὸς
νυκτὸς τε πηγὰς οὐρανοῦ τ'ἀναπτυχὰς
Φοίβου παλαιὸν κῆπον —.

[Far over all the sea, to the ends of the earth, and to the springs of the night and the opening out of heaven, the old garden of Phoebus.]

Lines 125–7 of the Elegy seem also to invoke Fragment 298a:

Ἐν Διὸς κήποις ἀροῦσθαι μόνον εὐδαίμονας ὄλβους.
['Tis only in Jove's gardens that we reap
The blessings of true happiness.][14]

But the primary reference is plainly to the heavenly garden where night and day grow. In Swinburne's poem, however, the growths "deep as depth of dawn or night" are brought forth (a suitably ambiguous phrase) and perceived by "thought"; they seem to symbolize all the faiths – possibly, in a broader sense, all the intellectual opinions – ever produced by men. All faiths were studied by Burton and related in such works as the *Kasîdah* (a versified study in comparative religion), and so combined in the "garnered sheaf / His strenuous spirit bound and stored aright." Thus Swinburne honours Burton's ambition to establish an all-comprehensive system on eternal principles, to be attained, in Burton's terms, through belief in all things – combined with belief in nothing.[15]

For this very attempt to attain permanent truth through the eclectic study and synthesis of transient opinions is a quixotic endeavour. Burton's *Kasîdah* admits that absolute Truth is unknowable in this world: "Truth may be, but 't is [sic] not Here; mankind must seek and find it There, / But Where nor *I* nor *you* can tell ... Enough to think that Truth can be."[16] The second half of Swinburne's Elegy evokes a "life incognisable" that may "perchance" exist "Beyond the bounds of sensual sight" (87, 78, 86), but declarations of faith here are balanced precariously on the fulcrum of a conditional clause ("If life have eyes ...," 85–8; "If death's deep veil by life's bright hand be rent," 134). "What loftier heaven, what lordlier air" now yields to Burton? "No dream, no faith can tell us" (113–20). We cannot even conceive of the triumph in which we long to trust.

For this reason, Swinburne desperately needs the kind of symbol provided by the "garden of the Sun." If the speaker cannot himself conceive of a transcendent "Truth," he nevertheless knew Burton, and saw that even in life the explorer and free-thinker had attained to a lofty freedom "above the coil about us" (97–8). He had seen Burton's "trust in time," his confidence that, by the path "That breasts ... the steep, the crag," man may reach at least some confidence that "Truth can be" (*Kasîdah*, ix.iv, vi.xviii). By a leap of faith which is at once an act of personal loyalty and an attempt to emulate Burton's aspirations, the mourner declares that all the intellectual "growths" of time, from Burton's luminous syncretism to the "Far-shadowing" Tree of Christian Mystery, spring from one "unwithering root" within the "old garden of the Sun." Burton has always sought this source of thought. But thought cannot "see" its own root, cannot conceive of that which alone conceives it. As the agnostic theologian Mansel put it, we cannot "be conscious without variety, or discern without differences"; difference is "inherent in our mental constitution."[17] The image of the unwithering root, suggesting as it does that the variations of thought are grounded in an "incognisable" organic unity, embodies and sums up the elegist's desperate act of Romantic faith.

By contrast with Herbert Spencer's "Unknowable," or Arnold's "Eternal, not ourselves, that makes for righteousness," Swinburne's "garden of the Sun" is no "blank counter," but an extremely evocative image. We may think of the radiant vitality of Spenser's Garden of Adonis, with its Ovidian god "that living gives to all";[18] we must think of the more frightening fertility evoked fifteen years before the Elegy in Swinburne's own *Erechtheus*, where Praxithea recalls Oreithyia's ravishment

Beyond the wild ways of the unwandered world
And loud wastes of the thunder-throated sea,
Springs of the night and openings of the heaven,
The old garden of the Sun; whence never more

From west or east shall winds bring back that blow
From folds of opening heaven or founts of night
The flower of mine once ravished ... (P4:379)

In this earlier exploitation of Sophocles' Fragment 655, the person loved and mourned seems to be swept beyond, rather than to, the garden of Apollo; and the Sun's garden is not differentiated from the garden of time. In the Elegy, Swinburne leaves it an open question whether the old garden of the sun is purely temporal or only contains – or produces – the temporal world. The "garden of the Sun" passage, in fact, is a fragment of a sentence without either subject or main verb; it is an elaborately developed adverbial phrase ("Still toward the old garden of the Sun ..."), modifying nothing. The passage describes the quality and direction of Burton's spiritual ambition; this "indomitable ascent" sunward (136, 121, 133) is Swinburne's more audacious version of the "quest" after a "fugitive and gracious light" which closes Arnold's elegy ("Thyrsis," 201–40). It is this "ascent" which gives value to Burton's life; and if "death's deep veil" is to be torn at all, it will be "rent" by the "bright hand" of such a life, to show us the continuation of that ascent toward an apocalyptic dawn (133–6).

Unlike Arnold in "Thyrsis," Swinburne in the Elegy maintains his focus to the end on the dead man mourned; he does not say farewell, nor turn to the world of the living mourner to contemplate the mourner's own quest. He raises transcendental possibilities, but not to provide the kind of consolation which traditionally concludes examples of the elegy. In the last stanza, indeed, he suggests that Burton's hypothetical triumph would not lessen the mourner's grief: we may see the soul's ascent "through the shadow of death withdrawn," "But not the soul" itself, not the beloved personality (135–40). The speaker says very little of his own feelings; he is concerned less to console himself than to praise the dead. And it is only through such selfless praise that he passes from the concept expressed in the topographical section – the concept of transcending time and change through death – to the concept of an unknowable, "unwithering" principle which may transcend space and time, but can certainly be perceived in space and time, through its operation as the source of "thought".

Only through his long, difficult, loving struggle to praise the dead worthily can the speaker even begin to resolve the painful dualities of his experience; and the resolution he finally posits is threatened on every side. Can any art catch "From darkness light"?

The Elegy for Burton says little explicitly about the status of language; but the poem as a whole constitutes a rather desperate gesture "toward the old garden of the Sun"; it is not, like "The Last Oracle", an invocation charged with confidence in the power of words. And, just as Swinburne divests the elegy of much of its traditional consolatory force, so when he turns to the Greater Romantic Lyric in *Astrophel* he calls into question both the reconciliation of mind and nature with which a poem in that sub-genre traditionally concludes, and the Apollonian synthesis proclaimed in "On the Cliffs," his own first experiment in the genre.

"A Nympholept," which Swinburne in 1901 justly called "one of the best and most representative things I ever did" (L6:153), is a splendid example of the sceptical Romantic meditation as developed in *Astrophel*. Composed circa 1893, this lyric evokes an incognizable deity, an "Unknown sweet spirit" radiant and vital as the "garden of the Sun" in the Elegy; but this spirit enters the temporal world to transfigure it. After exposing nature and language, in the first half of the poem, to a critique as devastating as anything in Swinburne's work since *Atalanta*, the poet goes on to describe this unknown god's transforming advent or epiphany. The conclusion, in which the speaker and the unknown spirit unite like two lovers, is really more ambitious than the kind of resolution traditional within the Greater Romantic Lyric; but Swinburne's triumph here, as in the Elegy, demands that he first undermine all the easier, more conventional paths to reconciliation, union, and victory.

"A NYMPHOLEPT" AND THE UNKNOWN SPIRIT

In Part I, I discussed Swinburne's criticism of sacramental theology and sacramental linguistics at some length; in Part II, so far, I have shown how he justifies and reinforces this criticism through his experiments in creating new gods, and new theories of language. Sacramental language incorporates and sanctifies the violent divisions of the temporal world – the world of "things." And "things" must inevitably seem divided, and divisive, until man comprehends his own centrality as the medium through which the temporal world makes sense of itself. At different times Swinburne defines this medium as consciousness, freedom, or creative action; but always the principle which makes for order and meaning constitutes the essence of humanity, even when (as with the Apollonian Logos) it is also more than that. It is by discovering his own nature that man sees through "This double seeming of the single world" (Tennyson, "The Ancient Sage," 105).

When "words, like Nature, half reveal / And half conceal the Soul within" (*In Memoriam*, v.3-4), words are involved in this "double seeming"[19] – or so Swinburne seems to imply. Swinburne manipulates the conceal-and-reveal topos as he does eucharistic imagery; that is, with audacious originality. We saw in Chapter 3 that "The Triumph of Time" uses this topos as part of the relapse into dualism at the end of the sea-vision: "Thou art strong for death and fruitful of birth; / Thy depths conceal and thy gulfs discover" (302–3). These alternations are part of "The sound of time, the rhyme of the years" (310). In the first chorus of *Atalanta*, concealing and revealing are yet more plainly part of the lust and violence which dominate in the dualistic world of time. Nature's supposedly sacramental function is reduced to the hide-and-seek of the Bacchic revel.

And soft as lips that laugh and hide
The laughing leaves of the trees divide,
And *screen from seeing and leave in sight*
    The god pursuing, the maiden hid.

The ivy falls with the Bacchanal's hair
    Over her eyebrows *hiding* her eyes;
The wild vine slipping down *leaves bare*
    Her bright breast shortening into sighs ... (109-16; italics mine)

Conveying Hugo's agnostic theism in 1880, Swinburne presents a more nearly traditional vision of the temporal world as an ambiguous revelation of deity. Of course this is by no means a Christian vision; God may be "force or thought, / Nature or fate or will" – Swinburne calls idealists, materialists of Büchner's ilk, pantheists, and the followers of Schopenhauer into the Hugolian fold, but Christians are not invited. The poet describes an immanent deity, but with a genuinely Hugolian emphasis on concealment.[20] This god is "the unknown of all time,"

Veiled and revealed of all things and of nought,
Hooded and helmed with mystery, girt and shod
With light and darkness, unapparent God.
Him the high prophet o'er his wild work bent
Found indivisible ever and immanent
At hidden heart of truth,

In forms of age and youth
Transformed and transient ever; masked and crowned ...
       (Birthday Ode, 281–91, P3:350)

There is perhaps an unresolved tension between this deity's im-
manence and his inaccessibility. The oppositions of light and darkness, of good and evil (283), are only the vesture of this god, who
exists beyond good and evil, "At hidden heart of truth." But perhaps
he is inaccessible only because he moves so swiftly through the years'
alternatives, an Ovidian deity in constant metamorphosis, "In forms
of age and youth / Transformed and transient ever." Swinburne does
not examine the question in detail here; but he raises it again, thir-
teen years later, in the Pan-poems of *Astrophel*.

"The Palace of Pan" (1893) also evokes a pantheistic deity which
is, somewhat paradoxically, beyond human conception, simply because of its size. Pan's "sanctuary" is pure of the ceremonies by
which men attempt to shadow forth a transcendent reality: "no
music beguiles" the temple's "musical silence," and "No festivals
limit its feast" (9, 39, 40). This temple or "palace" is formed by the
"infinite" pine-forest; thought cannot measure the height of the
pines' "indivisible roof," which forms a net to catch and shred the
sun (9–10, 16–30; cp. Pan's "palace roof," which "doth hang / From
jagged trunks," in Keats's *Endymion*, 1.232–3).[21] The immeasurable
forest, like the "Démesuré" figure of Hugo's Pan, confounds our
perceptions – is "the unimaginable lodge / For solitary thinkings;
such as dodge / Conception" (*Endymion*, 1.293–5). Noon, night, and
dawn pass, but all the process of temporality "Conceals *not*, reveals
not for man ... / Some track of a nymph's or some trail of a faun's"
to the presence of Pan, the immanent and yet invisible god (41–5;
italics mine). The shadowing forth of the infinite through the limited
and temporal, which is the essence of sacramental mediation, is
impossible when the infinite and the temporal are not distinguished.

Only "Thought, kindled and quickened by worship," can discern
even a "token or trace" of this "godhead terrene" (46, 50, 53). And
even when the speaker's "spirit" has been "made one with the spirit"
of Pan, Pan is too great to be comprehended or described. He "saith
/ Things" – the whole temporal world is his utterance – but the world
which is his speech and his dwelling-place is likewise too large for
human comprehension. The "Things" he says are "Triumphant and
silent as time" (61-5). In the world of this truly pantheistic lyric,
"things" have a unity and a meaning which are independent of
human action and almost entirely beyond human conception. The

"sunlight of human thought or imagination" (*L*3:137) is baffled and dissipated in the vastness of temporality: "As the shreds of a plumage of gold on the ground / The sun-flakes by multitudes lie, / Shed loose as the petals of roses discrowned" (26–8).

Here, it seems, Swinburne at last dethrones "human thought or imagination," removes it from the privileged position which it has occupied in his mythology for some fifteen years. Only six years earlier, in "Pan and Thalassius" (1887), the poet had presented Urania, the sunny articulate "Muse" working through human creativity, as the god beyond Pan's understanding; hers was "the word, the token, / The song," that gave "kingdom and glory, / And grace" to Pan (*P*3:218–21). Has Swinburne really jettisoned Urania and Apollo, and all that Promethean defiance of the "God of Time" ("By the North Sea," *P*5:104)? Only for the moment. "A Nympholept" (*P*6:127–40) – written at about the same time as "The Palace of Pan," or shortly after, to judge from the strong verbal similarities and the identity of the setting within the two poems – places both Pan and Apollo in a new light. The sun itself "Conceals and reveals" Pan "in the semblance of things that are" (104–5); but, instead of providing a "faint transcript" or analogy of an "Infinite Mind which is the origin of all truth, beauty, goodness,"[22] nature here presents by her alternations the character of a dualistic godhead.

> The fierce mid noon that wakens and warms the snake
>   Conceals thy mercy, reveals thy wrath; and again
> The dew-bright hour that assuages the twilight brake
>   Conceals thy wrath and reveals thy mercy... (106–9)

Throughout the first half of the poem, language and nature, Apollo and Pan, can express only the double seeming of the temporal world. With the utmost difficulty, the speaker defines this doubleness and denounces its insufficiency; the dualities of light and darkness, good and evil, rapture and fear, would make life meaningless if there were not a *tertium quid*, a rapture that casts out, absorbs, or transfigures dread. And as the speaker defines the need for this *tertium quid*, he begins to apprehend it; he becomes a nympholept indeed, as the "Unknown sweet spirit" whom he has invoked (255) takes shape and catches him up into herself. In this nymph, or through her power, nature and language are transformed. Divisions and dualities vanish, not through exclusively human activity, but through the intercourse of man and nymph and through their ultimate union.

"A Nympholept" can be roughly divided into eight sections. (1) The speaker first evokes the natural setting, which is, as in "The Palace of Pan," a forest at noon (1–35). (2) He then expresses, and discusses, an expectant dread (36–84) which (3) culminates in his direct experience of Pan's presence; this experience I shall call the First Vision (85–98). (4) Next follows a long argumentative section upon the ambiguous moral nature of Pan: he is the lord "of life and of light and of all things fair," but also the lord "of ravin and ruin and all things dim" (99–182). (5) These dualities are intolerable; the speaker yearns for their resolution (183–94), and (6) resolution comes with the Second Vision, at the advent of the unknown spirit (195–230). (7) But the speaker doubts for a moment if the Second Vision can possibly be valid; it may, perhaps, be explained by the operation of physical causes on the senses (231–49). (8) In the last stanzas, however, he turns to the unknown spirit in faith and hope, and is rewarded by perfect union with her, as "rapture ... casts out fear," and heaven and earth are made one (250–73).

From the beginning the problems of temporality and its violent divisions are established as central to the poem.

> Summer, and noon, and a splendour of silence, felt,
>   Seen, and heard of the spirit within the sense.
> Soft through the frondage the shades of the sunbeams melt,
>   Sharp through the foliage the shafts of them, keen and dense,
>   Cleave, as discharged from the string of the God's bow, tense
> As a war-steed's girth, and bright as a warrior's belt.
>   Ah, why should an hour that is heaven for an hour pass hence? (1–7)

The emphatic placing of "felt" in the first line indicates that this lyric, like "On the Cliffs," will be essentially dramatic rather than didactic; the syntax of the first sentence (a main verb is lacking) and the slow, stately movement of the stanza (seven pentameters, with an ABABBAB rhyme-pattern) suggest that the dramatic development will be gradual and subtle. This is a meditation rather than a rhapsody. Who is meditating? We know nothing of the speaker; although "the presence or the emotion of a spectator" is clearly felt throughout the poem, this spectator lacks individual characteristics altogether. The result is that, as in Herbert's religious poems, the reader is silently invited to thrust his heart into the lines. The "spirit within the sense" in line 2 might well be ours.

Such a phrase "suggests a condition where thought and sensation are merely ... aspects of a single, identical activity."[23] The first two lines of the poem seem to evoke a unified sensibility, which can blend heat, light, and sound into a single synaesthetic impression; and the third line suggests another kind of blending or melting. Instead of "shades of the sunbeams," we would ordinarily say, "shades cast by the leaves which intercept the sunbeams"; but Swinburne, by implying that the shadows belong to the rays, reminds us that light makes shadow possible, and by light shadow is defined. This is ominous; and yet these contraries melt into one another in a gentle harmony – until the next line. As in "On the Cliffs," a mild peace is opposed to a "Sharp" image of shooting and cleaving. The arrows of Apollo pierce the foliage; here the sun-god is decisively the "warrior," and the imagery of attack, invasion, destruction will be prominent until the advent of the unknown spirit.

The faint uneasiness created by this shift from the soothing to the militant increases in the last line of the stanza. The persona's deep delight in the summer noon is tainted by the anticipation of its own transience. Throughout this opening section, delight is dominant, but the imagery creates an undercurrent of repressed anxiety. Ridenour has pointed out that Plato in the *Cratylus* (408d) defines Pan as "the declarer of all things," and, more simply, as "speech"; the second stanza of "A Nympholept" goes further, coolly amalgamating Hugo's satyr with the Apollonian Logos as

> the word that quickened at first into flame, and ran,
> Creative and subtle and fierce with invasive power,
> Through darkness and cloud, from the breath of the one God, Pan.
>   (12–14)[24]

Because Pan was already associated with "Summer, and noon," Swinburne can develop this identification of Pan with the sun-god in a way which seems natural and casual. The sun is both warrior and lover; it possesses the earth (15), and the noon is "strong as desire that prevails and fades" (17). This love is transient, though it "impregnates" life with a peculiarly deep delight (19). In the same way, Pan has the "invasive" ferocity of a warrior, and his advent is anticipated by the persona and the surrounding wood as that of a divine lover. The beauty of the setting encourages the speaker to expect some revelation of "the deep mid[25] mystery of light and of heat that seem / To clasp and pierce dark earth, and enkindle dust" (33–4). Accordingly, he calls on the gods about him (42), and joins the forest in its anguish of yearning (52–61).

This longing for Apollo-Pan seems a purely temporal, physical alternation of contraries: "Each pulse that awakens my blood into rapture fades, / Each pulse that subsides into dread of a strange thing near / Requickens with sense of a terror less dread than dear" (59–61). It is appropriate that at this point Swinburne alludes to "The Palace of Pan," with its celebration of pure temporality: the trunks of the conifers, and the "roof sublime" which they uphold (and which screens the "floor" of the wood from the sun) are "silent, splendid, and perfect and calm as time" (64–6). For the moment the speaker is entirely satisfied with the phenomenal world: "The dense ferns deepen, the moss glows warm as the thyme: / The wild heath quivers about me: the world is good" (69–70). But this confidence is contradicted by the surrounding imagery; this Eden contains its serpents.

The wood's "desire" for Pan "would fain find tongue / And palpitates, tongueless as she whom a man-snake stung, / Whose heart now heaves in the nightingale" (53–5). Plainly, the nightingale is no longer Sappho the singing-goddess, but Philomela of the "tongueless vigil" (Atalanta, 72); not victor over time, pain, and dread, but victim of the man-snake's rape. And Apollo-Pan is uncomfortably like Tereus. The god's kindling breath moves fiercely through "the tremulous maidenhair" as the "snake" of fear creeps, "felt … In the stress of the sun" (71–4); Apollo seems to be one with the Python that he was supposed to have shot. The alternations of time, day and night, both rouse serpents, but it is noon especially that "wakens and warms the snake" (106–11). We are moving rapidly toward the old concept of a tyrannical god, whose kiss is a snake's; we may also recall the tyrant Love in "Thalassius," as the archer-Pan of "A Nympholept" sends "shafts" of love, as of anger (75). Above all, we should remember the fiery God of Atalanta; for Apollo-Pan's wrath and his love are each "as fire to the darkness its breath bade melt" (76–7): the creative deity and his Word form a single searing flame.

Yet all this is so far implied only by Swinburne's manipulation of the imagery. As yet the speaker is tremulous with an unstable mixture of rapture and terror (57, 78) as he prepares to "Receive the God"; as yet he does not know whether Pan's advent will bring love or dread (80–4). Then the "naked noon" leaps upon the persona – and the First Vision has brought dread, not love: "the fierce dumb spell, / The fearful charm of the strong sun's imminent might, / Unmerciful, … / Pervades, invades, appals me with *loveless* light" (85–8; italics mine). Now we see in what manner the physical sun "Conceals and reveals" Apollo-Pan. At night all but the wicked find release from the knowledge of Pan's cruelty: "then … [we] know not if blood for [his] lips be wine" (113–19). The implication is that in daylight we do see him as the diabolical God of the Cannibal Catechism.

In the "loveless light" of the First Vision, the speaker's dim mis-givings become explicit; his experience of an "Intense, invasive, intolerant, imperious" god (95) makes possible the intellectual rec-ognition of Pan's dualism in the fourth section of the poem. This deity expresses his nature not only in doves' "murmuring" (cp. the "faint sweet speech" and "murmur" which the speaker hears in his lovely grove, 46, 238), but also in "the clamouring of winds that call / And wolves that howl for their prey" (123–4). Echoing Psalm 148.8 ("stormy wind fulfilling his word"), the speaker declares to the god that "The tempests utter thy word, and the stars fulfil" (133). Like the Apollonian Logos, Apollo-Pan is the "word," and is incarnate in human speech as well.

> Smiling and singing, wailing and wringing of hands,
>   Laughing and weeping, watching and sleeping, still
> Proclaim but and prove but thee, as the shifted sands
>   Speak forth and show but the strength of the sea's wild will
>   That shifts and grinds them as grain in the storm-wind's mill.
> In thee is the doom that falls and the doom that stands ... (127–32)

The internal rhymes of 127–8 recall the cadences of the early lyric, "Anima Anceps," which proclaimed that the contraries of language, like those of life, would be swallowed up in death and emptiness, "Where earth is hollow / Under the earth."

> For all your weeping,
> Waking and sleeping,
> Death comes to reaping
>   And takes away.
>   ....
> Grief, when days alter,
> Like joy shall falter;
> Song-book and psalter,
>   Mourning and mirth. (P1:101)

So in "A Nympholept" the contradictions of nature and language "Proclaim" the god, but proclaim him as "doom." He is the destruc-tion that falls upon the wretched, and the "secret and speechless law" (143) that stands for ever, constituting the order of nature's alternations (cp. *OED*, "Doom," 4b and 1). He is also an imprisoning enchanter, like the ominous sorcerers at the beginning of "Off Shore" and "By the North Sea," or the dread lady with her "strong magic" in "Thalassius," 389–92. By his "fearful charm," "Death seals up life,

and darkness the sunbright air" (86, 150); and his "fierce dumb spell"
is the effect of a "dumb fierce mood" which rules earth and sky "as
with fire and invasion," with the oppression of a "tyrannous weight"
(85, 206–9).

Increasingly, this Apollo-Pan, this "word," reveals himself as a
"dark dumb godhead" (176). To elucidate this point, Swinburne
plays with the view developed in "Pan and Thalassius" (and in "Le
Satyre"): even if Pan is "God, more than shadows conceived and
adored of man," man has a peculiarly privileged position within
nature, since only man's soul can "conceive and perceive ... Pan, /
With sense more subtle than senses that hear and see" (156–61). Yet
even this "sense" cannot really "say" what the "spirit" that moves
Pan is like (162–5); and if it could, that would not do away with the
contradictions of change. The more clearly the speaker "conceives"
the god, the more obvious it becomes that, when language and
nature express only a set of balanced contraries – light and dark,
good and evil, and so forth – then nature and language express no
enduring value; we are left with the meaningless silence of an amoral
universe.

Yet then should God be dark as the dawn is bright,
    And bright as the night is dark on the world – no more.
Light slays not darkness, and darkness absorbs not light;
    And the labour of evil and good from the years of yore
    Is even as the labour of waves on a sunless shore.
And he who is first and last, who is depth and height,
    Keeps silence now, as the sun when the woods wax hoar. (169–75)

The double antimetabole in the first three lines (*dark/bright/bright/
dark, light/darkness/darkness/light*) intensifies the sense of senseless
alternation (cp. *mercy/wrath/wrath/mercy* in 107–9). To man, search-
ing for a divinity with power to give meaning and value to these
alternations, Apollo-Pan exists in a wintry silence, "splendid and
sterile" as Dolores herself ("Dolores," 71, P1:156). As in *Atalanta*, the
very fact of change hopelessly vitiates the rapture which is one
element among time's alternations: the god's nature "Imbues the
rapture of dawn and of noon with dread, / Infects the peace of the
star-shod night with strife" (176–8). Much even of the aural harmony
through these first four sections of the poem is organized around
the alliterative assonances by which *fair* is transmuted to *fierce, fear,*
or *fire* (71–7, 120–1, 144–6). If the joy which the speaker feels in the
forest has, as he thinks and hopes, any enduring value, it must be
a value which somehow transcends or "absorbs" the dread Pan
brings. Otherwise,

What helps it man, that the noon be indeed intense,
  The night be indeed worth worship? Fear and pain
Were lords and masters yet of the secret sense,
  Which now dares deem not that light is as darkness, fain
  Though dark dreams be to declare it, crying in vain.
For whence, thou God of the light and the darkness, whence
  Dawns now this vision that bids not the sunbeams wane? (190–6)

Riede observes that Swinburne adapts a characteristically Victorian perception of nature's violence to his purpose of "salvaging the visionary nature poetry of [R]omanticism."[26] We saw that "On the Cliffs" corresponded exactly to the model of the Greater Romantic Lyric in every important respect save one : the speaker addresses neither himself, nor (for the most part) the "outer scene," nor, strictly speaking, a "silent human auditor." He addresses Sappho, and as we hear her song and see his reaction to it, we come to realize that she is more than human. In the same way, "A Nympholept" develops into an explicitly religious lyric, in the sense that it addresses divine beings. Besides this, however, "A Nympholept" is further from the pattern described by Abrams than is "On the Cliffs," in two ways. I have already mentioned the fact that the persona in the later lyric is not individualized – a point which also helps to establish "A Nympholept" as a religious poem of sorts. A more striking innovation is that the speaker suffers from no "dejection," no sense of alienation, "isolation, or inner death."[27] On the contrary, he is filled with delight, and his effort throughout the poem is to explore the true implications of that delight – not to rest in it, but not to deny it either.

The dread Pan brings does not cancel this rapture: "fear [is] less than delight" at the moment (141). But doggedly the speaker insists that the rule of Pan would make his rapture valueless; the conviction he feels that his delight at this moment has enduring value pushes him to the belief that there must be something beyond the "God of the light and the darkness" (195). It is difficult for him to hold to that conviction. In the last few stanzas of the fourth section, statement after statement is qualified or denied: "Yet ... and yet ... Yet then ... And yet ... And yet ..." (163–88). As Baum observes, Swinburne's visions are "inwoven and overlaid with ... questioning, reservation, reluctance."[28] And this is true of the Second Vision, as of the First.

Precisely what is this crucial "vision that bids not the sunbeams wane"? "What light, what shadow, diviner than dawn or night ...?" It would seem clear, at least, that this vision represents some sort of triumph over time and change – over the senseless alternating light and darkness of Pan's world. Yet, of the critics who have dealt with "A Nympholept," two fail even to distinguish between Pan and the "Unknown sweet spirit" whose advent the Second Vision describes. And Riede identifies the new spirit of the "nymph" as "Pan's wife, change itself." According to Riede's ingenious interpretation, "A Nympholept" begins in a unity imposed by the Apollonian power of man's thought; the vision of the nymph is "the shadow of mortality" that separates the human mind from nature and enables the speaker to realize that "the perceiving mind *creates* the harmony of man and earth" (italics Riede's).[29] The problem with this reading is that, as I have shown at length, Swinburne identifies Apollo and Pan throughout the first four sections as one god, violent and divisive; while the Second Vision is introduced in such a way as to imply that light and shadow are *united* in the nymph.

McGann and Ridenour, I think, come closer to the truth when they suggest that the Second Vision is a saving transformation of the First. To McGann, the "visionary maiden" is one of the "metamorphic images" making up a "triple divinity" whose other two members are Pan and the "noontide landscape"; while Ridenour presents the "visionary nymph" as a revised, "gentler" version of Pan. She is a fiction who embodies our own "human, organic capacities that make 'apprehension' ... possible," for these continuing capacities make up the only kind of "permanence" open to us.[30] Like Pan, then, she would represent the perceiving and conceiving powers of the "spirit within the sense," but these are viewed in a new way, so that we can now see these powers as making, not for division and destruction, but for unity and a kind of permanence.

The interpretations of McGann and Ridenour both imply a close relationship between the First and the Second Vision, and a transformation of perception in the second. It will be helpful to consider these elements in more detail. At the outset of each Vision, the speaker feels a mixture of fear and longing (57–84, 203). The deity approaches slowly (71–84, 197–8), while, in the First Vision, "the silence trembles with passion of sound suppressed," and in the Second "the shadow ... trembles and yearns with light" (50, 212). The word, "suppressed," in the First Vision is significant. Apollo-Pan is a Logos which "Keeps silence"; the unknown spirit is a bright shadow which "bids not the sunbeams wane," and which therefore affirms enduring light (175, 202, 196). Here the two Visions are decisively opposed.

The doubts with which the First Vision is "inwoven and overlaid" ("Is it rapture or terror," 57) anticipate the sombre discussion of Pan's dualism after this advent; for they are doubts about the moral status of the god. The doubts which plague the Second Vision are alto-gether different: simply, is this vision possible? The speaker must reassure himself that he is not indulging in an escapist dream: "I sleep not ... I sleep not: ... may I dream that I dream not ...?" (211–31). The alliterative antimetabole of *die/dream/dream/die* in 218–19 emphasizes the contrast between transient dream and enduring vision: this is not one of the peaceful illusions engendered by the ignorant innocence of the night. In this vision, noon is purged of its savagery, and darkness of its ignorance: "Light wounds not, darkness blinds not, my steadfast eyes" (224). Yet surely it is im-possible so to transcend the conditions of temporal perception. Echoing St Clement of Alexandria, perhaps, the speaker reminds himself that he is "An earth-born dreamer, ... / Held fast by the flesh" (232–3).[31] The fluctuations of "rapture or wrath" are physically deter-mined (233–4); and, after all, is not the physical joy of the moment sufficient in itself? Is not the "sense" completely "fulfilled of the joys of earth" (237)?

> I lean my face to the heather, and drink the sun
>   Whose flame-lit odour satiates the flowers: mine eyes
> Close, and the goal of delight and of life is one:
>   No more I crave of earth or her kindred skies.
>   No more? But the joy that springs from them smiles and flies;
> The sweet work wrought of them surely, the good work done,
>   If the mind and the face of the season be loveless, dies. (246–52)

McSweeney calls this "the most radiantly joyous moment in all of Swinburne's poetry,"[32] and so perhaps it is; but the speaker resists this easy joy, damns it with a but (250). Delight in the natural world is not enough, unless love moves in the "mind and the face" of the passing moment. The invasive power of Pan appalled the persona with its "loveless light"; but, hoping that the unknown spirit em-bodies the love Pan lacks, the speaker chooses to "cleave to" her, in the biblical phrase associated with marriage (253). The intensity of his love and longing here ("Thee, therefore, thee would I come to, cleave to, cling") contrasts sharply with his cautious address to Pan, at the corresponding point in the First Vision: "Thee, thee ... / We scarce dare love, and we dare not fear" (99–101). The use of the first person plural in the fourth section, and of the singular in the eighth, should also be noticed. Pan's nature (in "A Nympholept," though not in "The Palace of Pan") can be apprehended by the ordinary exercise of human perceptive powers, and can be discussed in general terms, as it is in the argumentative fourth section. The unknown spirit, on the other hand, can only be experienced, through a condition of "ecstatic absorption" which does transcend, or transform, the ordinary categories of perception.[33] It is not by accident that the eighth section echoes the sea-vision of "The Triumph of Time," with its momentary transcendence of time's divisions: "I will go down to her, I and none other, / Close with her, kiss her and mix her with me; / Cling to her" ("The Triumph of Time," 259–61).

But the sea-vision in the earlier poem is in some respects what the Second Vision of "A Nympholept" emphatically is not: an escapist dream. The speaker of the earlier poem never does go down to the sea; but we see the unknown spirit take shape and interact with the speaker. She does not like Pan subject the persona to a loveless rape; she develops hesitantly, until the speaker perceives her; and then he comes to her, cleaves to her, clings to her, so that in their union each exercises freedom and love. It is important to recognize this pattern of reciprocal activity, which is drawn directly from Christianity: "the soul in my sense … receives the soul / Whence now my spirit is kindled" (225–6). So the Christians in Acts (8.17, 19.2) receive the Holy Ghost, the kindling Paraclete. But, whereas the Christian deity is the Bridegroom of the human soul (as of the Church), the unknown spirit is the soul's bride, a Diana to this Endymion. Nevertheless, through her love "rapture" finally "casts out fear" (261; cp. John 4.18).[34] And, unlike Pan, she is associated with "heaven."

Invoking Pan earlier, the speaker refused to seek "heaven" with "worship and prayer," but called on "the gods hard by" (40–6). In the Second Vision, the distinction between earth and heaven is erased with a firm hand: the nymph, though "Earth-born," brings "heaven" about her, and at the climax of the poem "Heaven is as earth, and as heaven to me / Earth" (264–6, 271–2). Behind such lines as these we may feel the shadowy presence of Keats's *Endymion*, where Pan is "the leaven, / That spreading in this dull and clodded earth / Gives it a touch ethereal – a new birth" (1.296–8); like Keats's Pan, and indeed like his Cynthia, Swinburne's nymph is "An Unknown – but no more" (1.302; cp. 2.739, 3.301).[35] But Swinburne and Keats, I suspect, use the word "unknown" in different ways, with different purposes. Cynthia is "known" at last through the concrete forms of the moon (with her "starry sway," 3.142–79) and the mortal Indian maid. Swinburne's nymph takes shape as the moon does (216), but she is "More pure than moonbeams," just as she is "More soft than shadow, more strong than the strong sun's light" (199–200). The "stately sway" of the moon (24–5), like the piercing violence of the sun and the transient peace of night, is too much a part of time's contraries to be an adequate image of the saving nymph. "Heaven" – the enduring joy and the love which the speaker sensed in the noon from the beginning (7), but failed to discover in the All – must be not the denial of these contraries, but the synthesis of their perfected strength, softness, and purity.

To reach this heaven, then, we must see through the double "Time-vesture of the Eternal."[36] This vesture of the unknown spirit is "soft in spring, / In summer splendid, in autumn pale" as with shame and fear, and "In winter bright as the mail of a war-worn king / Who stands where foes fled far from the face of him stood" (255–9). With its implications of difficult triumph, the military metaphor here (the only one associated with the unknown spirit) contrasts both with the fierce invasive energy of Apollo-Pan and with the easy triumph of Pan's firs, which, "perfect and calm as time, / Stand fast as ever in sight of the night they stood" (66–7). "Suppressed and elate and reluctant" (213; Swinburne uses "reluctant" in its obsolete sense of "struggling"), "heaven" struggles into realization.

> The terror that whispers in darkness and flames in light,
>   The doubt that speaks in the silence of earth and sea,
> The sense, more fearful at noon than in midmost night,
>   Of wrath scarce hushed and of imminent ill to be,
>   Where are they? Heaven is as earth, and as heaven to me
> Earth: for the shadows that sundered them here take flight;
>   And nought is all, as am I, but a dream of thee. (267–73)

The dualities of Apollo-Pan are dissipated in the crashing paradox of the last line. The line can be interpreted in two ways, each partially correct. It is possible to read "of thee" as a subjective genitive: the unknown spirit, like the Red King in *Through the Looking-Glass*, may be the mind in whose dream "all" (i.e., Pan) plus "I" (the individual human consciousness) are held. This interpretation is valuable less for its Berkeleyan metaphysics than because it suggests that both the external universe and the inner consciousness of the individual are dependent on the same living force. We can then identify the unknown spirit, tentatively, with the power called "life," by whose "grace," as we were told in 101–3, Pan rules "for a span." As Setebos to the Quiet, so Pan to "life": there is a superior power which may one day overcome the capricious and morally ambivalent power that rules the world; or the capricious god may one day "grow into" the character of the superior, the perfect god. And this brings us to the other possible reading of line 273.

If we read "of thee" as an objective genitive, the unknown spirit more nearly resembles Tennyson's "divine event, / To which the whole creation moves."[37] We live truly only insofar as we envision and yearn for this spirit, through whom Pan, the kindler and creator (12–14), is himself kindled and created anew, transformed and filled with new life as at the approach of that apocalyptic spring which Swinburne had long prophesied (262–3). The unknown spirit thus has a strong resemblance to the force which Swinburne, in the Prelude to *Tristram of Lyonesse*, had called Love, "The body spiritual of fire and light / That is to worldly noon as noon to night" (*P*4:5). This self-actuating force creates and brings forth all living things, preserves and transforms them, and arouses the free human consciousness which is the beginning of intelligent activity and love. In "Hertha," Swinburne had formulated a somewhat similar concept, in dogmatic terms; but the unknown spirit is dramatically present.

If we combine these two readings of the final line, we can see that the unknown spirit is a living force central to both the temporal world and the individual consciousness, but central as the apocalyptic transformation and unification of these. The extent of this transformation is summed up in the words, "Nought is all ..." It would have been more natural to write, "All is nought ... but a dream of thee"; but that would have been to denigrate the "all," the temporal world of Pan, which Swinburne in this poem is concerned to redeem rather than to cast off. By his reversal of the conventional phrasing, he allows us to see the void transformed to the infinite potency and richness of the transfigured Pan. As McGann expresses it,

What was initially encountered as a problem – separations, changes, disappearances, silence – is now experienced as fullness ... Transformational faculties correspond to a metamorphic universe ... Almost a joke, [the final line] is the poem's ultimate moment of silence which ..., like all the other emptinesses and silences in the work, "thrills with the whisper of secret streams" [243] ... The poem has no messages, only a subject: transformation. The final line, like the whole poem, is an action, a *tour de force* if you will, which sets an example. It is an image of the idea of speech.[38]

But then what of the severe criticism to which language (as personified in Apollo-Pan) had been subjected earlier in the poem?

There, we remember, Swinburne had not only elaborated on the identification of Pan and language as supplied by Plato's *Cratylus*, but also suggested a view of language which is very much like Socrates' view of names in that dialogue. Socrates lightheartedly assures Hermogenes that many nouns are formed on the assumption that "there is nothing stable or permanent, but only flux and motion, and that the world is always full of every sort of motion and change" (411c); therefore, he says, "no man of sense will like to put himself or the education of his mind in the power of names: neither will he so far trust names or the givers of names as to be confident in any knowledge which condemns himself and other existences to an unhealthy state of unreality" (440c).[39]

Swinburne seems throughout "A Nympholept" to sympathize with this deep dissatisfaction at the notion of pure temporality, and at the philosophical assumptions and linguistic structures which express and reinforce it. The unknown spirit, when she arrives, is not explicitly related either to human speech or to the Logos. Does she then represent an incommunicable transcendence of the temporal flux? Early in the poem, Swinburne declares that, if anyone glimpses the "dreams that last" which are conveyed through the "mystery" of noon, "His lips shall straiten and close as a dead man's must, / His heart shall be sealed as the voice of a frost-bound stream"; "Shall a man's faith say" what the mystery is (27–35)?

But, of course, as McGann has pointed out, the whole lyric is an attempt to convey this "unutterable experience" (*Swinburne*, 188). When language and the Logos are perceived as conveying a "nought," a blank silence, the speaker tries obstinately at least to imagine an alternative to that silence. In the process of conceiving this alternative, the speaker forces language into strange explosive paradoxes by which the indefinable is, if not defined, at least evoked; as the "reluctant" nymph transforms Pan, at the level of myth, so the speaker transforms language as he struggles with it. In the second section of the poem, the wood yearns to speak, but is "tongueless" as Philomela – and yet Philomela, once mute, now sings as the nightingale, "never at rest / Nor satiated ever with song" (52–6). So by the transforming power of the unknown spirit Pan's silent word will quiver with song, as the shadow trembles with light (cp. "Loch Torridon," P6:174, where, just before the climax of the poem, the speaker enjoys "Shadow, kindled with sense of light" and "Silence, laden with sense of song"). The long-desired nymph is the speaker's Stella, as he is her Astrophel; through her, "long-needy Fame / Doth even grow rich, naming my *Stella's* name."

At stake is the nature of language generally. The poet may subvert that language, words in their general naming function, but only to save and serve the possibilities of his language, a language created *pour l'occasion* out of its own general incapacities. This is the stuff that the rarest of dreams, of visions, are made of – the rarest since, in their ultimate immediacy, they are not transferable, can occur nowhere but here in this work ... By denying that words can say anything, these specially empowered words can say it all.[40]

It is clear now that the Second Vision does constitute the kind of resolution which is said to be characteristic of the Greater Romantic Lyric: it dissolves a deep sense of the divisions within the temporal world; it presents a perfect union between sense and spirit within the speaker, and also between the speaker's "soul in [the] sense" and the "spirit" which he apprehends via the interplay between mind and nature. It even offers a quasi-apocalyptic union between earth and heaven. The action of the speaker's mythic or visionary imagination (and here the distinction between myth and vision is surely a distinction without a difference, since "A Nympholept" is so plainly a religious lyric) produces the redemptive climax of the poem. The main difference between "A Nympholept" and such poems as "Tintern Abbey" or Shelley's "Stanzas Written in Dejection" is that for Swinburne in this poem the landscape does not exist at all as an object. From the very beginning, and throughout the poem, we are dealing with a kind of diffused personification: a militant sun that possesses earth and soothes "The chaster air" (16); silence and twilight that feel longing and pain; a wood yearning to speak. Every part of the "landscape" is involved emotionally in the complicated erotic relationship connecting the speaker with Pan and the unknown spirit, and every part "yearns, reluctant in rapture that fear has fed, / As man for woman, as woman for man" (79–80). The antimetabole here anticipates the perfect reciprocity, the entire union between the speaker and the unknown spirit: "My spirit or thine is it, breath of thy life or of mine, / Which fills my sense with a rapture that casts out fear?" (260–1).

This treatment of landscape is doubtless one of the points on which Swinburne was affected by the French Symbolists; like Mallarmé, he evokes "the horror of the forest, or the silent thunder afloat in the leaves; not the intrinsic, dense wood of the trees."[41] But a more direct influence on "A Nympholept" may be a work which we know that Swinburne had read and admired as early as 1869: Gasperini's *La nouvelle Allemagne musicale* contains, among other things, an elaborate discussion, partly critical and partly sympathetic, of Wagner's

Tristan und Isolde, and in this discussion the account of the second act takes pride of place. After quoting Wagner's *Lettre sur la musique* on "la grande, l'unique mélodie de la forêt," Gasperini continues: "Cette mélodie sans fin comme l'éternelle voix de la nature, retentissant en nous à certaines heures, sans que nous en puissions rien retenir, ces ténèbres qui sont la lumière, cette confusion qui est ordre, ce silence qui est sonorité et harmonie, voilà son idéal, le dernier mot de ses aspirations d'artiste, l'alpha et l'omega de son esthétique!"[42]

The opening of the second act in *Tristan* is Wagner's attempt to realize this ideal.

Quand il s'agit ... de faire parler la nature, de l'associer au tourbillon des passions déchaînées, Wagner est dans son élément ... Iseult attend Tristan dans la nuit. Bien longtemps avant que Tristan ne soit arrivé, longtemps avant qu'il n'ait quitté la chasse royale, il est là devant nous. Nous entendons sa voix qui se rapproche, s'éloigne, pour se rapprocher encore; la forêt est dans l'angoisse; cette lumière vacillante brille comme la dernière lueur du monde réel ... Pendant que le coeur d'Iseult bondit d'impatience, la scène tout entière s'agite; une mélodie passionnée circule dans l'air; le feuillage bruit, la terre se soulève, le bien-aimé arrive à pas précipités; les deux amants, réunis enfin, s'étreignent avec emportement. Cette imprégnation de la nature entière par la vie du drame est un des plus puissants moyens de l'art dramatique.[43]

Though Swinburne's is a noontide rather than a midnight idyll, many of the most striking elements in "A Nympholept" are already here: the silence that trembles with sound, the shadow that quivers into light, the impregnation of nature with human eroticism; the anguish of the wood and the twilight, "wrung / With love as with pain" (51–2); the palpitating impatience for the lover (and Apollo-Pan is, like Tristan, both warrior and harpist); the leaves' murmur, the lover's tread (238, 82). The unknown spirit "Draws near, makes pause, and again ... draws near" (198), almost as Tristan approaches and moves away, to approach again; and the speaker's union with the spirit is anticipated as a rapturous embrace (253). Further, Gasperini emphasizes (and sharply criticizes) Wagner's mysticism and idealism: "nulle voix ne chante le couplet sans fin que Wagner a entendu dans la forêt. La mélodie que nous aimons commence et finit," insists the critic, adding that Tristan's escape into the void of night is unnatural and intolerable. Instead of descending "dans les ténèbres et l'anéantissement," we should adore the cyclicity of life, as revealed in the wholesome daylight of reason.[44]

In "A Nympholept," Swinburne seems to be reconciling the attitudes respectively ascribed to Wagner and expressed by Wagner's critic. The atemporal transcendence which Tristan finds in the "holy darkness" is a transient illusion (108–19); but the daylight world of clear vision and the mystical eroticism of the *Liebestod* coalesce in the nympholept's noontide vision. The solipsism of Tristan and Isolde's cry, "C'est moi-même qui suis le monde,"[45] is repudiated, as the world and the speaker become merely a dream centred upon the nymph's luminous reality. The nymph subsumes the natural cycle, instead of transcending it; but she can subsume it because the natural world, like the speaker, is established from the beginning of the poem as her waiting lover, as a soul that yearns for the advent of the Unknowable. Thus, whereas in the Greater Romantic Lyric the great consummation is mind's marriage with nature, in "A Nympholept" mind and nature, indistinguishable from the first, wait to marry with the godhead. And, although the "sweet spirit" seems initially to be beyond conception or expression, by declaring his love and longing for her the speaker learns to express her perfection, exploiting the very limitations of transient words. As Swinburne wrote in his last important elegy, "Barking Hall: A Year After" (1897),

> Night and sleep and dawn
> Pass with dreams withdrawn:
> But higher above them far than noon may climb
> Love lives and turns to light
> The deadly noon of night.
> His fiery spirit of sight
> Endures no curb of change or darkling time.
> Even earth and transient things of earth
> Even here to him bear witness not of death but birth. (P6:332–3)

"THE LAKE OF GAUBE" AND THE PASSING MOMENT

Was it a vision, or a waking dream?
(Keats, "Ode to a Nightingale")

The end of "A Nympholept" can usefully be contrasted with the conclusion of Mallarmé's "L'Après-Midi d'un Faune," which the French poet had sent to Swinburne in 1876 ("Merci mille fois," Swinburne replied, "de votre merveilleux petit joyau de poésie ... [u]ne chose si belle de toutes parts" [L3:193]). Mallarmé's faun sees two nymphs, as in a vision, and (like Swinburne's speaker) yearns for an erotic union with these luminous figures; unlike Swinburne's speaker, however, the faun fails to achieve his desire. At the beginning of the poem, reflecting on this failure, the faun accuses himself of an errant idealism:

Aimai-je un rêve?

Mon doute, amas de nuit ancienne, s'achève
En maint rameau subtil, qui, demeuré les vrais
Bois mêmes, prouve, hélas! que bien seul je m'offrais
Pour triomphe la faute idéale de roses. (3–7)[46]

And in the end the diffused eroticism of the faun's imagined sin ("un souhait de [ses] sens fabuleux," 9) gives way to an evocation of the ponderous physical world and its silent power:

Non, mais l'âme

De paroles vacante et ce corps alourdi
Tard succombent au fier silence de midi:
Sans plus il faut dormir en l'oubli du blasphème,
Sur le sable altéré gisant et comme j'aime
Ouvrir ma bouche à l'astre efficace des vins!

Couple, adieu; je vais voir l'ombre que tu devins. (104–10)[47]

The formidable silence of the noon, like Pan's silence in "A Nympholept," exerts a tyrannical influence over the soul and over "ce corps alourdi." The "beauté d'alentour" (46) has excited, but has also suppressed, the blasphemy of a visionary eroticism. That art which entertains "des confusions / Fausses" between the divine mystery and the singer, or the song, reveals itself as "un chant crédule" (45–7). For the radiant, transfiguring power of the Romantic mind-as-lamp, Mallarmé substitutes a helpless submission to experience. The sunlight is the "source of the wine of life,"[48] but we can only drink the sun "As though it had been wine," in Wilde's phrase; we cannot communicate the "transmitted effluence" of the Apollonian flame as poets do in "Adonais" (407) or in "The Last Oracle" – we cannot shed light from the radiance that the singing-god has kindled within us. This, at least, seems to be the superficial meaning of the myth; if the poem triumphs over our limitations (and the ambiguity of the final line certainly leaves the way open for a more hopeful reading), it must be through a subversion of the narrative structure by wordplay.

"A Nympholept" deals with the epistemological and semantic doubts raised by Mallarmé, yet resolves these doubts through its evocation of the "rapture" raised by the speaker's union with the unknown spirit. The nymph in Swinburne's poem resembles the "unknowable" deity of Mansel and Spencer, in that she is apprehended as that which is beyond the dualities that condition all human perception. Again, she kindles the universe of Pan as Shelley's "Light" does in "Adonais"; she too is all-embracing "Beauty" and "sustaining Love" ("Adonais," 477–81). Yet she is apprehended, not as a transcendent entity upon whom the world of phenomenal appearance depends for its continued existence, but as the transformation by which the meaningless silence of nature and the mind, the self-contradictions of human perception, apocalyptically become a living and united song. She is the Romantic miracle, the "vision" or "waking dream" which alone makes sense of the world – if sense can be made.

Krieger's analysis of Keats's "waking dream" is useful here: "The poem ... is, then, self-demystifying, but as such it does not fall outside the symbolist aesthetic so much as it fulfills what that aesthetic, at its most critically aware, its most self-conscious, is able to demand: nothing less than a waking dream."[49]

"A Nympholept" ends by emphasizing the power and necessity of the dream, rather than the "self-demystifying" implications of the word "dream" itself (although these implications are discussed earlier in Swinburne's poem). As Mansel put it, "the limits of positive thought cannot be the limits of belief" (xi). Yet in still later works, such as "The Lake of Gaube" or The Tale of Balen, Swinburne's emphasis shifts toward a "demystifying" scepticism. The difficulties so triumphantly surmounted at the end of "A Nympholept" are declared insurmountable in the concluding section of "The Lake of Gaube."

In "The Lake of Gaube" (1904; P6:284–7), the earth – like Mallarmé's faun at the end of "L'Après-Midi" – is at first overwhelmed by the "compulsive silence" of the sun, which imposes on earth a "rapture, fair / As dreams that die and know not what they were" (8, 4–5). The opening section of the poem evokes a world of non-human life in which life, song, and rapture all disappear like a lightning-flash, leaving no illumination, knowing and explaining nothing of their own nature. In the next section, with its driving anapestic heptameters, Swinburne aspires to a superior rapture, a mythic experience in which he may confront the void imaginatively and move "through meaninglessness to signification."[50] An animal like the salamander may delight in the "blind" (3), unthinking rapture of physical existence, that fiery sunlight which is the salamander's native element; but the human speaker delights in a waking dream of perfect freedom which apocalyptically fuses the physical and the spiritual.

> As the bright salamander in fire of the noonshine exults and is glad of
>   his day,
> The spirit that quickens my body rejoices to pass from the sunlight away,
> To pass from the glow of the mountainous flowerage, the high multitu-
>   dinous bloom,
> Far down through the fathomless night of the water, the gladness of
>   silence and gloom.
> Death-dark and delicious as death in the dream of a lover and dreamer
>   may be,
> It clasps and encompasses body and soul with delight to be living and
>   free ... (33–8)

Line 37 evokes the Wagnerian *Liebestod* only to dismiss it. This passage is often read as if it referred primarily to the void of death, but, as lines 53 and 56 indicate, the darkness of the lake is "The darkness of life" as well as that "of death." Instead of losing his identity in the flowing darkness, or being rapt up in the "dream" like the speaker in "A Nympholept," the persona here defines himself as a centre of intellectual and physical consciousness, sporting in the freedom of the void, which is the native element of consciousness. Yet he can attain only to "rapture, a passionate peace in its blindness blest" (42); it is not at all clear that this rapture is, after all, superior in kind to the unthinking rapture of the salamander, or of "earth and air" (2–5). The dreamlike quality of this experience lies precisely in the fact that the gulf of our ignorance is apprehended as a love sustaining such blind rapture; the speaker is "glad as a bird whose flight is impelled and sustained of love" (48).

> As a sea-mew's love of the sea-wind breasted and ridden for rapture's
>   sake
> Is the love of his body and soul for the darkling delight of the soundless
>   lake:
> As the silent speed of a dream too living to live for a thought's space
>   more
> Is the flight of his limbs through the still strong chill of the darkness from
>   shore to shore.
> Might life be as this is and death be as life that casts off time as a robe,
> The likeness of infinite heaven were a symbol revealed of the lake of
>   Gaube. (49–54)

Like the speaker in the "Ode to a Nightingale," the swimmer is "darkling"; but, where Keats's darkness (like Wagner's) is flowing with music, this darkness is "soundless," "silent," "still"; this dream is too vivid to endure "for a thought's space more." As Swinburne wrote in "A Nympholept," "sleep would die of a dream so strange" (218). The swimmer seems to be in love with an experience which is transient, incommunicable, valuable in and for itself alone. Yet the hypothesis expressed in the last two lines gives this experience, potentially at least, the kind of visionary resonance which "L'Après-Midi d'un Faune" doggedly resists. If life were a dreamlike "rapture," and death a timeless rapture, then the "likeness of infinite heaven" would be "a symbol revealed of the lake of Gaube." The metaphorical power of the dive may convert the meaningless silence of the void into a "deep heaven" (27) of radiant significance.

But how are we to read line 54? Like the final line of "A Nympholept," this verse must be read in two ways at once. If the second "of" is read as the equivalent of "by," then the lake of Gaube has revealed the "likeness" of heaven as a "symbol." These terms are suggestive. A "likeness" has a superficial similarity to the object it represents, but may be essentially different, as a mirror-image differs in nature from the object mirrored; a symbol, although apparently different from the object which it represents, "partakes of the Reality which it renders intelligible; and while it enunciates the whole, abides itself as a living part in that Unity, of which it is the representative." It does not seem excessive to relate Swinburne's "likeness" and "symbol" to Coleridge's "allegory" and "tautegory," respectively.[51] For, if the "rapture" of the dive has the kind of universal validity which Swinburne would like to ascribe to it, it follows that we need not talk about the divine in terms of "likeness" – i.e., allegorically; for that sign which is the dive "partakes of the Reality which it renders intelligible." Allegorical language can be transformed into symbolic language. And, more radically, silence can be charged with the harmonies of eternity.

Yet, if we read "of the lake" as an objective genitive, the line implies that "The likeness of ... heaven" is only an appropriate symbol *for* the lake of Gaube. The theological concept of heaven and the physical experience of the dive are still bound together in the mysterious intimacy of the symbolic relationship, but the former is now subservient to the latter. Experience is the centre of this structure of faith, whereas with Keble the structure of faith and the sacramental system which serves it are organized around a stable theological concept, and experience is only the book in which "Pure eyes and Christian hearts" can read "heavenly lore." The universe of divine analogy is turned inside out, as in "A Year's Carols" (1894; *P*6:185), where Christmas itself becomes only a "sacramental sign" of spring.

And even this impudently reversed system of analogy is invoked, in "The Lake of Gaube," in one couplet only, in which the syntax is conditional and the diction is most carefully and ambiguously "worked." The triumph is temporary and uncertain; and Swinburne promptly drops into allegorical language, with a resounding thud, as if to call into question the very possibility of a "symbol." After the sweeping, ambitious energy of the second section's heptameters, the singsong trimeters of the third section are as deliberately flat as the abstract language they contain, and the dive itself becomes a mere likeness of the impossible act of fathoming the "fathomless" (36), seeing in "blindness" (42). There is no longer any essential connection between the dive and the unattainable bright "glory / We dream of."

> Whose thought has fathomed and measured
>   The darkness of life and of death,
> The secret within them treasured,
>   The spirit that is not breath?
> Whose vision has yet beholden
>   The splendour of death and of life?
> Though sunset as dawn be golden,
>   Is the word of them peace, not strife?
> Deep silence answers: the glory
>   We dream of may be but a dream,
> And the sun of the soul wax hoary
>   As ashes that show not a gleam. (55–66)

The dream apparently incarnate in the unknown spirit and in the heavenly revelation of the dark lake is, perhaps, "but a dream"; the mythopoeic faculty may be a self-consuming brand like Meleager's, collapsing, in the end, into a wintry dust. The lake of Gaube retains its "Deep silence." No word, either of "peace" or of "strife," comes to relieve, or even to illuminate, our apparent subjection to temporality. As McGann puts it, "In this poem, explicitly, experience is silence."[52] Only the lies of fear speak (26, 70). And fear's lies have to do, not with fact, but with the evaluation of experience. Fear "saith / That heaven, the dark deep heaven of water near, / Is deadly deep as hell and dark as death" (25–8). As Swinburne's repetitions insist, the lake is indeed deep and dark, "Death-dark" (37); fear lies, not in perceiving the gulf of life and death, the gulf of our blindness, but, precisely, in perceiving it as fearful. To let "faith [bid] fear take flight" (21), to discard the speech of fear, and live in "kindly trust" (20) of the silent darkness, is the moral imperative with which Swinburne concludes.

But this imperative levels us with the salamander of the first section, who listened to faith and developed a "kindly trust" in what was apparently alien. The leap of loving faith which sea-mews and salamanders take unreflectingly is the only leap we can take, even as the transient rapture of earth is the only rapture we can certainly feel. To leap into heaven, as the swimmer attempts to do symbolically, is another matter. "The Lake of Gaube" is a radically sceptical lyric in two ways. First, Swinburne implicitly rejects all myths that do not centre on the darkness and silence of immediate experience; second, by suggesting that all experience is essentially dark and silent (that is, that it reveals nothing), he expresses a deep scepticism about the validity of "mythical thinking" itself. Even the radically humanist myth of the second section "may be but a dream."

Of course, this scepticism is in some ways as Romantic as "mythical thinking" itself. Shelley's Demogorgon refuses to define his version of what Browning, in "Caliban upon Setebos," calls "the Quiet":

> *Demogorgon.*   If the abysm
> Could vomit forth its secrets ... But a voice
> Is wanting, the deep truth is imageless;
> For what would it avail to bid thee gaze
> On the revolving world? What to bid speak
> Fate, Time, Occasion, Chance, and Change? To these
> All things are subject but eternal Love.
> *Asia.* So much I asked before, and my heart gave
> The response thou hast given; and of such truths
> Each to itself must be the oracle.
>   (*Prometheus Unbound*, ii.iv.114–23)

Even here, however, Shelley insists that a "deep truth" exists beyond our limited perception. The scepticism of this passage is intimately connected with the transcendentalism of "Adonais": "Heaven's light forever shines, Earth's shadows fly" (461). Asia's declaration that "of such truths / Each to itself must be the oracle" expresses not a confidence in the inner light but an agnostic faith in something "infinitely distant," as Wasserman implies: "Mind ... cannot gain knowledge from external institutions pretending to ultimate truths, but must derive its knowledge from itself, even though that self-examination reveals, skeptically, the mind's ignorance of what lies outside Existence" (322–3).

The distinction between this sceptical faith and the attitudes expressed in "The Lake of Gaube" lies in the fact that Swinburne keeps the moment of experience at the centre of his religious hypothesis. And, like Mallarmé, Swinburne focuses on the immediate in a manner which is "demystifying" as Shelley's scepticism is not; for the immediate may be apprehended in its transiency, as a centre "Où notre ébat au jour consumé soit pareil."[53] But the immediate may also be apprehended as, possibly, filled with that apocalyptic value which seems to be rejected in "L'Après-Midi." It is significant that both "A Nympholept" and the second section of "The Lake of Gaube" use the present tense, with its hopeful evocation of an eternal present, while Mallarmé moves fitfully between present and preterite, and places peculiar emphasis on the words "contez" and "souvenirs" (25, 52). Mallarmé's passing moment has already passed, or is present only as a fiction created by the artist. Shelley's "deep truth" permits of no manifestation but one: the "destined hour" of the apocalypse, when Jupiter, *in illo tempore*, is flung down from heaven (and this is a purely negative manifestation: whatever the "deep truth" may be, it is not the divine tyrant that we have conceived). But Swinburne's dive into the dark combines the potential mythic resonance of Shelley's apocalypse with the self-conscious temporality of Mallarmé's "faute idéale." At the end of his life, Swinburne is in effect mediating between the Romantic symbolists (both English and French) and the French *symbolistes* – and constructively criticizing both.

Conclusion

Swinburne's career is a demonstration of the vigour and flexibility of Romanticism. At the beginning of his poetic career, Swinburne's relationship to the Romantic tradition was ambivalent: his admiration for the artistic achievements of Blake, Shelley, and Byron was tempered by a distrust of their visionary confidence. To him the radical Romantics were by definition "philanthropic" reformers. The aestheticism inculcated by "Gabriel and his followers in art (l'art pour l'art)" made him disapprove of any poem in which the didactic impulse was predominant; hence, in 1865, he felt that Shelley's *Prometheus Unbound* was "spoilt ... by the infusion of philanthropic doctrinaire views and 'progress of the species'" (L1:195, 115). And the profound pessimism of his late twenties made him sceptical about reform: no doubt certain social injustices could be remedied, but evil was no "skin disease" to be removed from the world by "moral surgery" (B13:163). At that time, the central focus of Swinburne's concern was the kindling and devouring fire of temporality itself, the dark central power in a world of pain.

To be sure, Swinburne's pessimism itself exploits, as Mario Praz has demonstrated, certain Romantic assumptions and strategies. The "mistaken Demon of heaven," the "ruling principle of Hate," is a Romantic bogey – but is no more; except by Sade (whose status as a Romantic is far from clear), the Demon of heaven is usually not taken very seriously.[1] Byron and Shelley use this figure as an emblem of the cruelties entailed by Christian error, or as an excuse to endow their religious views with the moral grandeur they ascribed to Milton's Satan. So Byron's Lucifer prefers "an independency of torture / To the smooth agonies of adulation, / In hymns ... and self-seeking prayers."[2] This rhetorical strategy proved invaluable to later generations of free-thinkers, anxious to display their heroic devotion to objective truth, or righteousness, or human dignity; from J.S. Mill to Anthony Froude, from Winwood Reade to T.H. Huxley, Victorians exploit the strategy of stoicism in the face of a malicious deity, without really believing in the "wayward, fierce, unrighteous, merciless" deity they defy.[3] Even Blake's Urizen is only one among many fallen powers, although perhaps the most formidable and most hateful of these. The diabolical deity and the deified Whore of Swinburne's early poetry and drama are something more.

In developing the dark vision of *Atalanta* and *Poems and Ballads*, First Series, Swinburne was indebted less to the English Romantics than to the examples provided by Hugo and Baudelaire in their Satanic moments, and by Sade. Yet Swinburne's chief debt at this stage is to the Church of England, and to the literature associated with that Church – from the King James Bible and the Prayer Book to the High Anglican texts of Neale and Trench. For this literature supplies Swinburne with the system which he inverts and distorts to express his pessimism; or, to put it more precisely, he manipulates sacramental and typological imagery in a style which, in itself, constitutes a radical criticism of High Church Christianity. The universe of "immediately *felt*" analogies, celebrated by an Oxford Movement heavily influenced by Romanticism,[4] becomes a universe of dark correspondences made evident by pain. And in this darkness (as the studies of Meyers and Murfin have demonstrated) Romanticism itself seems insufficiently radical.

The despair, violence, and black humour of the early works bear fruit in the works of Hardy and Hughes, Stevie Smith and Plath.[5] But, as Swinburne experiments with alternatives to the "turbid nihilism" of his own early vision, he begins to align himself more closely with various forms of radical Romanticism. In *William Blake* (1862–7), Swinburne had urged that a Shelley or a Hugo, "poets whose work is mixed with and coloured by personal action or suffering for some cause moral or political," can be none the greater as artists because they attempt to offer "doctrine, philanthropy, reform, guidance, or example" to their readers; but in 1872 he added that "the poetic supremacy ... of Milton and of Shelley" is not diminished because of their "moral or religious passion": "the doctrine of art for art is ... sound as an affirmation, unsound as a prohibition." There is clearly no inconsistency between this view and Swinburne's earlier aestheticism, but there is an important shift of emphasis: once the influence of "Gabriel and his followers" had lapsed, Swinburne was able to explore Romantic solutions to the problem of temporality.[6] After William Rossetti's 1869 edition of Shelley had stimulated Swinburne to a fresh examination of radical Romanticism, Shelley seemed not the "ineffectual angel" of Matthew Arnold's later essay, but "a son and soldier of light, an archangel winged and weaponed for angel's work" ("Notes on the Text of Shelley," 1869).[7] By 1875, Swinburne could pronounce himself a member of "the Church of Blake and Shelley," and in both *Songs before Sunrise* and *Songs of the Springtides* the "philanthropic" reformer – the bard who is also a political martyr – is a part of deity.

Swinburne identifies himself as the disciple of Shelley and Hugo throughout his political verse. In the humanistic ideology developed through the Romantic prophecies of *Songs before Sunrise*, time is conquered through time; the apocalyptic Republic, to be attained through the self-sacrifice of political radicals working in time, is the true meaning of the apparently meaningless world of changing "things." Thus, if Paul de Man is right in associating allegory with "the unveiling of an authentically temporal destiny," and symbol with a non-temporal concept of "simultaneity" (190), it is perhaps not surprising that Swinburne's prophecies should employ both modes. In any case, Swinburne is frankly adopting the tradition of Romantic political verse as he understands it. More subtly, the conquest of time through time is achieved in the Apollonian mythopoeia of Swinburne's next period. To celebrate another artist's triumph over time is to reenact it – to replay it, but in a different key. The technique of celebration, as developed in *Songs of the Springtides*, makes it possible for the dead letter of another's text to become a new song. Swinburne's conflation of Sappho's text with the song of the living nightingale, like his image of the oceanic song as a living architecture, implicitly reconciles the aestheticism of a Gautier with the organicism of a Coleridge. Yet Sappho, "More miracle than bird or handiwork,"[8] conquers time by enduring its "Fire everlasting"; and the reconciliations of *Songs of the Springtides* depend on a two-edged word which can curse as well as bless.

The ambiguity of the word illuminates the ambiguity of time. Is a triumph over time really possible? In *Astrophel* this question is answered with the utmost difficulty; in "The Lake of Gaube" it is declared, in effect, unanswerable, for we cannot be sure that such a triumph is possible at all. At the end of his career, Swinburne's scepticism turns every divinity within his last volumes into what one might call a nonce-god, a god created for the moment only. At the same time, Swinburne resists Mallarmé's youthful reduction of scepticism to a dogma: "je veux me donner ce spectacle de la matière, ayant conscience d'être et, cependant, s'élançant forcenément dans le Rêve qu'elle sait n'être pas, chantant l'Âme et toutes les divines impressions pareilles qui se sont amassées en nous depuis les premiers âges et proclament, devant le Rien que est la vérité, ces glorieux mensonges!"[9]

Swinburne, in contrast to the young Mallarmé, is genuinely ambivalent in his attitude to nature and to "le Rêve" as an epistemological tool. Dream may be vision or illusion; the swimmer in the dark, the nympholept in the grove, may or may not be "united to a creative power greater than his own because it includes his own."[10] Five years after Mallarmé proclaimed his "poétique très nouvelle" to Henri Cazalis – "Peindre, non la chose, mais l'effet qu'elle produit"[11] – Swinburne was writing of Shelley, "His aim is rather to render the effect of a thing than a thing itself; the soul and spirit of life rather than the living form, the growth rather than the thing grown" (B15:380). The explanatory phrases which Swinburne attaches to the Mallarméan formula imply that to capture an "effect" is not to limit oneself to the sensuous impression of the moment (after the manner prescribed in Pater's Conclusion to *The Renaissance*); rather, it is to subordinate such impressions to the evocation of a *motion* which is "life" and "growth." Even in "The Lake of Gaube," pure experience is conceived less as a succession of Paterian "moments" than as a single flowing motion, a curving dive. The sense of motion in Swinburne's poetry appears sometimes as a violent manifestation of temporality, sometimes as a triumph in the creative *action* of the political or poetic mind; and even in a lyric as deeply sceptical, and as sharply focused on the immediate, as "The Lake of Gaube," the immediate is invested with a "powerful rushing flame of life"[12] which makes the dream of meaning potentially, at least, more than a dream.

> All aflower and all afire and all flung heavenward, who shall say
> Such a flash of life were worthless? This is worth a world of care –
> Light that leaps and runs and revels through the springing flames of
>   spray. ("The Sunbows" [1884], P6:22)

Thus even Swinburne's "naturalism" (to borrow McSweeney's term) is visionary and subjective. It evokes the intellectual beauty of a bird "Like a cloud of fire," a forest like a lyre, rather than the more familiar naturalism of Tennyson's black ash-buds and yellow seas.[13] For this reason, Swinburne's landscapes often seem abstract and – as it were – "thingless"; they differ markedly from, say, the landscapes of Browning and Meredith, which are rank with particular life. Yet at the same time Swinburne's universe is vigorously active, precisely because his central concern is with the power of imaginative action, as it resists, exploits, or conquers time.

It is possible, then, to set Swinburne "in the center of the path that leads from Shelley to Hardy" – in the "mainstream" of a tradition of "agnostic mythmaking" which culminates in Lawrence, Yeats, and Stevens.[14] But it must be added that Swinburne's work also embodies the conjunction of French Romanticism and *symbolisme* with the English tradition. The sceptical and the allegorical strains already in English Romanticism receive a powerful reinforcement from the influence of Hugo and Mallarmé; while we have seen how even the mythic triumphs invoked in "The Garden of Cymodoce" and "A Nympholept" depend on strategies adapted from the French tradition. And these strategies make it possible for Swinburne to reply to his own early criticism of the Romantic tradition. In such poems as "The Garden of Cymodoce" and "A Nympholept," the pessimism of *Atalanta* is confronted and transmuted; it does not fade, but suffers a sea-change.

The development of Swinburne's religious attitudes is an extremely complex process, and should not be reduced to a graph of ascent or decline, either on the moral or on the aesthetic level. "Thalassius" and the Prelude to *Songs before Sunrise* are valuable as poetry, and they illuminate Swinburne's changing ethical and aesthetic emphases; but, as literary criticism, or as a chart of his poetic development, these lyrics are thoroughly misleading. Still more misleading is the popular concept (too widely accepted, even now, by scholars unaware of recent critical developments) of Swinburne as a rocket that flashed up in 1863–6, exploded in one sensational burst of lyric energy, and faded almost at once. It is interesting and useful to pursue the way in which the poet's views and interests flowed (or unfolded) one into another; but there is no need to praise *Songs of the Springtides* at the expense of *Songs before Sunrise*, or *Atalanta* at the expense of *Astrophel*. The most helpful way of viewing Swinburne's career is to see it as a connected series of brilliant experiments in Romantic art.

A careful reading of his verse effectively refutes the superstition that "his insights seem always to move towards the peripheral, the immature."[15] We have seen that his criticism of Christian thought is well-informed and intelligent, however virulent it may become under the stress of political controversy; and his subtle manipulation of typological and eucharistic imagery constitutes a profoundly original exploitation of High Church sacramentalism. The intellectual vigour of his Romantic visions and revisions owes much to his imaginative anticlericalism. If we are prepared to dismiss European anticlericalism and Neo-Romantic Idealism as "peripheral" to the history of nineteenth-century thought, then, perhaps, Swinburne's "insights" may also be dismissed as peripheral. Yet his poetry cannot be dismissed. And that poetry shows a comprehensive understanding of the Romantic tradition – its mythopoeic and allegoric impetus, its organicism and its profoundly ironic sense of temporality – which contemporary criticism is only beginning to match. Moreover, it is becoming increasingly clear that Swinburne has helped to shape the Romantic tradition inherited and exploited by the twentieth century.

But the experience of reading Swinburne's poetry is its own reward, and is Swinburne's best justification. To appreciate his work fully, we must understand the typological and sacramental systems that he exploits; we must also be able to recognize the conventions of form and genre with which he experiments. Above all, it is necessary to grasp the complexity of the Romantic tradition. Only an eclectic approach, therefore, can begin to do Swinburne justice. Swinburne's poetry is unsettling, deeply moving, intellectually rewarding at every level; and, as Swinburne himself said of Blake, "it is not for his sake that we should contend to do him honour."[16]

Appendix

MYTH AND ALLEGORY IN *WILLIAM BLAKE*

It is in *William Blake* that Swinburne's views on the relationship of allegory and myth are most clearly expressed. Riede has suggested that Swinburne, as a late Romantic, simply condemns allegory in favour of myth (*Swinburne*, 30–40); but the matter is more complex than that. If Swinburne at one point distinguishes between "mere allegory and creative myth," he also refers impatiently to "the mere mythologic fancy ... without curb or guide" (*WB* 250, 241). "Allegory," as he uses the term, seems to refer to any tale of which the meaning is clear, coherent, and limited, and in which the system of figures is worked out with a "logical patience" that Blake lacked: "of allegory pure and simple there is scarcely a trace in Blake" (*WB* 178, 265).

As Swinburne's understanding of myth was shaped primarily by his early devotion to Greek and Roman literature, he subscribed to certain assumptions which had been questioned even in his own time. A myth, he implies, exists only in literary form; it can be created by an individual (such as Blake or Hugo); it describes a fantastic action, perhaps a very simple one (the world-tree grows and buds, a goddess gives birth), but one of large significance (*WB* 234–6, 269–70).[1] Above all, myth is "creative" and free. Swinburne follows Coleridge and Wordsworth in his characterization of allegory. Coleridge calls it "but a translation of abstract notions into a picture-language," and Wordsworth, in relation to classical fables and allegories, laments "the bondage of definite form." So Swinburne speaks of "the house of allegoric bondage" (*WB* 191).[2] The mythmaker, unlike the allegorist, does not bind himself to an abstract scheme worked out beforehand. Swinburne finds both "allegories" and "myth" in Blake's *Jerusalem*:

Thus much for the scheme of allegory with which the prophet sets out; but when once he has got his theogony well under way and thrown it well into types, the antitypes all but vanish: every condition or quality has a god or goddess of its own; every obscure state and allegorical gradation becomes a personal agent: and all these fierce dim figures threaten and complain, mingle and divide, struggle and embrace as human friends or foes. (*WB* 286-7)

It is the freedom of myth that makes possible not only this fierce drama, but also true "imaginative vision." In Blake's "Memorable Fancy" of the Abyss and the pit (*The Marriage of Heaven and Hell*, Plates 17–20),

direct allegory and imaginative vision are indivisibly mixed into each other. The stable and mill, the twisted root and inverted fungus, are transparent symbols enough: the splendid and stormy apocalypse of the abyss is a chapter of pure vision or poetic invention. (*WB* 218)

Although Swinburne does not use the word, "myth," here, the relationship of "imaginative vision" to allegory precisely parallels the relationship of myth to allegory in the discussion of *Jerusalem*; it is clear that "vision or poetic invention" supplies us with symbols of large and complex resonance, as opposed to the "transparent symbols" – images with a single obvious meaning – which are characteristic of "direct allegory." Yet, without the discipline of the allegoric impulse, the inventive power or "mere mythologic fancy" may fail to create any coherent structure of meaning; according to Swinburne, much of Blake's prophetic work exemplifies this failure (*WB* 241–3). Blake the mythmaker, Swinburne implies, was not quite enough of an allegorist. (We should not be surprised, then, that in *Songs before Sunrise* Swinburne uses allegory more freely than Blake ever did: the Prelude, for instance, is emphatically allegorical; and in sections of "Before a Crucifix" and "Hertha" Swinburne provides the verbal equivalent of a labelled diagram in a book of emblems.)

Nevertheless, as the tone of the passage on Blake's Memorable Fancy suggests, the power that Blake did possess is more valuable and important than the power he lacked. We can relate the distinction here developed to Meredith B. Raymond's discussion of Swinburne's broader critical principles. That art which exhibits a "clear, orderly," conscious subordination of all detail to an obvious purpose looks "rigid and bare" ("John Ford" [1871], *B*12:386-7) beside the art which fuses complexities in "the mystery of its unity" (*A Study of Shakespeare* [1880], *B*11:3).[3] Yet we should notice that "the *mystery* of its unity" is a phrase coined in 1880. Up to 1871, at least, Swinburne seems to think of the allegoric and mythic impulses, and of control and "invention," generally, as opposing impulses which can and should be deliberately harmonized; it is later that he learns to conceive of the transcendent poetic imagination as a crucible in which these impulses are inexplicably fused.[4]

Notes

INTRODUCTION

1 Miller, *The Disappearance of God*, 3.
2 Rosenberg, "Swinburne"; McGann, *Swinburne: An Experiment in Criticism*. Of course, no Swinburne industry on any substantial scale will be possible until a reliable scholarly edition appears.
3 9 September 1866, L1:182.

CHAPTER ONE

1 "I trample underfoot the prejudices of my childhood, I annihilate them, [and] that excites me." All translations from French into English are my own, except where I have indicated otherwise.
2 Abrams, *Natural Supernaturalism*, 65. On Swinburne's Romanticism, see Murfin, *Swinburne, Hardy, Lawrence and the Burden of Belief*; Riede, *Swinburne: A Study of Romantic Mythmaking*; and McSweeney, *Tennyson and Swinburne as Romantic Naturalists*.
3 Gosse, *The Life of Algernon Charles Swinburne*, 9; L4:166, 214. To Swinburne, even in 1873, Keble and Newman were names "synonymous with genius and worship" within the religious body (or bodies) to which they belonged (L2:246). The period during which Swinburne himself experienced "very strong ... religious feelings" appears to have been "from the age of fifteen to eighteen or so" (W.M. Rossetti, *Diary*, 8).
4 Elizabeth Swinburne Bowden, in 1881, in J.H. Newman, *Letters and Diaries*, 29:360n1. The gift to Newman was a reliquary and crucifix.
5 For Nichol's influence on Swinburne's free thought, see Suiter, 179–83 and 203.
6 Keble, *The Christian Year*, 52–4.
7 Trench, *On the Study of Words*, 29, 69–70, 109–10.

8 Henry Mortimer Luckock in his introduction to *The Great Commission* shows how Woodford's "strong belief in the ineffable grace of Orders" expressed itself in an elaborate preparation of candidates for ordination (with Communion daily) and an unusually impressive performance of the rite of Ordination (xi–xxx). Quotations in my text are from Woodford, *The Great Commission*, 117, 155–6, 13, 163. Elsewhere Woodford speaks of the "mighty mystery of the Presence of Christ" vouchsafed in the Eucharist, but does not define that Presence ("S. Peter's Shadow," *Sermons on Subjects from the New Testament*, 89). Woodford's enduring reverence for the sacramental system in the larger sense is expressed in "The Call of God" (*The Great Commission*, 12) and in "Entrance through the Veil of Christ's Humanity" (*Sermons on Subjects from the New Testament*, 139–51).

9 J.H. Newman, "The Resurrection of the Body," *Parochial and Plain Sermons*, 1:275, and letter to Hurrell Froude, 2 February 1836, in *Letters and Diaries*, 5:226 (cp. Härdelin 150, 187).

10 Clara Watts-Dunton, *The Home Life of Swinburne*, 127–8.

11 Gosse, *Life*, 116.

12 Northrop Frye, *The Great Code*, 140ff.

13 Woodford, "The Act of Ordination," in *Great Commission*, 169. Woodford supports his arguments by reference to typology in "The Power of Absolution" (ibid., 61–2), and in "Entrance through the Veil ..." (*Sermons on Subjects from the New Testament*, 142–3). William Sewell, formally severing his connection with Newman and Hurrell Froude, adapts and justifies the typological polemic of the Reformers, perceiving in Popery "the foreshadowed form of the Antichrist" (Sewell, "Divines of the Seventeenth Century," 478ff). On Sewell's relationship with the Swinburne family in Bonchurch, see Hutchings and Turley, *Young Algernon Swinburne*, 2–10. As a freshman at Oxford, Swinburne was allowed to visit the boy's college, of which Sewell was then warden; in late 1856 or early 1857, however, Sewell declined further visits from one who had adopted the "'sinister tenets'" of free thought (Gosse, *Life*, 338, quotes Woodgate, then a prefect at the college). According to G.C. Boase, "Sewell, William," *DNB* (1897), this school was "conducted on mediaeval principles; the fasts of the church were strictly kept, and full services held in the chapel night and morning." The Swinburnes' connection with the Sewells affords some clue as to the religious climate within Swinburne's immediate family.

14 Landow, *Aesthetic and Critical Theories of John Ruskin*, 351 (italics Landow's).

15 Landow, *Aesthetic and Critical Theories*, 339; Tennyson, *Victorian Devotional Poetry*, 145–8.

16 The link between Catholicism and sadism is made all the more effectively because the choir-boy's hymn is an excellent pastiche, on the model of "Ut jucundas cervas undas" in a volume which Swinburne exploited frequently (*L*3:309, 323; 5:108): Archbishop Trench's edition of *Sacred Latin Poetry*, 213–

16. Trench splits each eight-stress line into two, and Swinburne character-istically extends the number of end-rhyming lines in each stanza from two to four, with the same rhyme used throughout each stanza; but the basic pattern is the same. Leith (*Boyhood*, 32–4) testifies to Swinburne's deep interest in the mediaeval Latin hymnody which was then being popularized by such High Churchmen as Trench and J.M. Neale: in 1864, she reports, she and Swinburne read together the Rhythm of St Bernard de Morlaix, in Neale's adaptation and also in the original Latin; and Swinburne's own partial adaptation of the Rhythm, which she supplies, compares favourably with that in Neale (46–8, 34–5). It seems appropriate that Mary Gordon – identified (somewhat questionably) as Swinburne's Dolores by Fuller (*Swinburne*, 114, 270) – should also have played the rôle of Polyhymnia.

17 Robert Browning, *The Ring and the Book*, 11.2426–7, *Works*, 6:295.

18 Darnley's dramatic fluctuations, both theological and emotional, suggest that his views should be taken critically. In his mean terror, Darnley can perceive only one aspect of this "god in woman's flesh." But she is more than the Demon of heaven; so much is implied when he ceases to see her as one with the cruel God of his scripture, and calls upon that god to deliver him from her: "Out of her hands, God, God, deliver me!" This is a staring dramatic irony; for these are his last words. And within the context of his earlier quotations from the Prayer Book, the irony is still keener: "I will call upon God: and the Lord shall save me" (Ps. 55.17; The Book of Common Prayer, ed. Richard Mant, 602–3; hereafter cited as Book/Mant). Mary de-feats this kinder deity, and stands alone as supreme being.

CHAPTER TWO

1 Prickett, *Romanticism and Religion*, 104.

2 Abrams, *Natural Supernaturalism*, 17–140, 463–9.

3 "Merry black Mass," "L'Imprévu," *Oeuvres*, 1:171. For Baudelaire's influence on Swinburne's art and reputation, see Walder, *Swinburne's Flowers of Evil*; Betz, "Baudelaire, Swinburne and the Legacy of Greece"; and Clements, *Baudelaire and the English Tradition*, 10–76.

4 "The ideal of infinite spirit through the torture of limited matter"; "nothing is real except for physical sensations ... parts of a vile and crude material [world] ... [to make] of one oblong bit of matter three or four thousand round or square bits." *Justine*, 1st ed., in Sade, *Oeuvres*, 2:71, 81; 3:91.

5 Gosse, "The First Draft of Swinburne's 'Anactoria,'" 277; McSweeney in-terprets the poem as a "Triumphant and unqualified" assertion of "natural and creative immortality" (*Tennyson and Swinburne*, 129–30) – a reading which does not give sufficient weight to the last ten lines. Baird suggests that "Anactoria" reveals Sappho as a sadistic "product of the torturing vio-lence created by the acceptance of a belief in a 'God of nature'" ("Swinburne,

Sade, and Blake," 74–5). But "Anactoria" is not a dramatic monologue with a specific setting and audience; Sappho's agony is not rooted in particularities, and is therefore not distanced from the reader as is the agony of Tannhäuser in "Laus Veneris" or of the speaker in "The Triumph of Time." Moreover, Sappho can look forward to the undoing of that "bondage of the gods" for which the God of nature is responsible (89–94, 300); Sappho is therefore not truly "trapped in a theistic conception of the world" (Baird, 63), and her vision should be taken seriously. Morgan offers an interpretation of "Anactoria" very similar to the one I outline: "In short, Sappho reasons, the dominant partner behaves toward the submissive partner in so-called perverse acts in exactly the same manner as God treats mankind"; "the Christian religion ... promises 'caritas' while supporting a spectacle of 'cruelty'" ("Swinburne's Dramatic Monologues," 181). For the text of "Anactoria," see P1:57–66.

6 "A spiritual being, uncreated; eternal, imperishable; ... the most wicked, most ferocious, most appalling of all beings." Sade, qu. Praz, *The Romantic Agony*, 105 (translation mine); see also Lafourcade, *Jeunesse*, 2:401–3, 355–6.

7 Cancelled lines from the fourth chorus, qu. Baum, "The Fitzwilliam Manuscript of Swinburne's 'Atalanta,' Verses 1038–1204," 163.

8 My interpretation of this chorus is drawn in part from Lafourcade, *Jeunesse*, 2:388–403. Lafourcade also discusses the influence of Shelley, Blake, and Sade on the passage. Throughout my discussion I shall use "Chorus," capitalized, to refer to the virgins (58) who make up the group, and "chorus," uncapitalized, to describe each song that these maidens sing.

9 God breaks (1173) and rends (1186); the gods break (688), rend (1506), and divide (292, 869, 1506, 2171); Love breaks (838) and divides (212, 721, 783, 839); Artemis divides and is divided (43, 4); Apollo breaks (21) and divides (1989). In revising the text Swinburne brought out the theme of division more carefully than in the original draft; see Lougy, "Thematic Imagery and Meaning in *Atalanta in Calydon*," 20n3.

10 On fire-imagery in *Atalanta*, see Lougy, 21–3; Mathews, "Heart's Love and Heart's Division," 35–48; and McGhee, *Marriage, Duty, & Desire*, 179–83. The association of love and fire, which is positive in *Prometheus Unbound*, II.v.48–57 (Shelley, *Poetical Works*, 241), is pessimistically reworded in the third chorus of *Atalanta* and in 1978–83; hence Meyers deduces that Swinburne is criticizing "Shelley's faith in love" ("Shelley's Influence on *Atalanta in Calydon*," 153–4).

11 Jordan, "The Sweet Face of Mothers," 107; Vickery, *The Literary Impact of The Golden Bough*, 35.

12 "Artemis's Revenge," 699.

13 Jordan, "The Sweet Face of Mothers," 107; Riede finds only positive implications in this word (*Swinburne*, 90 and n7).

14 Mathews, 46–7; Frye, *Anatomy*, 270–2, 268–9.

15 For instance, Fate is Althaea's son, bedfellow, and brother, just as Jesus is Mary's father, son, brother, and husband in mediaeval lyric. See nos. 43 and 47 in Mone, *Lateinische Hymnen*, 1:59–60, 62; and no. 548 in 2:343.

16 Frye, *Anatomy* 272, 271; cp. 294.

17 "Notes on Poems and Reviews" (1866; B16:359); WB 195, 215; "Charles Baudelaire" (1862; B13:424).

18 Discussed in Peckham, *Victorian Revolutionaries*, 293.

19 On the weakness of "fair words," see also Prendergast, "'Time and Fruitful Hour'," 69–70.

20 Cassidy, *Algernon Charles Swinburne*, 91.

21 Siegchrist, "Artemis's Revenge," 703–4, 707–9. Yet it is hard to see why Toxeus and Plexippus would have attacked Atalanta, or why the Messenger says that they would have "rent *her* spoil away" (1541, italics mine), if she had refused the spoil.

22 Here another parodic biblical reference appears: Elisha "stretched himself" upon the child of the Shunnamite to revive him (2 Kings 4.34); but, if Atalanta performs the same rite, it can only be a vain gesture of pity for a death without remedy. I am indebted to Professor Cecil Y. Lang for drawing my attention to this reference.

23 Miller, *The Disappearance of God*, 13.

24 Lentricchia, *After the New Criticism*, 242; Cassirer, *Philosophy of Symbolic Forms*, 2:68 (italics Cassirer's).

25 Cf. Brisman, "Swinburne's Semiotics," 582. W.D. Shaw discusses Hopkins's use of "allotropes of being" to present this "mystery" ("Poetic Truth in a Scientific Age," 256).

26 Baum traces the history of 1040–1, showing how in Swinburne's manuscript we "can almost watch the first *word* ... become *the word* with its connotation of *logos*" ("Fitzwilliam Manuscript," 163–4; italics Baum's). "The sacred 'centre' is found to be an absence: the only reconciliation is obliteration, the only *logos* death" (Snodgrass, "Swinburne's Circle of Desire," 85; italics his).

27 Cp. the later denunciation of priests "Who drink and eat God, and who kiss and stroke / Satan" (*Marino Faliero*, T5:339–40). Jibes at the materialism of the eucharist are common in Protestant literature; Robert Browning's Bishop longed to "see God made and eaten all day long" ("The Bishop Orders His Tomb at Saint Praxed's Church," 82–4). But the sadistic element added in Swinburne's images is less common.

28 See Landow, *Victorian Types, Victorian Shadows*, 153–62, for a discussion of some instances in which Swinburne employed sacramental or typological imagery for political purposes. This chapter, and the following one, owe much to the inspiration of Landow's example.

29 *In Memoriam*, xxxvii.19, in Tennyson, *Poems*, 896 and n.; "Love's Redemption," later "Love's Testament," in D.G. Rossetti, *Poems*, 105–6 and 105n4.

30 *Songs of Innocence and of Experience*, Plate 51, in Blake, *Complete Poetry and Prose*, 29–30; lines 1–4 are entirely in italics, which I have silently normalized.

31 On 9 October 1866 Swinburne wrote to William Rossetti, "After all, ... it is nice to have something to love and to believe in as I do in Italy ... I'd rather be an Italian stump-orator than an English prophet" (*L1*:195–6).

32 Landow discusses Swinburne's other uses of this type (*Victorian Types, Victorian Shadows*, 163–4); another example appears in "Lucifer" (1904), where Voltaire, as Lucifer-Christ, crushes the snake he called "l'infâme" (*P6*:397).

33 "We must have him visible and edible ... Earthworm, give up creating the sun." Hugo, *Oeuvres*, 14:764, 799.

34 Ctr. *The Tale of King Arthur*, Bk. II.16, in Malory, 1:85.23–7.

35 This point is reinforced by both brothers: Balen says that in this deadly castle "' death makes night of day,'" and Balan, "'here / Light is as darkness'" (*P4*:227, 225, 229, 230).

36 *B10*:386–7, 389, 394, 387, 405–7.

37 "Of old, I set the first woman with the first man in a charming, well-chosen spot; in spite of my prohibition, they ate an apple; that is why I am punishing men forever ... Nothing could be fairer than that. But, since I am very kind, this distresses me. Alas! What is to be done? An idea! I shall send my son into Judaea to them; they will kill him. Then – this is why I agree to it – having committed a crime, they will be innocent. Seeing them thus commit a real fault, I shall pardon them for the one which they did not commit ..." Hugo, *Oeuvres*, 14:770, qu. "Religions et Religion" (*B13*:198).

38 Tennyson, *Poems*, 988, 986; Rosenberg, "The Two Kingdoms of *In Memoriam*," 240.

CHAPTER THREE

1 "All my life I have concerned myself with the form of the flask, never with the quality of its contents." Gautier, *Mademoiselle de Maupin*, 191.

2 D.G. Rossetti, "Songs of One Household, No. 1. My Sister's Sleep," 11. 15–16; *Poems*, 97.

3 D.G. Rossetti, *Poems*, 270–1 and 270n2.

4 Ibid., 11–13.

5 McGann, "Rossetti's Significant Details," 45. McGann's defence of Rossetti develops Swinburne's view that Rossetti deliberately gives "the mere physical charm of Christianity" (*B15*:24).

6 Villon, *Oeuvres*, 1:214; D.G. Rossetti, *Poems*, 102; Swinburne, *New Writings*, 15.

7 D.G. Rossetti, *Poems*, 105–6, 107, 213. Of course, in *The House of Life* such views characterize the *early* stages of love.

8 According to Lang, we can be sure only that "The Triumph of Time" was written between 1862 and 1866 ("Swinburne's Lost Love," 125). The date at

which "Love's Redemption" was composed is still more problematic. William Michael Rossetti, in *The Collected Works of Dante Gabriel Rossetti*, places the poem between 1848 and 1869 (1:517); Tisdel suggests on the basis of internal evidence that the sonnet was probably composed between 1853 and 1862 ("Rossetti's 'House of Life'," 266). In the absence of more definite evidence, one cannot say for certain whether Rossetti's eucharist of love has influenced Swinburne's, or the reverse. Fallis discusses some of the eucharistic imagery in "The Triumph of Time," but suggests that this imagery is "traditional" in style ("The Sacred and the Profane," 157–64); Gitter correctly interprets the poem as a criticism of Rossetti's visionary eroticism ("Arnold and Rossetti," 51–7).

9 The text of "The Triumph of Time" appears in *P*1:34–7.

10 See Friar William Herebert, *"Quis est iste qui uenit de Edom?"* in Carleton Brown, ed., *Religious Lyrics of the Fourteenth Century*, 28–9; Mâle, *L'art religieux*, 115–22; and the discussion of Herebert's lyric in Gray, *Themes and Images*, 12–17 and 231, nn. 23–9.

11 Greenberg, "Gosse's *Swinburne*, 'The Triumph of Time,' and the Context of 'Les Noyades'," 105.

12 Carlyle, *Sartor Resartus*, III.viii (264, 260); II.vi (147).

13 J.H. Newman, *Apologia Pro Vita Sua*, 36.23–4, 37.7–13; Tennyson, *In Memoriam*, v.3–4, in *Poems*, 868. See chap. 6 below for further discussion of the way in which Swinburne manipulates this topos.

14 "Metaphorical Thinking," 129. Morgan also presents the sea-vision as a "successful alternative" to our ordinary perception of time (130–1).

15 "A Marching Song," "A New Year's Message," *P*2:159, 137.

16 Cp. Landow's discussion of this passage in *Victorian Types, Victorian Shadows*, 154–60.

17 *Swinburne*, 126.

18 See Abrams, *Mirror*, 160–1.

19 See p. 211n51 below.

20 Feuerbach, *The Essence of Christianity*, 60.

21 Cockshut, *Unbelievers*, 63–4.

22 Dante, *Paradiso*, 3.85.

23 *WB* 35–6; *The Marriage of Heaven and Hell*, Plate 12, in Blake, *Complete Poetry and Prose*, 38–9; quoted with approval in *WB* 214–15.

24 Blake, 562, 477 (ll. 53–6); also 709 (Letter 12, to Mrs Flaxman, 14 September 1800, and 13, to William Hayley, 16 September 1800); *WB* 34.

25 Book/Mant, 371; the text of "Ave atque Vale" appears in *P*3:50–7.

26 McGann, *Swinburne*, 302, 298; "great king of subterranean things, familiar healer of human pains." "Les litanies de Satan," 7–8, in Baudelaire, *Oeuvres Complètes*, 1:124.

27 Book/Mant, 365.

28 Feuerbach, *Essence of Christianity*, 277.

29 "The Day of the Daughter of Hades," 8.60–1, 64, in George Meredith, *Poems*, 1:221–38.

30 Ibid., 6.51, 55–6; Feuerbach, 278; cp. the God in "Phoebus with Admetus," in Meredith, *Poems*, 1:242–5.

31 The text appears in *P3*:295–310. The figure of the foster-father has been identified as Landor, Milton, "*any* visionary poet" (italics McGhee's), and the *pharmakos* of rationality whom the poet must exorcise (W.B.D. Henderson, *Swinburne and Landor*, 56ff; W. Wilson, "Algernon Agonistes," 384–5; McGhee, "'Thalassius'," 128; Stuart, "Swinburne," 118, 120). McSweeney declares that "the elder poet is simply a representative of the poetic life into which Thalassius is to be initiated" ("Swinburne's 'Thalassius'," 51), and I have interpreted the foster-father elsewhere as "a vast mythical figure composite of all poets present, past, and legendary" (Louis, *"Thalassius" and "On the Cliffs,"* 3–4, 29). The passage in "Thalassius" describing the eucharistic song echoes the words of two republican visionaries: Blake's "The Bread of Sweet Thought & the Wine of Delight" (see McGhee, 128), and Milton's "the clear *Hyaline*, the Glassy Sea" (*Paradise Lost* VII.619; see W. Wilson, 385).

32 Book/Mant, 365, 348; in the Prayer of Consecration, and at the administration of the sacrament, the phrases "a perpetual memory" and "in remembrance" emphasize the commemorative aspect of the Eucharist (364–7).

33 Book/Mant, 353.

34 "Algernon Agonistes," 393–4.

35 W. David Shaw, "The Agnostic Imagination in Victorian Poetry," establishes the concepts of "idolatrous," "analogical," and "agnostic" theories of language. To the "idolatrous" thinker or poet, the sign and the signified are identical; the signifier, then, is comparable to the transubstantiated Host. To an "analogical" thinker, like Keble, each sign may be an analogy of the divine reality; within a stable sacramental economy, it is possible to convey divine truth (as in Browning's "Saul") confidently and meaningfully. This attitude is expressed in the High Anglican view that the Eucharist is the type and shadow of Christ's sacrifice, and that through the signifying ritual we come into contact with the significance of the ritual, with Christ himself. Agnostics, such as Spencer, "focus cynically on empty signifiers" like "the Unknowable" (125); religious signs can only be "gestures in the direction of an unknowable Power" (121).

36 Carlyle, *Sartor Resartus* II.ix (187); Vivante, *English Poetry*, 264 ("It would betray, however, human pride, a one-sided, anthropomorphic view, to recognize this reviving power of *form* only in song or in speech," italics Vivante's), 286–9, 294–5.

37 Rosenberg, Introduction to *Swinburne*, ix–xiv; Empson, *Seven Types of Ambiguity*, 194–5.

38 Rosenberg, Introduction to *Swinburne*, xxx; Peters, *Crowns of Apollo*, 95–108.

39 Shaw applies the phrase, "Secret and eccentric," to the language of *Sordello*, which he relates to the Idealist tradition of the mind as "self-reflecting mirror" ("The Optical Metaphor," 303). We should observe that Swinburne early claimed *Sordello* to be "one of [his] canonical scriptures" (*L*1:16). *On Heroes, Hero-Worship and the Heroic in History*, iv, in Carlyle, *Works*, 5:115; *WB* 36, 35.

40 Swinburne even provides an image of false communion – a negative eucharist of brutal tyranny and vampirism – to elucidate the nature of Hugo's true communion, exactly as in *Songs before Sunrise*. Paraphrasing Hugo's *Ratbert*, x–xvi, Swinburne describes the emperor's murderous feast as an "inexpiable / Communion in the sacrament of hell," a "monstrous eucharist" (365–7); this expands on a hint of Hugo's ("Le souper de Satan," *Oeuvres*, 10:574), and the extravagant style of Swinburne's strophe is appropriate to the melodramatic extravagance of *Ratbert* itself.

41 In Leith, *The Children of the Chapel*, 103.

42 Wordsworth, *Poetical Works*, 5:15, *The Prelude*, 67.

43 Feuerbach, *Essence of Christianity*, 276. Feuerbach and Swinburne, like the vast majority of their contemporaries, habitually used "man" as a generic noun. In expounding Swinburne's views, I have silently followed his practice; in this respect I am concerned simply to elucidate his opinions and assumptions, which should not be confused with my own.

CHAPTER FOUR

1 John Morley, rev. *Poems and Ballads*, First Series, *Saturday Review*, 22, 4 August 1866, 145–7; rpt. in Hyder, ed., *Swinburne: The Critical Heritage*, 29. Unfortunately, Swinburne failed to shake off the placard: the *Edinburgh Review*, in its discussion of *Songs before Sunrise*, compared Swinburne to a satyr, and Marie Corelli, in *The Sorrows of Satan*, called the poet a "satyr-songster" (qu. Hyder, 138, xli).

2 For the text of the Prelude see *P*2:3–9; line-enumeration is my own.

3 *Swinburne's Hyperion*, 123; "Matthew Arnold's New Poems," *B*15:72.

4 Sidgwick and Widgery, 100 (Sidgwick's *Outlines of the History of Ethics* first appeared in 1886); Epictetus, qu. Marcus Aurelius Antoninus, 140 (*Meditations* 4.41); *P*1:173; Plato, *Dialogues*, transl. Benjamin Jowett, 2nd ed., 1:455; "The Higher Pantheism in a Nutshell" (*P*5:374). On Swinburne's admiration for Epictetus, see *L*1:xxvi, 5:132.

5 Epictetus, *Enchiridion*, xlviii, viii, in *Works*, 396–7, 378.

6 Plato, *Dialogues*, 2nd ed., 2:222.

7 Bruno, *Expulsion of the Triumphant Beast*, 79; Sorley, "Synderesis," 2:656; extract from *The Doctor and the Student*, qu. The Corrector, "Milton's Common-Place Book," *Athenaeum* (1877): i. 738; Inge, "Synderesis."

8 Bruno, 115–16, 120–7, and passim; on Swinburne's enthusiasm for Bruno as "philosopher and martyr," see "For the Feast of Giordano Bruno" (*P3*:48–9), where he ranks Bruno with Shelley and Lucretius as a champion of free thought. On Bruno as a popular hero for nineteenth-century freethinkers, see Chadwick, *Secularization*, 178–9.

9 ll. 39, 56, 58, 60, 65–6, 166–70; in 1865 Swinburne praised the cold "pluck" of Carlyle's Friedrich ɪɪ over the "'Dutch courage'" of a "'God-intoxicated man'" (*L1*:116). Cp. "Epicurus" in *Swinburne's Hyperion*, 162.

10 Fragment 57 (Nauck, *Tragicorum Graecorum Fragmenta*, 20); *Comus*, 550. This passage in the Prelude may also be related to Catullus' *Carmen LXIII* (Greenberg, "Swinburne and the Redefinition of Classical Myth," 179–80).

11 *L2*:162; Swinburne quotes from a speech delivered at the Church Congress in Nottingham and reported in the Supplement to the *Guardian* (18 October 1871).

12 The conceit that the Whore enrobes herself in another's nakedness may owe something to Blake's "The Chimney Sweeper," in the version quoted by Swinburne (*WB* 126n); cp. Blake, *Complete Poetry and Prose*, 23, 793: "God & his Priest & King … wrap themselves up in our misery."

13 Rosenberg, *Swinburne*, 184n.

14 Hugo, *Châtiments*, 62–3.

15 "The Exile to his Country," Massey, *Poetical Works*, 129.

16 "Lux," 236, 239 (Hugo, *Châtiments*, 248); "Notes of an English Republican on the Muscovite Crusade" (1876), *B15*:414. F.A.C. Wilson points out that the "gallows tree" of "Before a Crucifix" is Yggdrasil's "desolate antithesis" ("Indian and Mithraic Influences," 58). Greenberg relates this "contrary" of the life-tree to Blake's Tree of Mystery ("Swinburne and the Redefinition of Classical Myth," 177–8, 186).

17 Renan, *Vie de Jésus*, 116.

18 Charlton, *Secular Religions in France*, 12; italics his.

19 Introduction, 1.i (Michelet, 18).

20 See Gay, *The Enlightenment*, 1:332.

21 Clough, *Poems*, 199–203.

22 "Matthew Arnold's New Poems," *B15*:66, 71. Much later (1891), Swinburne echoed these sentiments in a jibe specifically aimed at Clough: "We've got no faith, and we don't know what to do: / To think one can't believe a creed because it isn't true!" ("Social Verse," *B15*:283). This couplet seems to point directly at lines 65–89 in "Easter Day."

23 Strauss, *The Life of Jesus*, Introduction, sections 10–15 (1:36–87; 48, 78 especially). Strauss, of course, views this fiction as "the shell of an *idea* – of a religious conception" which is the "absolute inherent truth" conveyed by the myth (1:48, italics his); Clough shares this view, as he shows in "Epi-Strauss-ion," but does not express it in the first "Easter Day."

24 Clough, *Poems*, 203–4, 163; Strauss, Concluding Dissertation, section 144 (3:396).

25 For the text of "Le Satyre," see Hugo, *Oeuvres*, 10:585–601; for this and for "Hymn of Man," line-enumeration is my own.

26 *Civiltà Cattolica*, serie VII, vol. v, 349–52, qu. Hales, *Pio Nono*, 285; *Syllabus Errorum*, qu. Vidler, *The Church in an Age of Revolution*, 151.

27 W.M. Rossetti, ed., *Rossetti Papers*, 390; Swinburne to William Rossetti, October 1869 (L2:35, 36, 43–4); to the Anti-Catholic Council, 10 November 1869 (L2:54).

28 *Times*, 19 January 1870; cp. the "Hymn of Man," 146–8.

29 Compare Swinburne's later translation of the relevant chorus, "The Birds (685–723)" (P5:41–5). See also, for this reading of the opening of the Hymn, McGann, *Swinburne* 193, 197, and Wexler, "Mythological Strategy," 119–20 (cp. also 105–8 on "Genesis").

30 *Collected Essays*, 5:256–7.

31 "All betrays him; all the unhearing [elements] conspire against him." "Le Satyre," iii. 556–8.

32 "Under the rustling tree, near the belling monster, someone is speaking. It is the Soul. She emerges from chaos. Without her, no winds, only miasma; no waves, only the mere; the soul, arising from chaos, dispels it; for chaos is only the rough sketch and the soul is the [animating, organizing] principle ... And yet without man horizons are dead ... He alone speaks; and without him the world is headless." Swinburne's emphasis on the concept of law in the Hymn anticipates his heartily expressed approval of John Tyndall's Belfast Address (which Swinburne read "with great care and greater admiration") three years later. To the vision of nature as controlled by "the caprices of the gods" – or of God – Tyndall opposes the assumptions of science, a discipline which "demands the radical extirpation of caprice and the absolute reliance upon law in Nature." Swinburne's comment that Theism "seems to introduce an element" of "disorder" reformulates this argument, the appeal of which is both moral and aesthetic. Tyndall makes scientific materialism seem compatible with the notion of a "cosmical life"; in its seventh edition the Address closes with a lengthy quotation (on "A motion and a spirit, that ... rolls through all things") from "Tintern Abbey," which Tyndall called a "forecast and religious vitalization of the latest and deepest scientific truth." Swinburne to Watts, 29 August 1874 (L2:334–5); "British Association for the Advancement of Science," *Times*, 20 August 1874, 4–5; Tyndall, *Address delivered before the British Association assembled in Belfast*, 97–8.

33 Mazzini, *Life and Writings*, 5:347. In his notes "On the Encyclica of Pope Pius IX," Mazzini had bitterly attacked the policy of quietism which Pio Nono had recommended. Save your own soul, says the pope; the misery

and injustice of the world should be nothing to you. "Right, equity, truth, reign in heaven; fact, force, and inevitable evil, upon earth ... No," cries Mazzini, "it is not true that there exists antagonism or separation between heaven and earth ... The earth is of God ... [and therefore] it should be rendered more and more the image of the kingdom of heaven ... For those who admit the *unity* of God, and the consequent unity of the human family, it is one of the truths of faith that we are all responsible for one another" (*Life and Writings*, 5:336–9). Swinburne refers to this doctrine when he insists that the man-god is "Indivisible spirit and blood, indiscernible body from soul" (50).

34 Book/Mant, 709. Fallis comments further on the biblical resonance of line 184 of the Hymn ("The Sacred and the Profane," 189).

35 For the text of "The Higher Pantheism," see Tennyson, *Poems*, 1204–5.

36 "Sang of the monstrous earth ... savage palpitation ... Someone speaks ... Air wishes to become Spirit, man appears."

37 "Trees are holy, animals are holy, man is holy." On the fall from freedom, see ii, 431–2; iii, 463–92. On submission to priests and kings, see iii, 476, 486, 493–529, 530–3, 552–69, and cp. overall ll. 91–120 of the Hymn. Abrams has pointed out that Romantic theories of history tend to exploit "the design of Biblical history" (*Natural Supernaturalism*, 32–70).

38 "Matter comes to devour man" until man masters "all that has formerly persecuted him."

39 "All will agree, all being harmony" (cp. 580–1, and ll. 128–30 of the Hymn).

40 "We shall see man become law ... for a spirit moves as a sphere does" (cp. ll. 130–2 of the Hymn).

41 "That black final god whom man calls Enough ... all the almosts ... O world, all evil comes from the form of the gods ... Make room for the effulgence of the universal soul! A king is of war, a god is of night. Liberty, life, and faith, on the ruins of dogma! Everywhere one light and everywhere one spirit! Love! all will agree, all being harmony! ... Make room for All! I am Pan; Jupiter, to your knees!"

42 *P3*:220, 6:131. Pan's boast that men "die, and behold, I am living, / While they and their dead Gods give / Place" ("Pan and Thalassius," *P3*:218), also echoes the satyr's cry, "Place à Tout"; while the idea that nature is dead unless given "sense and soul" by human speech appears again and again in Swinburne's later poetry (notably in "Pan and Thalassius" and in "The Interpreters," *P3*:218, 246).

43 "Monotones," *P2*:219; "To Walt Whitman in America," *P2*:122.

44 *Evolution and Poetic Belief*, 190.

45 Ridenour, "Swinburne on 'The Problem to Solve in Expression'," 131–2.

46 Cp. Rosenberg's notes in *Swinburne*, 174–5. Swinburne was fully conscious of the element of parody here (*L2*:46).

47 J. Cockburn Thomson, trans. *The Bhagavad Gita*, 51, 54.

48 Ibid. 51–2, 63–5; Emerson, *Complete Works*, 9:195 (see 9:465–6 on Emerson's own debt to the Bhagavad Gita). Hertha's assertion that she is "the search, and the sought, and the seeker" (25) has a somewhat surprising affinity with the word-play in Trench's version of the *Veni, creator spiritus*: "Tu dans, tu datus coelitus, / Tu donum, tu donator" (*Sacred Latin Poetry*, 155), which means literally, "Thou giving, thou given by heaven, / Thou gift, thou giver." The shift from giving to seeking is consonant with Swinburne's concept of a developing deity.

49 "It Will End in the Right," in Massey, *Poetical Works*, 74.

50 *On Heroes, Hero-Worship and the Heroic in History*, i, in Carlyle, *Works*, 5:21. Wendell Stacy Johnson points out Swinburne's debt to this passage ("Swinburne and Carlyle," 119–20).

51 Tillyard, *Five Poems*, 101; Abrams, *Mirror*, 171–4; Coleridge, *Statesman's Manual*, in *Lay Sermons*, 72. Cp. the discussion of J.G. Herder's Romantic plant imagery, and especially of his concept of history as "a single and marvelous tree," in Mandelbaum, *History, Man, & Reason*, 58.

52 Italics his; *Statesman's Manual*, in *Lay Sermons*, 71.

53 Perhaps the closest analogue to the final stanza of "Hertha" is T.H. Green's "idea of God as an object to himself" in his early essay on the development of Christian dogma (*Works*, 3:184). Swinburne had listened to this essay at Oxford, without enthusiasm (Gosse, *Life*, 40).

54 Riede, *Swinburne*, 113.

55 Keats, *Letters*, 1:224.

56 Wexler, "Mythological Strategy," 126.

57 "To Walt Whitman in America," *P2*:122, 124; Epilogue, *P2*:228.

58 Curtius, *European Literature and the Latin Middle Ages*, 84, in a rather different context.

CHAPTER FIVE

1 Shelley, *Poetical Works*, 613.

2 Harrison, "The Swinburnian Woman," 97.

3 Morgan, "Metaphorical Thinking," 149.

4 Italics Swinburne's. Swinburne to Theodore Watts, 8 February, and to Edwin Harrison, 13 February 1876 (*L3*:137, 142). Swinburne's enthusiasm for this poem took an unusually commercial form. On February 1 he offered the lyric (then "just finished") to the *Fortnightly Review*; but he withdrew his offer, because Morley refused to pay what Swinburne considered worthy of "The Last Oracle." "What do *you* think I ought to have – or to ask –," he wrote to Watts, "for the maidenhead of one of my most important lyric works?" But his chief tribute to the poem is the obvious excitement with which he describes and explicates it, at length, to Morley, to Watts, and (twice over) to Edwin Harrison (*L3*:130, 137, 142, 143–4).

5 This very summary account draws on Kerferd, "Logos"; Goodenough, *By Light, Light*, 7; and Ficino, *Marsilio Ficino's Commentary*, 230–2 especially. What knowledge Swinburne possessed of the Neoplatonic tradition would probably have come chiefly from such authors as Spenser and Shelley.

6 *L*3:137. For the text of "The Last Oracle," see *P*3:5–10; line enumeration is my own.

7 Greenberg, "Swinburne and the Redefinition of Classical Myth," 190.

8 *P*1:69; *Atalanta*, 1898.

9 Schelling, in Feldman and Richardson, *The Rise of Modern Mythology*, 326.

10 On the "spiral" pattern as a Romantic transformation of the Neoplatonic "Great Circle," see Abrams, *Natural Supernaturalism*, 179–87; see 207–17 on the connection between this pattern and the Christian concept of the *felix culpa*. One must not, however, assume that Swinburne has yet developed a concept of this spiral pattern similar in detail to the concepts developed by such Romantic Idealists as Schelling.

11 Ridenour, "Time and Eternity in Swinburne," 112; see 109–12 for a discussion of other echoes from the Bible and the Prayer Book in "The Last Oracle."

12 "Mr. Gilfil's Love-Story," vii, in George Eliot, *Works*, 4:176; "Dejection," 54, 62–6, in Coleridge, *Poetical Works*, 365.

13 Abrams, *Mirror*, 68; "Dejection," 136.

14 "Words are things ... The word devours, and nothing can resist its tooth ... The word, the expression, type come whence no one knows, face of the invisible, aspect of the unknown ... the word keeps the world under its feet ... Be the dawn; I am your equal, for I am reason ... Yes, all-powerful! such is the word. He is mad who mocks at it! When error ties a knot in man, the word disentangles it ... The word is life, spirit, seed, hurricane, virtue, fire; for the word is the Logos, and the Logos is God." Hugo, *Oeuvres*, 9:79–81.

15 "The creation of beings arose from the word of God; the community of the peoples will arise from the word of man." *Napoléon-le-Petit* 5.V, in Hugo, *Oeuvres*, 8:488.

16 Riede, *Swinburne*, 136ff; Murfin, *Swinburne, Hardy, Lawrence and the Burden of Belief*, 164–6.

17 The text of *Songs of the Springtides* used throughout this chapter is *P*3:291–361. On Swinburne's admiration for Trelawny as "the ancient monarch of the sea," and as a "magnificent old rebel, a lifelong incarnation of the divine right of insurrection," see *L*4:118, 3:16, 2:331.

18 See *L*6:252n, and also "At a Month's End" and "To a Seamew," *P*3:29–33, 211–14.

19 Cp. Abrams, *Natural Supernaturalism*, 75; Stuart, "Swinburne," 117, 119, 124. McSweeney, "Swinburne's 'Thalassius'," 50–1, provides a useful comparison of "Thalassius" and the Intimations Ode.

20 See chapt. 3, n31 above. Stuart suggests that the foster-father is a *pharmakos* who must be exorcised (120–6). But Swinburne always thoroughly admired

such old warrior-singers as the foster-father (*L*3:16), and the foster-father's republican principles are such as Swinburne applauded in Hugo, Landor, and Trelawny.

21 Hazlitt, *Complete Works*, 5:2.

22 The anagnorisis of the last stanzas recalls a similar passage in Blake's letter to Thomas Butts (2 October 1800): in the "sweet and singular" verses there enclosed (*WB* 33), Blake sees all the "Jewels of Light" along the seashore transformed into individual men; then, as his vision continues to enlarge ("My Eyes more & more / Like a Sea without shore / Continue Expanding / The Heavens commanding"), so these "Men" undergo a second transformation, and appear "as One Man / Who Complacent began / My limbs to infold / In his beams of bright gold" (Blake, *Complete Poetry and Prose*, 712–13). Thalassius' union with his father is much less vividly concrete, although "strange breath and light" are shed "all round" the sea-child, "and he knew / His father's hand ... / And the old great voice" (479–82).

23 *Swinburne*, 141; cp. Abrams, "Structure and Style in the Greater Romantic Lyric," 552.

24 Coleridge, "The Nightingale," 32, 69–74; for the text of this poem, see Coleridge, *Poetical Works*, 264–7. Swinburne's own early poem, "The Nightingale," shows the influence of Coleridge's lyric (*Swinburne's Hyperion*, 149–50).

25 McGann, *Swinburne*, 77, discussing the "moondawn" passage in "On the Cliffs" as it relates to another Romantic work, *Prometheus Unbound* (II.ii.24–40).

26 *Tennyson and Swinburne*, 146.

27 Peckham, Introduction, in his edition of *Poems and Ballads / Atalanta in Calydon*, xvii. For a discussion of the "worked" syntax in other passages of "On the Cliffs," see McGann, *Swinburne*, 159–66.

28 Aeschylus, 2:102–4; on the function of the Cassandra passage in "On the Cliffs," see Raymond, *Swinburne's Poetics*, 65–7, and Louis, 16–17.

29 Wharton, *Sappho*, 63n. The definition in Liddell and Scott is substantially the same. For the texts of the Hymn to Aphrodite and the Atthis-fragment, see Edmonds, ed., *Lyra Graeca* 1:182–5, 220–1.

30 This sense of "parcel," "emphasizing comprehension in the whole, rather than partitive character" (*OED*, "Parcel," *sb*. 1.1.b), appears in Swinburne's "Litany of Nations," 95: "Till the soul of man be parcel of the sunlight" (*P*2:68).

31 *Poetical Works*, 440–1.

32 Riede, *Swinburne*, 136.

33 Buckler, *Victorian Imagination*, 247; Ridenour, "Time and Eternity in Swinburne," 122; Keats, *Poems*, 371.

34 Abrams, "Structure and Style," 552–3.

35 I have found only one unrhymed line (.2 per cent) in "On the Cliffs" (398), as opposed to ten in *Lycidas* (5.2 per cent); but in the former, 68 out of 434

but their works seem to present interesting analogues to some of the ideas suggested in Swinburne's late poetry.

18 Shaw, "The Agnostic Imagination," 125; Spenser, *Faerie Queene*, 3.6.47, 1:431.

19 Tennyson, *Poems*, 1353, 868.

20 Swinburne seems to allude specifically to Hugo's poem "Lux" ("light's birth-song," Birthday Ode, 273), in which God is presented emphatically as "le grand mystérieux" (l. 100, *Châtiments*, 244).

21 For the text of "The Palace of Pan," see *P*6:178–80 (line enumeration mine). For *Endymion*, see Keats, *Poems*, 102–220.

22 Caird, *Sermons*, 132–3.

23 McGann, *Swinburne*, 188.

24 Ridenour, "Swinburne in Hellas," 4; Plato, *Dialogues*, trans. Jowett, 3rd ed., 1:198. In 405a–406a, Plato offers a discussion of the name *Apollo* during which the god is defined as "the single one" and the "master archer," among other titles (1:348–9).

25 Meaning "at the centre of the universe," as when Delphi is described as Apollo's "dark mid shrine" in "The Last Oracle," 4.

26 *Swinburne*, 197.

27 Abrams, "Structure and Style," 527, 553; on "A Nympholept" as a "basically religious poem," see Buckler, *Victorian Imagination*, 252–4, and also Pauline Fletcher's insistence that the poem presents "a non-Christian mystical experience" (*Gardens and Grim Ravines*, 220).

28 "Swinburne's 'A Nympholept'," 59.

29 Baum, "Swinburne's 'A Nympholept'," 58–68; McSweeney, *Tennyson and Swinburne*, 172–82; Riede, *Swinburne*, 193, 195–6; McGhee identifies the "second lover" as Apollo (*Marriage, Duty, & Desire*, 205), a reading which would make the poem's title pointless.

30 McGann, *Swinburne*, 186; Ridenour, "Swinburne in Hellas," 7–8.

31 Clement, one of the Fathers whom Mansel quotes to support his own agnostic version of Christianity, declares that God cannot be described or rightly named; we can only conceive of him imperfectly, "fettered as we are by the flesh" (Mansel, *Limits*, xx).

32 *Tennyson and Swinburne*, 182.

33 Baum, "Swinburne's 'A Nympholept,'" 64.

34 Ridenour mentions this allusion ("Swinburne in Hellas," 8).

35 Ridenour also makes this connection, briefly (ibid.). In his essay, "Keats" (1882), Swinburne described the hymn to Pan in *Endymion* as "golden grain amid a garish harvest of tares" (*B*14:296).

36 Carlyle, *Sartor Resartus*, I.xi, 74.

37 *In Memoriam*, Epilogue, 143–4. Ridenour interprets the final line of "A Nympholept" as meaning that "It is only in dreaming of the nymph ... that anything is," because the nymph "is the form of our experience of the world"

("Swinburne in Hellas," 8). I am not sure that this reading fully takes into account either the fact that the nymph is "Unknown" or the erotic passion with which the speaker addresses her.

38 McGann, *Swinburne*, 188–90.

39 Plato, 3rd ed., 1:355, 388.

40 Sidney, "What may words say, or what may words not say," and Krieger, "Mediation, Language, and Vision in the Reading of Literature," in Singleton, ed., *Interpretation*, 222–3.

41 Stéphane Mallarmé, trans. and qu. Symons, 73.

42 "This endless melody like nature's eternal voice, resounding within us at certain times though we can recall nothing of it, these shadows which are light, this chaos which is order, this silence which is resonance and harmony – here is his ideal, the final statement of his artistic aspirations, the alpha and omega of his aesthetic!" Gasperini, 101–2; translation mine.

43 "When he has to make nature speak, to associate it with the whirlwind of unchained passions, Wagner is in his element ... Iseult is waiting for Tristan in the night. Long before Tristan arrives, long before he has left the royal hunt, he is there before us. We hear his voice which draws near, moves away, only to draw near again; the forest is in anguish; this unsteady light glows like the last light of the real world ... While Iseult's heart bounds with impatience, the whole scene is perturbed; a passionate melody floats on the air; the leaves rustle, the earth stirs, the beloved arrives with hasty steps; the two lovers, reunited at last, embrace in rapture. This penetration of all nature by the spirit of the drama is one of the most potent techniques of dramatic art." Gasperini, 157–8. Swinburne read and praised *La nouvelle Allemagne musicale* in 1869 (L2:38). Sypher ("Swinburne and Wagner," 179–80) considers Gasperini's influence on *Tristram of Lyonesse*.

44 "No voice sings the endless couplet that Wagner has heard in the forest. The melody we love begins and ends ... [we should not descend] into darkness and annihilation." Gasperini, 104, 148–9.

45 "Selbst dann bin ich die Welt," qu. and trans. Gasperini, 148: "I myself am the world."

46 *Oeuvres*, 1:264–7. "Did I love a dream? My doubt, heap of old night, ends in many a subtle branch, which, remaining the true woods themselves, prove, alas! that alone I offered myself the ideal error of roses for triumph." Trans. Anthony Hartley, ed., *Mallarmé*, 51.

47 "A desire of [his] fabulous senses ... No, but the soul empty of words and this heavy body succumb slowly to the proud silence of noon: with no more ado we must sleep, forgetting blasphemy, lying on the thirsty sand and as I love to open my mouth to the effective star of wine! Couple, farewell; I go to see the shadow you become." Hartley, 56.

48 Cohn, *Toward the Poems of Mallarmé*, 30.

49 "'A Waking Dream'," 21–2.

50 Morgan, "Metaphorical Thinking," 208.

51 Coleridge, *The Statesman's Manual*, in *Lay Sermons*, 30; cp. *Aids to Reflection*, 1:160.

52 *Swinburne*, 185.

53 "L'Après-Midi d'un Faune," 74; I have omitted Mallarmé's italics. Hartley translates this line as follows: "Where our sport may be consumed like to the day" (*Mallarmé*, 55).

CONCLUSION

1 Blake, *Visions of the Daughters of Albion*, 5: 3, in *Complete Poetry and Prose*, 48; Byron, "Prometheus," 20, in *Works*, 4:49.

2 Byron, *Cain* i.i.385–88, in *Works*, 5:227; cf. *Prometheus Unbound* i.262–81, 395–402, and *Queen Mab* vii.192–5, and (on Milton) the Preface to *Prometheus Unbound* (Shelley, *Poetical Works*, 213–14, 216–17, 790, 205).

3 The quotation is from *Marino Faliero*, T5:359. Cp. Mill, *An Examination of Sir William Hamilton's Philosophy*, chap. 7, in *Collected Works*, 9:103 ("I will call no being good who is not what I mean when I apply that epithet to my fellow creatures; and if such a being can sentence me to hell for not so calling him, to hell I will go"); Froude, *The Nemesis of Faith*, 17 ("I would sooner perish for ever than stoop down before a Being ... whom my heart forbids me to reverence"); Winwood Reade, *The Martyrdom of Man*, 427 ("... you [i.e., God] can send me to hell-fire, but you cannot obtain my esteem"); Huxley, *Collected Essays*, 5:318 ("... if you cannot [give us rational grounds for believing Christian doctrine], we must respectfully refuse, even if that refusal should wreck morality and insure our own damnation"). Swinburne's own late play, *Marino Faliero*, uses this strategy in the same spirit, scorning "the prostrate noise of praises": "if God be, / Let God do justice: if he be not, then / Man's righteousness rebukes him" (T5:369–70, 344, 367). By 1885, even for Swinburne, God must be nothing if not moral, and Faliero's "if he be not" is almost certainly a syntactic pun: if God is not just, he does not exist.

4 Prickett, *Romanticism and Religion*, 108.

5 See especially Stevie Smith's "God the Eater," and her Fulleresque tribute to Swinburne, "Seymour and Chantelle" (*Collected Poems*, 339, 514–15) and Plath's "Lady Lazarus" (*Collected Poems*, 244–7; this lyric might well be compared with "Dolores"). In Hughes's "Skylarks" (*Selected Poems*, 102–6), the Romantic birds express a torment inherent both in the natural world and in the act of creation, as do Swinburne's fiery nightingales. Murfin, in *Swinburne, Hardy, Lawrence, and the Burden of Belief*, passim, and Sacks in *English Elegy* (227–34) have both discussed Swinburne's relationship with Hardy; but much remains to be done in this area.

6 WB 87; B13:243–4. Swinburne's views on the doctrine of *l'art pour l'art* have been discussed in detail in Rosenblatt, *L'idée de l'art pour l'art*, 121–67; Suiter,

"Swinburne," 248–74; Connolly, *Swinburne's Theory of Poetry*, 3–24; Peters, *Crowns of Apollo*, 55–73; Raymond, *Swinburne's Poetics*, 116–23; and Shmiefsky, "Swinburne's Anti-Establishment Poetics," 261–76.

7 *B*15:377; Arnold, "Byron," in *Complete Prose Works*, 9:237.3–4.

8 Yeats, "Byzantium," in *Collected Poems*, 280.

9 "I wish to give myself the pleasure of seeing this spectacle of matter, conscious of being and, nevertheless, springing frantically into the Dream which it knows does not exist, singing of the Soul and all the similar divine impressions which we have piled up since the earliest times, and which proclaim these glorious lies in the face of the Nothingness which is truth!" *Correspondance*, 1:207–8.

10 Frye, "The Drunken Boat," in *Romanticism Reconsidered*, 14.

11 "To paint, not the thing itself, but the effect it produces." *Correspondance*, 1:137.

12 D.H. Lawrence, discussing Swinburne's poetry generally, *Collected Letters*, 474.

13 "To a Skylark," 8, and "Ode to the West Wind," 57; "The Gardener's Daughter," 28, and "The Marriage of Geraint," 829 (Tennyson, *Poems*, 509, 1550); and see Gaskell, *Cranford*, chap. 4, *Works*, 2:42; Swinburne, in "Tennyson and Musset" (*B*14:340), praises the "fidelity" to fact of the line from "The Marriage of Geraint," but he also acclaims Coleridge and Shelley as "the two coequal kings of English lyric poetry" in "Wordsworth and Byron" (*B*14:170–1).

14 Riede, *Swinburne*, 219–20; see also Sacks, *English Elegy*, and Richardson, *Vanishing Lives*, passim.

15 Ian Fletcher, *Swinburne*, 7.

16 *WB* 304.

APPENDIX

1 Ctr. Strauss's view, above; ctr. also the view of Johann Gottfried Herder that "most national fictions spring from verbal communications, and are instilled into the ear," and that such orally developed mythology expresses "the way of life and genius of each nation" (Burton and Feldman, *The Rise of Modern Mythology*, 232–3). At no time does Swinburne show any interest in the developments which made the theory of myth the domain of linguists and anthropologists by the turn of the century.

2 Coleridge, *The Statesman's Manual*, in *Lay Sermons*, 30; Wordsworth, Preface of 1815, in *Prose Works*, 3:34.317–18. Abrams quotes these passages in *Mirror*, 295.

3 Raymond employs these quotations (94–5, 92) in her fine discussion of the principle (*Swinburne's Poetics*, 87–104).

4 Ibid. 157–63; cp. 96 and passim.

Bibliography

PRIMARY SOURCES

Aeschylus. *Aeschylus*. Translated by Herbert Weir Smyth and Hugh Lloyd-Jones. 2 vols. London: Heinemann 1926.

Antoninus, Marcus Aurelius. *The Meditations*. Translated by George Long. New York: Lovell 1885.

Arnold, Matthew. *The Complete Prose Works of Matthew Arnold*. Edited by R.H. Super. 11 vols. Ann Arbor: University of Michigan Press 1960–77.

– *The Poetical Works of Matthew Arnold*. Edited by C.B. Tinker and H.F. Lowry. London: Oxford University Press 1950.

Baudelaire, Charles. *Oeuvres Complètes*. Edited by Claude Pichois. 2 vols. Paris: Gallimard 1975–6.

Blake, William. *The Complete Poetry and Prose of William Blake*. Edited by David V. Erdman. Rev. ed. New York: Anchor/Doubleday 1982.

The Book of Common Prayer. Edited by Richard Mant. Oxford: J. Parker and F.C. and J. Rivington 1820.

Browning, Robert. *The Poems*. Edited by John Pettigrew and Thomas J. Collins. 2 vols. New Haven: Yale University Press 1981.

– *The Works of Robert Browning*. Edited by F.G. Kenyon. Centenary Edition. 10 vols. London: Smith, Elder 1912.

Bruno, Giordano. *The Expulsion of the Triumphant Beast (Lo spaccio de la bestia trionfante)*. Translated and edited by Arthur D. Imerti. New Brunswick, NJ: Rutgers University Press 1964.

Burton, Sir Richard. *The Kasîdah of Hâjî Abdu El-Yezdî*. 1880. Portland, Maine: Thomas B. Mosher 1896.

Byron, George Gordon, Lord. *The Works of Lord Byron*. Rev. ed. 13 vols. London: Murray 1905.

Caird, John. *Sermons*. New York: Robert Carter & Brothers 1865.

Carlyle, Thomas. *Sartor Resartus*. Edited by Charles Frederick Harrold. Indianapolis: Bobbs-Merrill 1937.

– *Works*. Edited by H.D. Traill. Centenary Edition. 30 vols. London: Chapman and Hall 1896–9.

Carroll, Lewis [Charles Lutwidge Dodgson]. *The Annotated Alice*. Edited by Martin Gardner. Rev. ed. Harmondsworth, Middlesex: Penguin 1970.

Catullus, Gaius Valerius, et al. *Catullus, Tibullus and Pervigilium Veneris*. Edited and translated by F.W. Cornish et al. 3rd ed. London: Heinemann 1962.

Clough, Arthur Hugh. *Poems*. Edited by F.L. Mulhauser. 2nd ed. Oxford: Clarendon 1974.

Coleridge, Samuel Taylor. *Aids to Reflection*. Edited by Henry Nelson Coleridge. 2 vols. London: William Pickering 1848.

– *Lay Sermons*. Edited by R.J. White. Vol. VI of *The Collected Works of Samuel Taylor Coleridge*. London: Routledge & Kegan Paul 1972.

– *Poetical Works*. Edited by Ernest Hartley Coleridge. 1912. Oxford: Oxford University Press 1967.

Dante Alighieri. *The Divine Comedy*. Translated by John D. Sinclair. 3 vols. New York: Oxford University Press 1961.

Edmonds, J.M., ed. *Lyra Graeca*. 2nd ed. 3 vols. London: Heinemann 1928.

Eliot, George [Marian Evans]. *Works*. Library Edition. London: Blackwood 1901. Vol. IV.

Emerson, Ralph Waldo. *Complete Works*. Edited by Edward G. Emerson. Centenary Edition. 12 vols. London: Archibald Constable 1903–4.

Epictetus. *The Works of Epictetus*. Translated by Thomas Wentworth Higginson. Boston: Little, Brown 1866.

Feuerbach, Ludwig. *The Essence of Christianity*. Translated by George Eliot. 1854. New York: Harper & Row 1957.

Ficino, Marsilio. *Marsilio Ficino's Commentary on Plato's Symposium*. Translated by Sears Reynolds Jayne. Columbia: University of Missouri, 1944.

FitzGerald, Edward. *The Variorum and Definitive Edition of the Poetical and Prose Writings of Edward FitzGerald*. Edited by George Bentham. 1902. New York: Phaeton Press 1967.

Froude, James Anthony. *The Nemesis of Faith*. 1849. Chicago: Belfords, Clarke 1879.

Gaskell, Elizabeth Cleghorn Stevenson. *Works*. Edited by A.W. Ward. Knutsford Edition. Vol. 2. 1906. London: Murray 1925.

Gasperini, Auguste de. *La nouvelle allemagne musicale*. Paris: Heugel 1866.

Gautier, Théophile. *Mademoiselle de Maupin*. Edited by A. Boschot. Paris: Editions Garnier 1966.

Green, Thomas Hill. *Works*. Edited by R.L. Nettleship. 2nd ed. 3 vols. London: Longmans, Green 1889.

Harrison, Frederick. *The Positive Evolution of Religion*. New York: G.P. Putnam's Sons 1913.

Hartley, Anthony, trans. *Mallarmé*. Harmondsworth, Middlesex: Penguin 1965.

Hazlitt, William. *Complete Works*. Edited by P.P. Howe. Centenary Edition. Vol. 5. London: Dent 1930.

Herbert, George. *Works*. Edited by F.E. Hutchinson. Rev. ed. Oxford: Oxford University Press 1945.

Hopkins, Gerard Manley. *The Poems of Gerard Manley Hopkins*. Edited by W.H. Gardner and N.H. Mackenzie. 4th ed. London: Oxford University Press 1967.

Hueffer, Francis. "Arthur Schopenhauer." *Fortnightly Review* n.s. 20 (1876): 773–92.

– "Richard Wagner." *Fortnightly Review* n.s. 11 (1872): 265–87.

Hugo, Victor. *Châtiments*. Edited by P.J. Yarrow. London: Athlone 1975.

– *Oeuvres Complètes*. Edited by Jean Massin et al. 18 vols. Paris: Le Club Français du Livre 1967–70.

Huxley, Thomas H. *Collected Essays*. 9 vols. 1893–4. London: Macmillan 1909.

Keats, John. *The Letters of John Keats: 1814–1821*. Edited by Hyder Edward Rollins. 2 vols. Cambridge, Mass.: Harvard University Press 1958.

– *Poems of John Keats*. Edited by Jack Stillinger. Cambridge, Mass.: Belknap, 1978.

Keble, John. *The Christian Year*. 10th ed. Oxford: J. Parker and C. and J. Rivington 1833.

Landor, Walter Savage. *The Complete Works of Walter Savage Landor*. Edited by T. Earle Welby and Stephen Wheeler. 16 vols. 1927–36. New York: Barnes & Noble 1969.

Lawrence, D. H. *Collected Letters*. Edited by Harry T. Moore. 2 vols. New York: Viking Press 1962.

Leith, Mary Gordon. *The Children of the Chapel: Including the Pilgrimage of Pleasure, A Morality Play by Algernon Charles Swinburne*. 3rd ed. rev. London: Chatto & Windus 1910.

Lucretius Carus, Titus. *De Rerum Natura*. Edited by Cyril Bailey. Rev. ed. Oxford: Clarendon 1922.

Mallarmé, Stéphane. *Correspondance*. Edited by Henri Mondor and Lloyd James Austin. 10 vols. Paris: Gallimard 1959–84.

– *Oeuvres Complètes*. Edited by Carl Paul Barbier and Charles Gordon Millan. Vol. 1. Paris: Flammarion 1983.

Malory, Sir Thomas. *The Works of Sir Thomas Malory*. Edited by Eugène Vinaver. 2nd ed. 3 vols. Oxford: Clarendon 1967.

Mansel, Henry Longueville. *The Limits of Religious Thought*. 5th ed. London: Murray 1867.

Massey, Gerald. *The Poetical Works of Gerald Massey*. Boston: Ticknor and Fields 1857.

Mazzini, Joseph. *Life and Writings of Joseph Mazzini*. 6 vols. London: Smith, Elder 1890.

Meredith, George. *The Letters of George Meredith*. Edited by C.L. Cline. 3 vols. Oxford: Clarendon 1970.

- *The Poems of George Meredith.* Edited by Phyllis B. Bartlett. 2 vols. New Haven: Yale University Press 1978.

Michelet, Jules. *History of the French Revolution.* Translated by Charles Cocks. Edited by Gordon Wright. Chicago: University of Chicago Press 1967.

Mill, John Stuart. *Collected Works of John Stuart Mill.* Edited by John M. Robson et al. 19 vols. Toronto: University of Toronto Press 1963–81.

Milton, John. *Complete Poems and Major Prose.* Edited by Merritt Y. Hughes. Indianapolis: Bobbs-Merrill 1957.

Mone, Franz Joseph, ed. *Lateinische Hymnen des Mittelalters.* 3 vols. Freiburg: Herder'sche Verlagshandlung 1853–5.

Nauck, Augustus, ed. *Tragicorum Graecorum Fragmenta.* 2nd ed. Leipzig: Teubner 1889.

Neale, John Mason, ed. and trans. *The Rhythm of St. Bernard de Morlaix, Monk of Cluny, on the Celestial Country.* 7th ed. London: J.T. Hayes 1865.

Newman, John Henry. *Apologia Pro Vita Sua.* Edited by Martin J. Svaglic. Oxford: Clarendon 1967.

- *The Letters of John Henry Newman.* Edited by Stephen Dessain and Thomas Gornall. Vols. 5, 29. Oxford: Clarendon 1981, 1976.

- *Parochial and Plain Sermons.* 2nd ed. 8 vols. London: Rivingtons 1882.

Pater, Walter. *The Renaissance: Studies in Art and Poetry.* Edited by Donald L. Hill. Berkeley: University of California Press 1980.

Plath, Sylvia. *The Collected Poems.* Edited by Ted Hughes. New York: Harper & Row 1981.

Plato. *The Dialogues of Plato.* Translated by Benjamin Jowett. 2nd ed. 5 vols. Oxford: Clarendon 1875.

- *The Dialogues of Plato.* Translated by Benjamin Jowett. 3rd ed. Vol. 1. Oxford: Clarendon 1892.

Reade, Winwood. *The Martyrdom of Man.* 1872. London: Watts 1925.

Renan, Ernest. *Vie de Jésus.* Paris: Michel Lévy 1863.

Rimbaud, Arthur. *Oeuvres complètes.* Edited by Antoine Adam. Paris: Gallimard 1972.

Rossetti, Dante Gabriel. *The Collected Works of Dante Gabriel Rossetti.* Edited by William Michael Rossetti. 2 vols. London: Ellis and Elvey 1890.

- *Poems.* Edited by Oswald Doughty. London: Dent 1961.

- "Songs of One Household, No. 1. My Sister's Sleep." *The Germ* 1 (1850): 21.

Rossetti, William Michael. *The Diary of W.M. Rossetti: 1870–1873.* Edited by Odette Bornand. Oxford: Clarendon 1977.

- ed. *Rossetti Papers: 1862–1870.* London: Sands 1903.

Sade, Donatien-Alphonse-François, Marquis de. *Oeuvres Complètes.* Edited by Jean-Jacques Pauvert. 35 vols. Paris 1955–70.

Schopenhauer, Arthur. *The World as Will and Idea.* Translated by R.B. Haldane and J. Kemp. 7th ed. 2 vols. London: Kegan Paul, Trench, Trubner 1910.

Sewell, William. "Divines of the Seventeenth Century." *Quarterly Review* 49 (1842): 471–550.

Shelley, Percy Bysshe. *Poetical Works*. Edited by Thomas Hutchinson. Revised by G.M. Matthews. Oxford: Oxford University Press 1970.

Sidney, Sir Philip. *Poems*. Edited by William A. Ringler, Jr. Oxford: Clarendon 1962.

Smith, Stevie. *Collected Poems*. Edited by James MacGibbon. London: Allen Lane 1975.

Sophocles. *The Dramas of Sophocles*. Translated by Sir George Young. Cambridge: Deighton, Bell 1888.

– *Sophoclis Tragoediae Superstites et Perditarum Fragmenta*. Edited by G. Dindorf. 3rd ed. 8 vols. Oxford: Oxford University Press 1860.

Spencer, Herbert. *First Principles*. 6th ed. New York: Appleton 1903.

Spenser, Edmund. *Spenser's Faerie Queene*. Edited by J.C. Smith. 2 vols. Oxford: Clarendon 1909.

Strauss, David Friedrich. *The Life of Jesus*. Translated by George Eliot. 3 vols. London: Chapman, Brothers 1846.

Swinburne, Algernon Charles. *The Cannibal Catechism*. London: privately printed 1913.

– *The Complete Works of Algernon Charles Swinburne*. Edited by Sir Edmund Gosse and Thomas James Wise. 20 vols. London: William Heinemann 1925–7.

– *Lesbia Brandon*. Edited by Randolph Hughes. London: Falcon Press 1952.

– *New Writings by Swinburne or Miscellanea Nova et Curiosa*. Edited by Cecil Yelverton Lang. Syracuse, NY: Syracuse University Press 1964.

– *Poems and Ballads / Atalanta in Calydon*. Edited by Morse Peckham. Indianapolis: Bobbs-Merrill 1970.

– *The Poems of Algernon Charles Swinburne*. 6 vols. London: Chatto & Windus 1904.

– *Selected Poems*. Edited by L.M. Findlay. Manchester: Carcanet 1982.

– *Selections from the Poetical Works of Algernon Charles Swinburne*. London: Chatto & Windus 1887.

– *The Swinburne Letters*. Edited by Cecil Yelverton Lang. 6 vols. New Haven: Yale University Press 1959–62.

– *Swinburne Replies*. Edited by Clyde Kenneth Hyder. Syracuse, NY: Syracuse University Press 1966.

– *Swinburne: Selected Poetry and Prose*. Edited by John D. Rosenberg. New York: Random House 1968.

– *Swinburne's Hyperion*. Edited by Georges Lafourcade. London: Faber & Gwyer 1927.

– *The Tragedies of Algernon Charles Swinburne*. 5 vols. London: Chatto & Windus 1905.

– *William Blake: A Critical Essay*. Edited by Hugh J. Luke. Lincoln: University of Nebraska Press 1970.

– *A Year's Letters*. Edited by Francis Jacques Sypher. New York: New York University Press 1974.

Tennyson, Alfred, Lord. *The Poems of Tennyson*. Edited by Christopher Ricks. London: Longman 1969.

Thomson, J. Cockburn, trans. *The Bhagavad-Gita: or, A Discourse between Krishna and Arjuna on Divine Matters*. Hertford: Stephen Austin 1855.

Trench, Richard Chenevix. *On the Study of Words*. 16th ed. rev. London: Macmillan 1876.

– ed. *Sacred Latin Poetry, Chiefly Lyrical*. London: John W. Parker 1849.

Tyndall, John. *Address delivered before the British Association assembled at Belfast*. 7th ed. New York: Appleton 1875.

– "British Association for the Advancement of Science." *Times*, 20 August 1874, 4–5.

Villon, François. *Oeuvres*. Edited by Louis Thuasne. 3 vols. Paris: Picard 1923.

Watts-Dunton, Theodore. *Aylwin*. London: Hurst and Blackett 1899.

Wilde, Oscar. *Complete Writings of Oscar Wilde*. Edited by Robert Ross. Vol. 1. New York: Nottingham Society 1909.

Woodford, James Russell. *The Great Commission*. Edited by Henry Mortimer Luckock. 2nd ed. London: Rivingtons 1887.

– *Sermons on Subjects from the New Testament*. Edited by Henry Mortimer Luckock. New York: Thomas Whittaker 1887.

– *Sermons Preached in Various Churches of Bristol*. 2nd ed. London: Joseph Masters 1860.

Wordsworth, William. *Poetical Works*. Edited by Ernest de Selincourt and Helen Darbishire. Rev. ed. 5 vols. Oxford: Clarendon 1959.

– *The Prelude*. Edited by Ernest de Selincourt. 2nd ed., revised by Helen Darbishire. Oxford: Clarendon 1959.

– *Prose Works*. Edited by W.J.B. Owen and Jane Worthington Smyser. 3 vols. Oxford: Clarendon 1974.

Yeats, William Butler. *The Collected Poems of W.B. Yeats*. 2nd ed. London: Macmillan 1950.

SECONDARY SOURCES

Abrams, M. H., ed. *English Romantic Poets: Modern Essays in Criticism*. New York: Oxford University Press 1960.

– *The Mirror and the Lamp: Romantic Theory and the Critical Tradition*. Oxford: Oxford University Press 1953.

– *Natural Supernaturalism: Tradition and Revolution in Romantic Literature*. New York: Norton 1971.

– "Structure and Style in the Greater Romantic Lyric." In *From Sensibility to Romanticism: Essays Presented to Frederick A. Pottle*. Edited by Frederick W.

Hilles and Harold Bloom. New York: Oxford University Press 1965. 527–60.

Baird, Julian. "Swinburne, Sade, and Blake: The Pleasure-Pain Paradox." *Victorian Poetry* 9 (1971): 49–75.

Bate, Walter Jackson. *John Keats*. Cambridge, Mass.: Belknap 1963.

Baum, Paull F. "The Fitzwilliam Manuscript of Swinburne's 'Atalanta', Verses 1038–1204." *Modern Language Review* 54 (1959): 161–78.

– "Swinburne's 'A Nympholept'." *South Atlantic Quarterly* 57 (1958): 58–68.

Beetz, Kirk H. *Algernon Charles Swinburne: A Bibliography of Secondary Works, 1861–1980*. Metuchen, NJ: Scarecrow 1982.

Betz, Dorothy M. "Baudelaire, Swinburne and the Legacy of Greece." *Canadian Review of Comparative Literature* 14 (1987): 1–24.

Bicknell, E.E. *The Channel Islands*. 2nd ed. London: Methuen 1923.

Bloom, Harold. *The Visionary Company: A Reading of English Romantic Poetry*. Rev. and enl. ed. Ithaca: Cornell University Press 1971.

Boase, G.C. "Sewell, William." *DNB*. 1897.

Brisman, Leslie. "Swinburne's Semiotics." *Georgia Review* 31 (1977): 578–97.

Brodie, Fawn M. *The Devil Drives: A Life of Sir Richard Burton*. New York: Norton 1967.

Brown, Carleton, ed. *Religious Lyrics of the Fourteenth Century*. 2nd ed. Rev. G.V. Smithers. Oxford: Clarendon 1957.

Buckler, William E. *The Victorian Imagination: Essays in Aesthetic Exploration*. New York: New York University Press 1980.

Cassidy, John A. *Algernon Charles Swinburne*. New York: Twayne Publishers 1964.

Cassirer, Ernst. *The Philosophy of Symbolic Forms*. Translated by Ralph Manheim. 2 vols. New Haven: Yale University Press 1955.

Chadwick, Owen. *The Secularization of the European Mind in the Nineteenth Century*. Cambridge: Cambridge University Press 1975.

Charlesworth, Barbara. *Dark Passages: The Decadent Consciousness in Victorian Literature*. Madison: University of Wisconsin Press 1965.

Charlton, D.G. *Secular Religions in France: 1815–1870*. London: Oxford University Press 1963.

Chew, Samuel C. *Swinburne*. 1929. Reprint. Hamden, Conn.: Archon 1966.

Clements, Patricia. *Baudelaire and the English Tradition*. Princeton: Princeton University Press 1985.

Cockshut, A.O.J. *The Unbelievers: English Agnostic Thought 1840–1890*. New York: New York University Press 1966.

Cohn, Robert Greer. *Toward the Poems of Mallarmé*. Berkeley: University of California Press 1965.

Connolly, Thomas E. *Swinburne's Theory of Poetry*. Albany: SUNY 1964.

Curtius, Ernst Robert. *European Literature and the Latin Middle Ages*. Translated by Willard R. Trask. New York: Harper & Row 1953.

Dalbanne, J., et G. Monmarché. *Auvergne et Centre*. Paris: Hachette 1924.

Diekhoff, John S. "Milton's Prosody in the Poems of the Trinity Manuscript." *PMLA* 54 (1939): 153–83.

Empson, William. *Seven Types of Ambiguity*. 3rd ed. 1961. Reprint. Harmondsworth, Middlesex: Penguin 1972.

Fallis, Jean Thomson. "The Sacred and the Profane: Transvaluation of Religious Symbol in Hopkins, Rossetti, and Swinburne." PHD dissertation, Princeton, 1974.

Fass, Barbara. *La Belle Dame Sans Merci & the Aesthetics of Romanticism*. Detroit: Wayne State University Press 1974.

Feldman, Burton, and Robert D. Richardson, eds. *The Rise of Modern Mythology: 1680–1860*. Bloomington: Indiana University Press 1972.

Fletcher, Ian. *Swinburne*. Harlow, Essex: Longman 1973.

Fletcher, Pauline. *Gardens and Grim Ravines: The Language of Landscape in Victorian Poetry*. Princeton: Princeton University Press 1983.

Frye, Northrop. *Anatomy of Criticism*. Princeton, NJ: Princeton University Press 1957.

– *The Great Code: The Bible and Literature*. Toronto: Academic Press 1981.

– ed. *Romanticism Reconsidered: Selected Papers from the English Institute*. New York: Columbia University Press 1963.

Fuller, Jean Overton. *Swinburne*. London: Chatto & Windus 1968.

Gay, Peter. *The Enlightenment: An Interpretation / The Rise of Modern Paganism*. 1966. New York: Norton 1977.

Gitter, Elisabeth G. "Arnold and Rossetti: Two Voices in Swinburne's 'The Triumph of Time'." *Pre-Raphaelite Review* 3 (1980): 48–57.

Goodenough, Erwin R. *By Light, Light*. Amsterdam: Philo 1969.

Gosse, Sir Edmund. "The First Draft of Swinburne's 'Anactoria'." *Modern Language Review* 14 (1919): 271–7.

– *The Life of Algernon Charles Swinburne*. London: Macmillan 1917.

Gray, Douglas. *Themes and Images in the Mediaeval English Religious Lyric*. London: Routledge & Kegan Paul 1972.

Greenberg, Robert A. "Gosse's Swinburne, 'The Triumph of Time', and the Context of 'Les Noyades'." *Victorian Poetry* 9 (1971): 95–110.

– "Swinburne and the Redefinition of Classical Myth." *Victorian Poetry* 14 (1976): 175–95.

Hales, E.E.Y. *Pio Nono*. New York: P.J. Kennedy 1954.

Härdelin, Alf. *The Tractarian Understanding of the Eucharist*. Uppsala 1965.

Harrison, Antony H. *Swinburne's Medievalism: A Study in Victorian Love Poetry*. Baton Rouge: Louisiana State University Press 1988.

– "The Swinburnian Woman." *Philological Quarterly* 58 (1979): 90–102.

Henderson, Philip. *Swinburne: The Portrait of a Poet*. London: Routledge & Kegan Paul 1974.

Henderson, W. Brooks Drayton. *Swinburne and Landor: A Study of Their*

and Psychology. 2nd ed.
a Self-Portrait." Victorian

of Victorian Poetic The-
59.
gner." Victorian Poetry 9

tarian Mode. Cambridge,

hatto & Windus 1948.
odern Philology 15 (1917):

Bough. Princeton: Prin-

1789 to the Present Day.
74.
he Knowledge of a Creative

udelaire's Influence on
Uppsala 1976. Uppsala:

timore: Johns Hopkins

London: A.M. Philpot

etry of Swinburne and

ane 1898.
winburne's Pantheism:
and Literature 8 (1972),

Visionary Poetry, and
ight'." Victorian Poetry

Spiritual Relationship and Its Effect on Swinburne's Moral and Poetic Development. London: Macmillan 1918.

Hutchings, Richard J., and Raymond V. Turley. Young Algernon Swinburne:
The Poet's Associations with the Isle of Wight. Brighstone: Hunnyhill Publications 1978.

Hyder, Clyde Kenneth. Swinburne: The Critical Heritage. New York: Routledge, Kegan Paul 1970.

Inge, W.R. "Synderesis." Encyclopaedia of Religion and Ethics. 1921 ed.

Jones, James Edmund. The Book of Common Praise. Toronto: Oxford University Press 1909.

Jordan, John O. "The Sweet Face of Mothers: Psychological Patterns in
Atalanta in Calydon." Victorian Poetry 11 (1973): 101–14.

Johnson, Wendell Stacy. "Swinburne and Carlyle." English Language Notes
1 (1963): 117–21.

Kerferd, G.B. "Logos." Encyclopedia of Philosophy. 1967 ed.

Krieger, Murray. "Mediation, Language, and Vision in the Reading of Literature." Interpretation: Theory and Practice. Edited by Charles Singleton.
Baltimore: Johns Hopkins 1969. 211–42.

– "'A Waking Dream': The Symbolic Alternative to Allegory." Allegory, Myth,
and Symbol, Harvard English Studies 9. Edited by Morton W. Bloomfield.
Cambridge, Mass.: Harvard University Press 1981. 1–22.

Lafourcade, Georges. La Jeunesse de Swinburne (1837–1867). 2 vols. Paris:
Publications de la Faculté des Lettres de l'Université de Strasbourg 1928.

–Swinburne: A Literary Biography. New York: Morrow 1932.

Landow, George P. The Aesthetic and Critical Theories of John Ruskin. Princeton,
NJ: Princeton University Press 1971.

–Victorian Types, Victorian Shadows: Biblical Typology in Victorian Literature,
Art, and Thought. Boston: Routledge & Kegan Paul 1980.

Lang, Cecil Yelverton. Introduction. Victorian Poetry 9 (1971).

– "Swinburne's Lost Love." PMLA 74 (1959): 123–30.

Leith, Mary Gordon. The Boyhood of Algernon Charles Swinburne. London:
Chatto & Windus 1917.

Lentricchia, Frank. After the New Criticism. Chicago: University of Chicago
Press 1980.

Lougy, Robert E. "Thematic Imagery and Meaning in Atalanta in Calydon."
Victorian Poetry 9 (1971): 17–34.

Louis, Margot Kathleen. "Thalassius" and "On the Cliffs": The Composition of
a Poet. Northampton: Smith College 1976.

McGann, Jerome J. "Rossetti's Significant Details." Pre-Raphaelitism: A Col-
lection of Critical Essays. Edited by James Sambrook. Chicago: University
of Chicago Press 1974. 230–42.

– "Shelley's Veils: A Thousand Images of Loveliness." Romantic and Victorian
Studies in Memory of William H. Marshall. Edited by W. Paul Elledge and

Richard L. Hoffman. Rutherford: Fairleigh Dickinso
1971. 198–218.
– *Swinburne: An Experiment in Criticism*. Chicago: Univers
1972.
McGhee, Richard D. *Marriage, Duty, & Desire in Victoria*
Lawrence: Regents Press of Kansas 1980.
– "'Thalassius': Swinburne's Poetic Myth." *Victorian Poet*
McSweeney, Kerry Mark. "Swinburne's 'Thalassius'." *Hi*
Bulletin 22 (1971): 50–5.
– *Tennyson and Swinburne as Romantic Naturalists*. Torc
Toronto Press 1981.
Mâle, Emile. *L'art religieux de la fin du moyen âge en Fro*
Armand Colin 1949.
Man, Paul de. "The Rhetoric of Temporality." *Interpretati*
tice. Edited by Charles S. Singleton. Baltimore: Johns I
209.
Mandelbaum, Maurice. *History, Man, & Reason: A Study in*
Thought. Baltimore: Johns Hopkins 1971.
Mathews, Richard. "Heart's Love and Heart's Division: T
in *Atalanta in Calydon*." *Victorian Poetry* 9 (1971): 35–48
Meyers, Terry L. "Shelley's Influence on *Atalanta in Calydc*
14 (1976): 150–4.
Miller, J. Hillis. *The Disappearance of God: Five Nineteen*
Cambridge, Mass.: Belknap 1963.
Morgan, Thaïs Elizabeth. "Metaphorical Thinking, Myth
Poetry of Algernon Charles Swinburne and Stéphan
dissertation, Brown, 1982.
– "Swinburne's Dramatic Monologues: Sex and Ideology
22 (1984): 1975–95.
Murfin, Ross C. *Swinburne, Hardy, Lawrence and the Burden*
University of Chicago Press 1978.
Peckham, Morse. *Victorian Revolutionaries: Speculations o*
Culture Crisis. New York: George Braziller 1970.
Peters, Robert L. *The Crowns of Apollo*. Detroit: Wayne Stat
1965.
Praz, Mario. *The Romantic Agony*. Translated by Angus L
London: Oxford University Press 1970.
Prendergast, Anne Marie. "'Time and Fruitful Hour': Pi
cerity in *Atalanta in Calydon*." *Journal of Pre-Raphaelite St*
75.
Prickett, Stephen. *Romanticism and Religion*. Cambridge:
versity Press 1976.
Pulos, C.E. *The Deep Truth: A Study of Shelley's Scepticis*
University of Nebraska Press 1962.

Sorley, W.R. "Synderesis." *Dictionary of Philosoph*
Stuart, Donald C. "Swinburne: The Composition
Poetry 9 (1971): 111–28.
Suiter, James E. "Swinburne and the Main Strea
ory." PHD dissertation, New York University
Sypher, Francis Jacques, Jr. "Swinburne and W
(1971): 165–83.
Tennyson, G.B. *Victorian Devotional Poetry: The Tr*
Mass.: Harvard University Press 1981.
Tillyard, E.M.W. *Five Poems 1470–1870*. London:
Tisdel, Frederick M. "Rossetti's 'House of Life'."
257–76.
Vickery, John B. *The Literary Impact of* The Golde
ceton University Press 1973.
Vidler, Alec R. *The Church in an Age of Revolutio*
3rd ed. Harmondsworth, Middlesex: Penguin
Vivante, Leone. *English Poetry and Its Contribution*
Principle. London: Faber and Faber 1950.
Walder, Anne. "Swinburne's Flowers of Evil:
Poems and Ballads, First Series." PHD dissertatic
Acta Universitatis Upsaliensis 1976.
Wasserman, Earl R. *Shelley: A Critical Reading*.
University Press 1971.
Watts-Dunton, Clara. *The Home Life of Swinbur*
1922.
Wexler, Eric Joseph. "Mythological Strategy in th
Meredith." PHD dissertation, Yale 1974.
Wharton, Henry Thornton. *Sappho*. London: Joh
Wilson, F.A.C. "Indian and Mithraic Influences o
'Hertha' and 'A Nympholept'." *Papers on Lang*
Supplement: 57–66.
Wilson, William. "Algernon Agonistes: 'Thalass
Swinburne's Critique of Arnold's 'Sweetness a
19 (1981): 381–95.

Index

PR 5513 .L6 1990

Louis, Margot Kathleen
  —

Swinburne and his gods

DEMCO